GRAPHIC DESIGN VISIONARIES

CAROLINE ROBERTS

LAURENCE KING

Published in 2015 by
Laurence King Publishing Ltd
361–373 City Road
London EC1V 1LR
e-mail: enquiries@laurenceking.com
www.laurenceking.com

A catalogue record for this book is available
from the British Library.

ISBN: 978-1-78067-484-1

Cover image: Portrait of Paul Rand by Herb Levart.
Photo courtesy Robert B. Haas Family Arts Library
Special Collections, Yale University Library, New
Haven, CT.

Design: TwoSheds Design
Picture research: Amanda Russell
Senior Editor: Peter Jones

Printed in China

GRAPHIC DESIGN VISIONARIES

CAROLINE ROBERTS

Laurence King Publishing

GRAPHIC DESIGN VISIONARIES

Introduction

The dictionary defines a visionary as 'a person with original ideas about what the future will or could be like'. It's a very forthright label, and it's unlikely that many of the designers featured here woke up one day and decided that they would try and change the world through graphic design. What links all of them – whether they are designing a single poster or a huge corporate identity – is a desire to break new ground, combined with a steadfast commitment to push standards higher. This book offers a glimpse into the personalities behind the work, but, as with most creative people, it's often impossible to separate the two.

Graphic design is everywhere. It surrounds us all on a day-to-day basis, but conversely it remains one of the least visible disciplines. Unlike ego-driven architects who take it in turns to ruin the skyline, or fashion designers who chase headlines with outrageous outfits in order to build their profitable fragrance and sunglasses brands, graphic designers work mainly for other people, providing solutions to problems large or small.

Whereas architecture and fashion tend to rely on the cult of personality, graphic design is much more low key. Over the years there has been a smattering of what might be described as 'superstar designers', but now these seem to be something of a dying breed. The general public would be hard-pressed to name any graphic designers, probably because the only time one appears in the national press is in an obituary. And while they might be on very familiar terms with their work, even graphic designers themselves would find it hard to identify some of the great and the good by their portraits alone (many of which are included here, but some of which unfortunately eluded us).

Compared to architecture and fashion, graphic design as we now know it is very much in its infancy. With its roots in the commercial art of the early twentieth century and in the printing and book trades, graphic design has undergone massive changes in the past 30 years. Many might say that it is still an industry in flux. In recent years it would appear to be suffering something of

an identity crisis, as not even those who practise it seem able to decide on what to call it. 'Commercial art', 'graphic communication', 'communication design' and 'visual communication' have all been mooted as more appropriate ways to describe graphic design. This confusion could be because the graphic designer's role has expanded hugely, and now encompasses that of art director, typographer, layout artist, photo retoucher and brand guardian. Some are authors, publishers, curators and entrepreneurs, too. As with any creative field, however, it is this reflexivity that drives things forward, questioning the status quo and the established rules.

One question which needs to be addressed here is: 'Where are all the women?' This book forms part of a series that aims to be a starting point for readers to go off and find out more about their chosen discipline. So the focus is, understandably, very much on the established design canon. Questions about who is responsible for writing design history aside, there's no denying that graphic design has been a male-dominated profession for many years, and a quick flick through this book will reveal a very narrow demographic. Things are changing rapidly, however, with more women than ever graduating from graphic design courses, working in key positions within the industry and setting up their own consultancies. Publications, conferences and awards schemes have a responsibility not simply to default to the same old faces, but to seek out the less visible – but equally talented – female designers. While there are some high-profile female designers, they are all too often the 'token female' on the panel or in the line-up. These women designers also have a responsibility to push for greater representation, no matter how boring it might be to answer endless questions about women and design.

Whether graphic design will ever be anything other than a primarily white and middle-class profession is somewhat in the hands of governments and education systems. On a much brighter note, one can imagine that any future editions of this book will look quite different, if not from a class, at least from a gender perspective.

60 50?, advertisement for cable supply
and operation, printed paper, 1927.

'The more uninteresting
the letter, the more useful
it is to the typographer.'

Piet Zwart

1885–1977

THE NETHERLANDS

Architecture was a major influence on Piet Zwart. Describing his design process as building pages with type, he often referred to himself as a 'typotekt' – a name he invented for his own particular typographer/ architect hybrid. Hugely influential for many post-war Dutch designers such as Wim Crouwel, Zwart was also an accomplished product designer. In 2000 he was posthumously named 'Designer of the Century' by the Association of Dutch Designers (BNO).

Zwart studied at the School of Applied Arts in Amsterdam. It was an education that encompassed many different disciplines, including architecture and the applied arts, as well as drawing and painting. Described by Zwart as 'a smashing school with no idea of a programme', the students were very much left to their own devices.

In 1919 Zwart was employed as a draughtsman by the architect Jan Wils, who was a member of the emerging De Stijl group (which included Theo van Doesburg, Gerrit Rietveld and Piet Mondrian), and would prove to be a big influence. While Zwart had a definite affinity with De Stijl, he was also interested in Constructivism and Dadaism, preferring not to attach himself to any one movement or set of rules.

One of Zwart's first major commissions was for the flooring manufacturer Vickers House. Despite (or perhaps because of) the unpromising subject matter, he created a series of exciting typographic adverts, playing around with scale and geometric shapes, and using the

black, white and red reminiscent of the De Stijl movement. In 1923 Zwart began working for a new client, the Dutch Cable Factory (Nederlandsche Kabelfabriek, NKF) at Delft. NKF would prove to be the perfect client. Over the next ten years Zwart designed hundreds of remarkable – mainly typographic – pieces for NKF, including advertisements and brochures. Further work for the Dutch Post Office (PTT) followed, and for the manufacturer Bruynzeel, for whom he designed calendars and other promotional material. Zwart also designed a kitchen for Bruynzeel. Taking three years to research and develop, this was one of the first mass-produced fitted kitchens, and could be configured in many different ways. A modified version is still in production by the company.

A keen educator, Zwart taught at the Rotterdam Academy of Fine Arts until, after voicing his outspoken views on its educational policy, he was asked to leave in 1933. In 1942, Zwart (along with hundreds of other artists) was arrested and held captive by the Nazis, and only released once the war was over. This had a profound effect on him, and after his release he concentrated mainly on industrial design. The Piet Zwart Institute at the Willem de Kooning Academie in Rotterdam (housed in the building in which he originally taught), is named after him.

Above Hot Spots, printed paper, 1923.

een kleine keuze uit onze lettercollectie

Trio-Reclameboek inside page,
*A small selection from our letter
collection*, poster, 1931.

Left Advertisement for rubber flooring, 1922.

Below Poster for film festival in The Hague, photolithograph, 1928.

Piet Zwart

1885 Born in Zaandijk, the Netherlands.

1890

1900

1902 Begins his studies at the School of Applied Arts in Amsterdam.

1910

1920

1923 Starts work at the Nederlandsche Kabelfabriek (NKF), Delft.

1929 Lectures at the Bauhaus School, Dessau.
1930 Employed by the Bruynzeel Company.

1933 Fired from the Rotterdam Academy of Fine Arts.

1938 The Book of PTT is published.

1940

1950

1960

1970

1977 Dies in Wassenaar, the Netherlands.

American Airlines: To New York,
poster, 1948.

'Personal contact with the men requiring advertising art in the exploitation of their products is an absolute necessity in obtaining good results.'

Edward McKnight Kauffer

1890–1954

USA

An American who spent most of his life in England, Edward McKnight Kauffer was one of the most influential poster artists of the 1920s and 1930s. Referred to as the 'Picasso of advertising design', he was influenced by art movements such as Cubism, Futurism and Vorticism, and saw no reason to differentiate between 'high art' and advertising. His relationship with the transport administrator Frank Pick in particular proved to be extremely fruitful – from 1915 onwards he designed over 100 posters for the London Underground, encouraging customers to experience the city's many attractions, its surrounding countryside, and the joys of travelling by public transport.

Growing up in San Francisco, Edward Kauffer worked in a bookshop by day, studying painting by night. Seeing great promise in the young artist, one of his customers, Joseph McKnight, sponsored Kauffer to study at the Académie Moderne in Paris, and as a mark of gratitude, Kauffer took on his name.

At the outbreak of World War I, Kauffer fled Paris. He arrived in London, where he was introduced to Frank Pick, at that time publicity manager for the Underground Electric Railways. Pick commissioned him to design four posters – *Oxley Woods*, *In Watford*, *Route 160: Reigate* and *The North Downs*. The results were masterful, and the first of 141 posters that Kauffer would eventually design for the company followed. These became progressively more sophisticated as he embraced techniques such as airbrushing and photomontage.

Kauffer is widely credited as pushing traditional poster art towards a more graphic sensibility. One of the pieces that made him famous was a striking poster for the Labour Party's *Daily Herald* newspaper, featuring one of his earlier designs, a Japanese-inspired woodcut of birds entitled *Flight*. Kauffer went on to design packaging, rugs, interiors and theatre sets too, although poster design remained his main passion, and he released a book on the subject – *The Art of the Poster* – in 1924. In 1930 Kauffer became art director at the publisher Lund Humphries, and after this he was commissioned by John Beddington to create a series of large-scale posters for Shell-Mex and BP.

At the onset of World War II, unable to contribute to Britain's war effort as an American expatriate, Kauffer returned to the US. Despite his reputation in the UK, and an exhibition at MoMA in 1937, Kauffer's work was not particularly well received by the US advertising industry. Between 1947 and 1953 he did, however, create a series of stunning posters for American Airlines promoting New York, California, Nevada, Arizona and New Mexico.

While Kauffer's work might not have been to the taste of NYC's ad men, he was a huge influence on its graphic designers, as Paul Rand explained: 'Many people were doing modern stuff in English. But Kauffer was doing the best stuff. There wasn't anybody anywhere near him except for Cassandre.'

Above Portrait of Kauffer.

Soaring to Success, redrawn by Peter
Branfield for the Poster Art 1915–40
exhibition, England, 1973 (original
poster 1919).

Soaring to Success !

DAILY HERALD

— the Early Bird.

Edward McKnight Kauffer

1890 — Born in Montana, US.

1900

1910 — Studies at the Académie Moderne in Paris.

1913 — Receives first commissions from Frank Pick for
London Underground Electric Railways.

1915

1920 — Writes and produces *The Art of the Poster*.

1924 — Appointed art director for Lund Humphries.

1930 — Elected Honorary Designer for Industry by the
Royal Society of Arts in London.

1936
1937 — Given a solo show at New York's Museum of
Modern Art.

1940

1950 — Dies in New York City, US.

1954

Above *Shop Between 10 & 4,* lithograph, 1921.

Right *Spring in the Village,* poster, 1936.

europa
1907

belgië

frankrijk   duitsland

engeland   nederland   spanje

noorwegen   oostenrijk   rusland

tschechoslowakije

zwitserland

stedelijk museum amsterdam   6 juli-30 sept

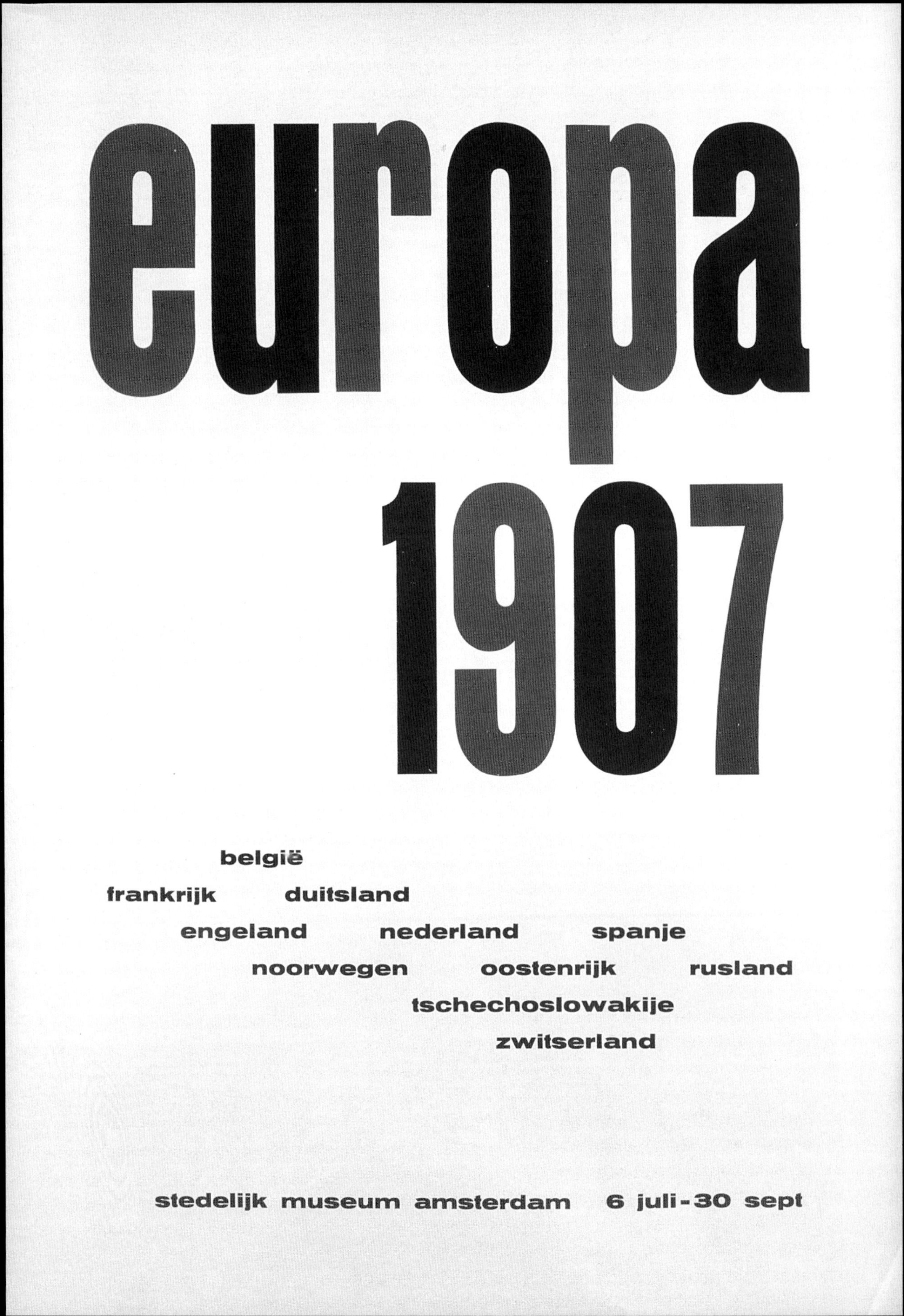

'Sandberg's work, characterized by modesty, presents a sensitive alternative to the Modernist quest for perfection.'
– Peter Bil'ak

Willem Sandberg

1897–1984

THE NETHERLANDS

Willem Sandberg enjoyed a long and fruitful relationship with the Stedelijk Museum in Amsterdam; however, it was not until after World War II that his influence was really felt. When he became the director of the museum in 1945, he started a radical programme of modernization that influenced both what was collected and how it was displayed. He was also responsible for the design of over 250 catalogues and 270 posters.

After a brief period at the State Academy of Fine Arts in Amsterdam, Sandberg travelled around Europe. While in Vienna he studied the Isotype system, developed by Otto Neurath (see p. 33). Back in Amsterdam, he started working for the Stedelijk as a designer, eventually becoming a curator in 1937, but only on the condition that he could continue to design the museum's exhibition catalogues. Often described as the man responsible for introducing contemporary art to the Netherlands, he staged an ambitious exhibition of abstract art, unlike anything seen there before.

In the years prior to World War II, Sandberg played an active part in the Dutch Resistance. Having visited Spain in 1938 and witnessed the wartime protection of the Prado Museum's treasures by the Republican government (who hid them in caves on the Costa Brava), he was then asked to secure the Stedelijk's art collection. Together with the city's chief engineer he designed a concrete bunker to house it: 'When the Germans overran Holland on May 10th 1940 the treasures of the Stedelijk and of the Rijksmuseum were safe – over 200 Van Goghs, Rembrandt's *Nightwatch*, *The Jewish Bride*, etc. were protected by 1.5 m of concrete and 10 metres of sand.'

In 1940 Sandberg and others started producing fake identity cards to enable Jews to avoid deportation.

The only way the fakes could be identified was through the local registry office, so a group including Sandberg decided to destroy the building in 1943. Most were caught and shot, but Sandberg escaped and went into hiding for over a year. It was during this period that he created his *Experimenta Typographica* catalogues – booklets featuring quotes, papers and carefully torn type. These would inform much of his later work for the Stedelijk.

Sandberg took the role of the museum very seriously and was a keen advocate of it reaching out to its audience. When he became director he whitewashed its gloomy interior, and expanded its remit to include photography, typography, industrial design and film. He was also acutely aware of the power of graphic material (posters, signage, catalogues, etc.) in attracting and connecting with the museum's audiences, and catalogues were issued several months before exhibitions. In 1940 Sandberg was the first designer to introduce the 'SM' logo for the museum, a device that was used for many years.

Above Portrait of Sandberg, 1955.

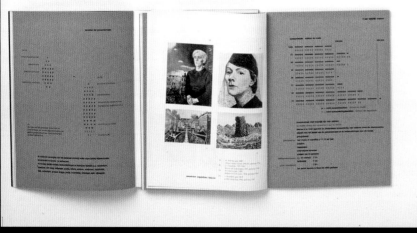

9 years at the Stedelijk Museum,
1945–54, exhibition catalogue, 1954.

Willem Sandberg

1890

1897 Born in Amersfoort, the Netherlands.

1900

1910

1920

1928 Begins working with the Stedelijk Museum.

Becomes a member of the Dutch Society for
Arts and Crafts (VANK).

1932 Inspects the treatment of the Prado's collection by the
Spanish Republican government during the Civil War.

1938 Prints and distributes fake identity cards for Jews.

1941 Involved in blowing up the civil registry office.

1943

1945 Becomes director of the Stedelijk Museum.

1950

1960

1970

1980

Dies in Amsterdam, the Netherlands.

1984

Right *The Poster*, exhibition poster for the Stedelijk Museum, Amsterdam, 1950.

Below *Franz Marc, Germaine Richier, Vieira de Silva*, exhibition poster for the Stedelijk Museum, Amsterdam, 1955.

Below right *For Daily Use*, exhibition poster for the Stedelijk Museum, Amsterdam, 1960.

Logo design for Griffin Books, 1950.

'Good visual design is serious in purpose. To inspire improvement and progress demands that the designer perform to the fullest limits of his ability. The designer must think first, work later.'

Ladislav Sutnar

1897–1976

CZECH REPUBLIC

Ladislav Sutnar is responsible for numerous iconic pieces of graphic design, many dealing with complex information, but it is his work for the US telecom company Bell that is particularly notable. By adding parentheses to the new area code – for which he was not credited – Sutnar was responsible for creating a format that became integral to the Bell System's identity, and had a positive impact on the everyday life of millions of American citizens.

After graduating from the School of Applied Arts in Prague, Sutnar became a professor, and then director, of the State School of Graphic Arts. Although often eclipsed by contemporaries Moholy-Nagy and El Lissitzky, he was a very successful designer, applying his Modernist sensibility to everything from magazine covers to glassware, textiles, porcelain and educational toys.

In 1938, with a raft of awards for exhibition designs already under his belt, Sutnar was appointed to design the Czech pavilion for the 1939 New York World's Fair. In 1938 Hitler had partitioned Sutnar's homeland, and when Sutnar was sent to officially remove the contents of the exhibit in April 1939, he decided to proceed with the exhibition, in collaboration with fellow expatriates, and with the funding of compatriot organizations. Sutnar – by now a marked man – chose to remain in the US, becoming one of many émigrés from Eastern Europe based in New York at the time.

One of Sutnar's most enduring relationships was with Knud Lönberg-Holm, the director of information research for Sweet's Catalog Service, where Sutnar became art director – a position he held for nearly 20 years. Described as 'the Rogers and Hammerstein of information design', the pair produced an immense body of work for the company, and also went on to write a series of highly influential design books.

In addition to his work for Sweet's and Bell, Sutnar created identities for clients such as Addo-X, Vera scarves and Carr's shopping plaza. In 1961, a travelling retrospective originating in Cincinnati and supported by his friends, 'Ladislav Sutnar: Visual Design in Action', provided the foundation for a book of the same name. Sutnar funded the book himself, and with a cover price of $15 (a considerable amount at the time), it did not become a best-seller; today, however, it is a much sought-after collector's item.

Above Portrait of Sutnar.

Addo-X, lithograph, 1958–59.

Below *Catalog Design,* book, 1944.

Bottom *Visual Design in Action,*
poster, 1961.

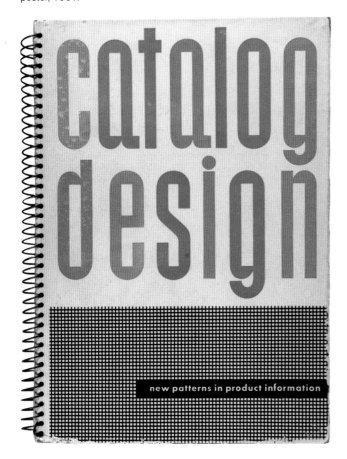

The American Institute of Graphic Arts presents "Sutnar : visual design in action", an exhibition on view – free at

the Pepsi-Cola Exhibition Gallery, 500 Park Avenue, NY, August 2 to 30 (Monday through Saturday, 9 am to 6 pm)

originated by The Contemporary Arts Center, Cincinnati, in cooperation with Champion Papers of Hamilton, Ohio

Ladislav
Sutnar

Ladislav Sutnar

1890

1897 Born in Pilsen, Czech Republic.

1900

1910

1920

1930

1932 Becomes the director of Prague's State School of Graphic Arts.

1934 His first one-man show, 'Ladislav Sutnar and the New Typography', opens in Prague.

1939 Travels to the United States for the New York World's Fair.

1941 Becomes the art director for Sweet's Catalog Service.

1944 Publishes Catalog Design: New Patterns in Product Information with Knud Lönberg-Holm.

1950

1961 Travelling retrospective 'Ladislav Sutnar: Visual Design in Action'.

1970

1976 Dies in New York City, US.

HARPER'S
BAZAAR

TRAVEL
CALIFORNIA
FLORIDA
CRUISES
WHITE
DRESSES
BATH

BATHING
SUITS
PRINTS
VEILS
HATS
FRANKLY FORTY

JANUARY 1936

50 ¢ 15 FR. IN PARIS. 2/6 IN LONDON.

A.B.

'A good picture must be a completely individual expression which intrigues the viewer and forces him to think.'

Alexey Brodovitch

1898–1971

RUSSIA

Overseeing the design of *Harper's Bazaar* magazine for 24 years, Alexey Brodovitch was the consummate art director. He set new standards in editorial design, combining photography and type to great effect, and commissioning some of the most exciting photographers, designers and artists of the day to create page upon page of exhilarating layouts. Constantly striving for perfection, Brodovitch understood the need to continually move forward. As he wisely observed, 'What is good today may be a cliché tomorrow.'

Despite receiving no formal art or design training, after fighting in World War I Brodovitch moved to Paris, where – designing everything from posters to packaging and fabric, as well as costumes for the Ballets Russes – he soon gained a reputation for his superlative design skills. There he also created his first layouts, for the art magazines *Arts et Métiers* and *Cahiers d'Art*.

Brodovitch moved from Europe to the US in 1930 when he was invited to set up an advertising and design department by the Pennsylvannia Museum and School of Industrial Art, Philadelphia. His experimental Design Laboratory class attracted huge numbers of students. In 1934, after visiting an exhibition curated by Brodovitch at the Art Directors Club in New York, Carmel Snow (then editor of *Harper's Bazaar*), asked him to become the magazine's art director. Brodovitch's subsequent redesign completed its transformation from straight fashion to lifestyle magazine.

At a time when illustration dominated fashion magazines, Brodovitch commissioned a raft of photographers (many of whom were former students), including Brassaï, Bill Brandt, Lisette Model, Richard Avedon and Henri Cartier-Bresson, as well as more traditional artists, such as Cassandre (p. 40), Dalí and Man Ray. He continually strove for new ways to entertain his readers, and was driven by the need to innovate: 'This disease of our age is boredom… The way to combat this is by invention – by surprise.' His playful approach, his wilful disregard for the grid and his use of techniques such as photomontage, hand-drawn type and cut paper elevated his magazine spreads to works of art in themselves.

While *Harper's Bazaar* is the magazine that will always be associated with Brodovitch, there is another publication that beautifully illustrates his masterful approach to editorial design. Created in collaboration with art director Frank Zachary and printer George S. Rosenthal, *Portfolio* set new standards for magazine design, and was unusual in that it featured exciting visual content, but made a strong design statement itself. Designed to appeal to visual artists, only three issues of *Portfolio* were ever published, between 1949 and 1950.

Opposite *Harper's Bazaar* cover, January 1936.

Above Portrait of Brodovitch.

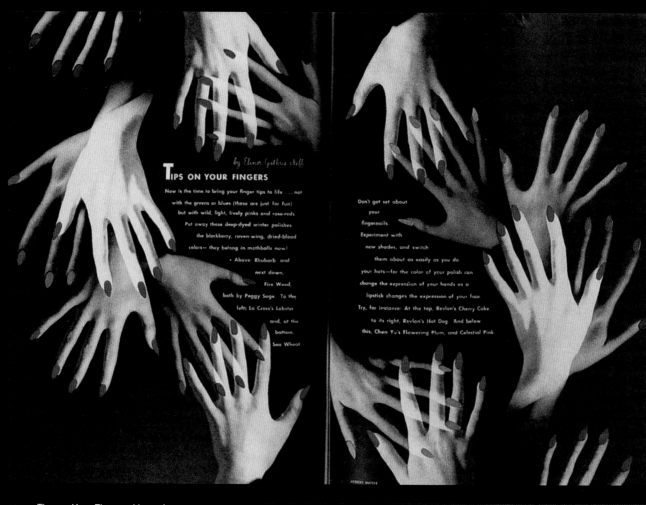

Above *Tips on Your Fingers*, *Harper's Bazaar* article, April 1941 (photography by Herbert Matter).

Right Cover of *Portfolio*, no 1, winter 1950.

Above Mock-up spreads for *Harper's Bazaar*, 1940s.

Alexey Brodovitch

1890

1898 Born in Ogolitchi, Russia.

1900

1910

1920 Moves to Paris, France.

1930 Moves to Philadelphia, US. Becomes art director of *Harper's Bazaar*.

1934 Becomes art director of *Harper's Bazaar*.

1940

1949 Becomes the art director of *Portfolio* magazine.

1958 Resigns from *Harper's Bazaar* after 24 years.

1960

1971 Dies in Le Thor, France.

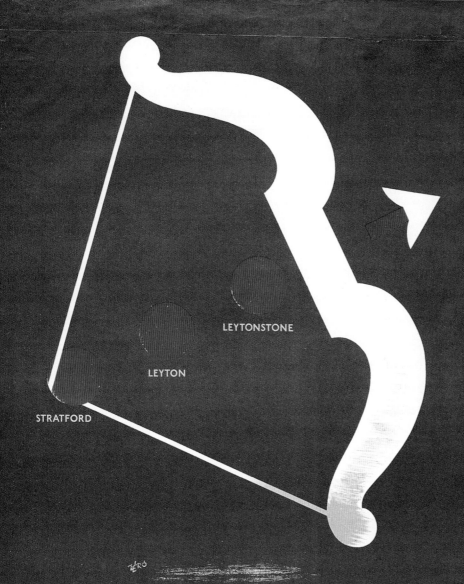

Central Line Eastern Extension, poster
for London Transport, 1946–47.

'The task itself is the vitalising element and no formula can fit two different projects.'

Hans Schleger

1898–1976

GERMANY

One of many European émigrés to arrive in Britain in the period leading up to World War II, Hans Schleger made a huge impact on its visual landscape with a range of public-service and commercial posters, and highly visible corporate identities for companies such as the British Sugar Corporation and the John Lewis Partnership.

After studying at the School of Arts and Crafts in Berlin, Schleger designed promotional pieces for the Hagenbeck film company, before moving to New York and setting up as a freelance commercial artist. He adopted the name 'Zéró' (a homage to the reductive qualities of Modernism), and when his work was embraced by the advertising industry, set up a studio on Madison Avenue. He returned to Berlin in 1929 after the Wall Street Crash, and worked for the English advertising agency Crawfords, until eventually fleeing to Britain to escape the Nazi movement in 1932.

In Berlin, Schleger had met fellow designer Edward McKnight Kauffer (p. 12) who took him under his wing, introducing him to a new artistic community and several clients, including Shell, BP and London Transport, for whom he designed many posters between 1935 and 1947. These covered subjects such as staying safe in blackouts, the new Central Line extension, and travelling by Tube. Schleger also produced a number of iconic instructional posters for the Ministries of Agriculture and Food – urging people to grow their own food and eat their greens – and a series for the Royal Society for the Prevention of Accidents and the GPO.

In 1935 Schleger received another important commission from London Transport – to redesign the humble bus stop sign. A rationalization of the existing roundel, Schleger's design set the tone for the standardization that was later instigated by Harold Hutchison after the organization's nationalization in 1947.

Schleger set up his own studio in the late 1940s, but between 1952 and 1962 he also worked part-time for the London-based advertising agency Mather & Crowther. It was during this period that he worked on corporate identities for high-profile clients such as Mac Fisheries, British Sugar Corporation, Finmar furniture and the John Lewis Partnership. His work had a light touch and a sense of fun, giving it mass appeal, while retaining a sense of integrity.

Ken Garland (p. 164) recalls being stunned to discover that the two different designers who he held in great esteem – Zéró and Hans Schleger – were in fact the same person: 'I know of no designer working at that time in this country who was equally at home with a hand-drawn poster, a complex corporate identity programme or an exacting piece of typographic design.'

Above Portrait of Schleger.

Address Your Letters Plainly, poster, 1942.

Hans Schleger

- 1890
- **1898** Born in Kempen, Germany.
- 1900
- 1910 Studies at the Berlin School of Arts and Crafts.
- **c.1919** Moves to New York and establishes Zéró studio.
- 1920
- **1924** Returns to Berlin to work in the German office of Crawfords.
- **1929** Moves to UK.
- **1932**
- 1940
- **1946** *The Practice of Design* published.
- **1948** Becomes Fellow of Society of Industrial Artists.
- 1950 Joins the ad agency Mather & Crowther.
- **1952** Becomes a member of the Alliance Graphique Nationale.
- **1955** Created Royal Designer for Industry.
- **1959** Speaker at World Design Conference in Tokyo.
- **1960**
- 1970
- **1976** Dies in London, UK.

'Words divide, images unite.'
– Otto Neurath

Gerd Arntz

1900–1988

GERMANY

Enlisted by the Viennese philosopher and social scientist Otto Neurath to visualize his International System Of Typographic Picture Education (Isotype), Gerd Arntz went on to oversee the production of thousands of unique symbols. Depicting everything from work and domestic life to politics and the economy, Arntz, Neurath and Neurath's wife, Marie Reidemeister, developed a universal language that aimed to help ordinary people foster a greater understanding of the world they lived in.

A successful artist prior to his association with Isotype, Arntz trained at the School of Arts and Crafts in Barmen. Politically active throughout his career, his early years were spent in the Prussian Army and working in his parent's factory. In 1920 he joined the Cologne Progressive Artists Group, creating a series of woodcuts that depicted subjects including war, the oppression of workers and the gap between rich and poor, reflecting the challenging economic conditions in Germany in the 1920s and 1930s.

Otto Neurath, the founder and director of the Gesellschafts- und Wirtschaftsmuseum (Museum for Social and Economic Affairs) in Vienna, spotted Arntz's work and asked him to move to Vienna to work on his ambitious information design project. Known at that time as the Vienna Method of Visual Statistics, it was a way of conveying complex information using a system of images that could be understood by anyone. These simplified pictorial representations both reflected, and acted as a tool to aid, the growing social change taking place in Vienna at the time. What distinguished Neurath's system was that greater numbers were represented by repetition of symbols, rather than symbols that had been scaled up proportionally.

In 1930, Neurath published *Gesellschaft und Wirtschaft*, an atlas illustrating 100 different sets of statistics using a series of woodcut symbols art-directed by Arntz. Isotype (as it became known) attracted attention from around the world; a similar institute was set up by Neurath in Russia, and exhibitions were held in New York, London, Berlin and The Hague. Arntz would eventually oversee the production of more than 4,000 different pictograms for Isotype.

In 1934 Arntz, Neurath and Reidemeister fled Nazi Germany for The Hague, setting up the Foundation for Visual Education there. In 1940, Neurath and Reidemeister escaped to Britain to set up the Isotype Institute in Oxford, which was employed by the Ministry of War to help with various wartime publications. Arntz remained in the Netherlands, but despite his anti-Nazi beliefs (as displayed in a series of hard-hitting woodcuts published in a Communist magazine), he was conscripted by the German Army in 1943. After the war, he returned to The Hague, continuing his work through the Foundation for Statistics.

Above Portrait of Arntz.

Economic Scheme

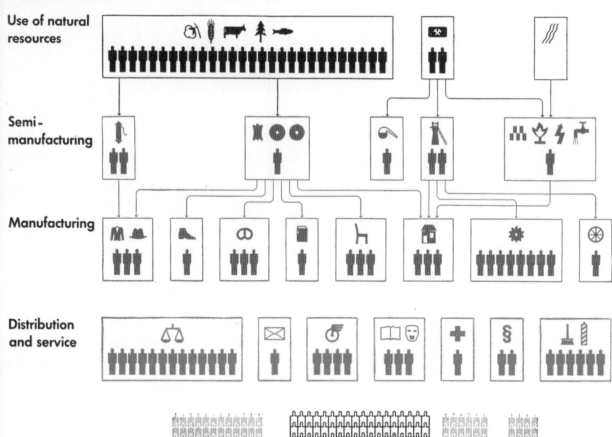

Use of natural resources

Semi-manufacturing

Manufacturing

Distribution and service

Each man symbol represents 5 per thousand population

young people

people working within economic scheme

housewives, students etc.

old people

Above Economic Scheme, published in *Modern Man in the Making*, 1939.

Right People, Isotype, 1928–65.

Opposite *Arbeitslose* [*Unemployed*], published in *Gesellschaft und Wirtschaft*, 1930.

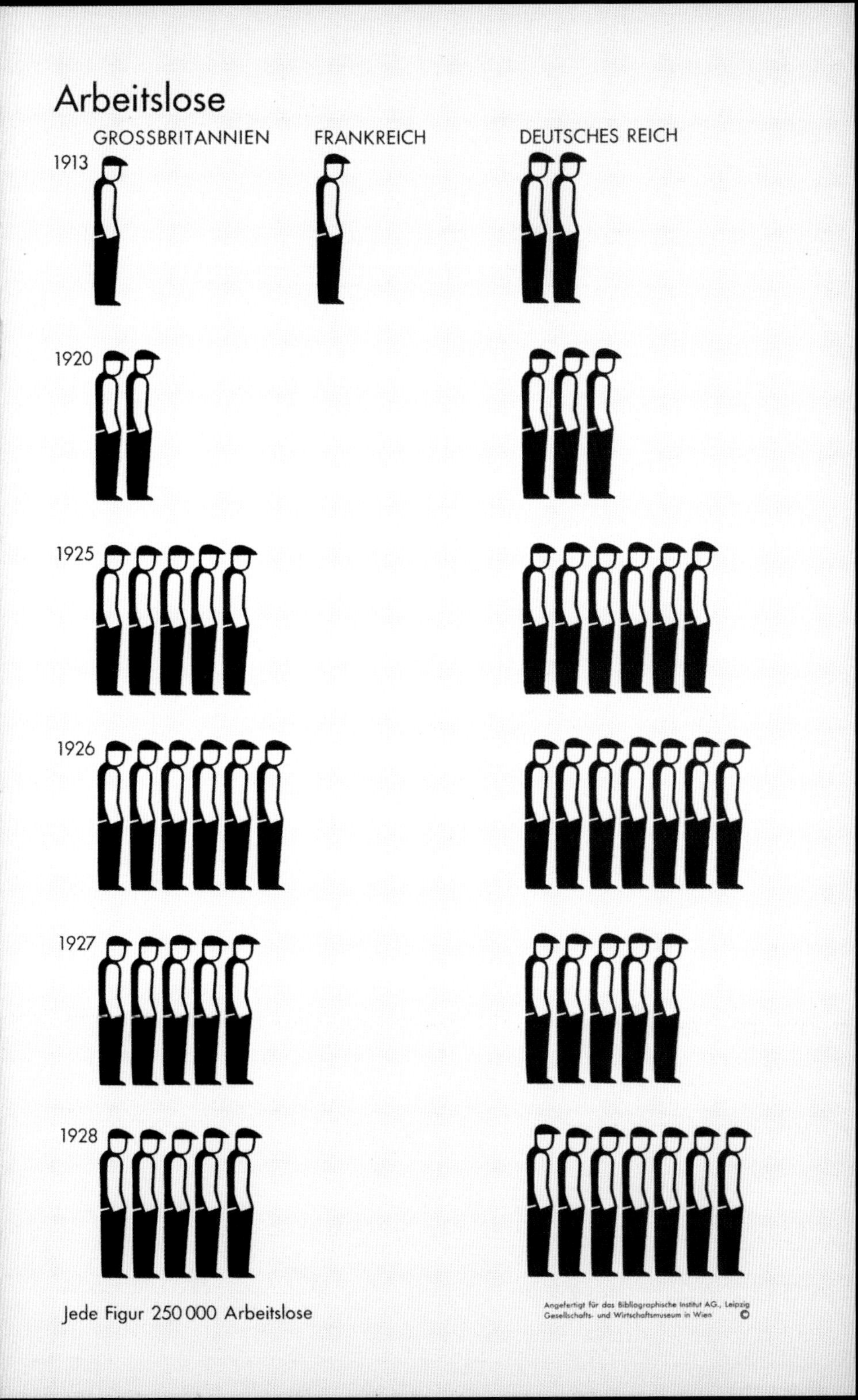

Arbeitslose

GROSSBRITANNIEN	FRANKREICH	DEUTSCHES REICH

1913

1920

1925

1926

1927

1928

Jede Figur 250 000 Arbeitslose

Angefertigt für das Bibliographische Institut AG., Leipzig
Gesellschafts- und Wirtschaftsmuseum in Wien ©

1900 — Born in Remscheid, Germany.

1910

1920

1928 — Introduced to Otto Neurath. Works at the Museum for Social and Economic Affairs, Vienna.
1929 — The atlas Gesellschaft und Wirtschaft is published.
1930 — Moves to The Hague.

1934

1940

1943 — Conscripted by the German Army.

1950

1960

1970

1980

1988 — Dies in The Hague, the Netherlands.

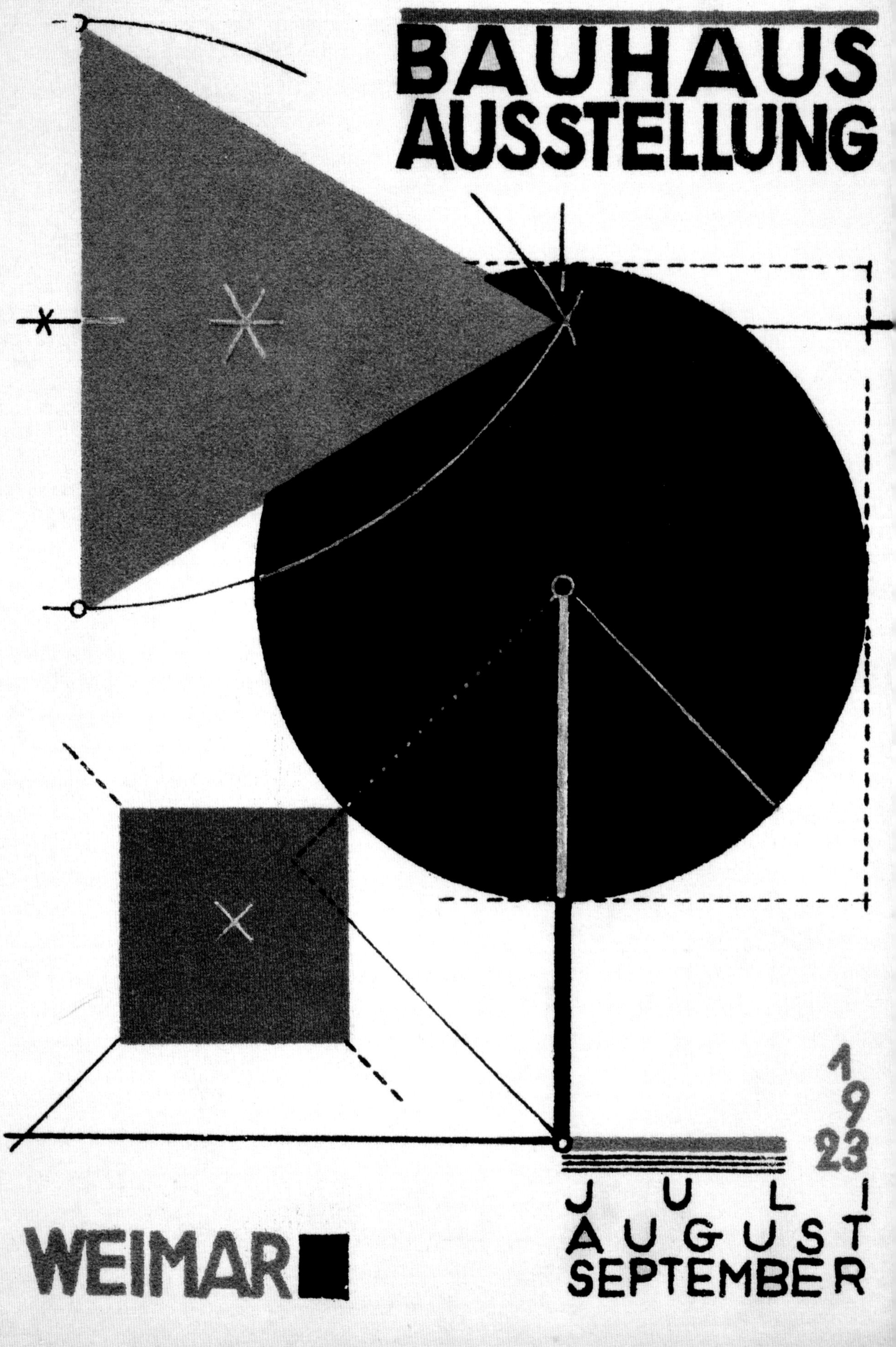

BAUHAUS
AUSSTELLUNG

1
9
23

JULI
AUGUST
SEPTEMBER

WEIMAR

> 'Is this pretense of the handwritten alphabet still justified at a time when almost all that is "written" is either printed on typewriters or on printing presses?'

Herbert Bayer

1900–1985

AUSTRIA

A key member of the Bauhaus and its last surviving master, Bayer studied in Weimar before becoming a leading member of the faculty in Dessau. His lower-case-only sans-serif typeface would define the school's visual language. The driving force behind the exhibition 'Bauhaus 1919–1928' at New York's Museum of Modern Art, Bayer is often credited as one of the first graphic designers to bring the school's Modernist philosophies to the corporate design culture of the US.

After a series of apprenticeships, Bayer joined the Bauhaus School in Weimar in 1921, studying under Johannes Itten and Wassily Kandinsky. He returned to teach at the Bauhaus' new home in Dessau in 1925, where he was appointed the head of its new print and advertising workshop. He also ran a lettering course, teaching his students the principles of the 'new typography', including that of Kleinschreibung, the use of solely lower-case characters. This was particularly radical in German, where every noun starts with an uppercase letter. Universal – Bayer's experimental circular-based typeface, comprised entirely of lower-case letters – was used in much of the school's printed material.

Bayer left the Bauhaus in 1928 and moved to Berlin to pursue his design work, photography and painting. As a director of the advertising agency Studio Dorland, he brought his Modernist aesthetic to *Paris Vogue* and *Die Neue Line* magazines, for which he worked as art director.

Despite the growing intolerance for Modernism (which was labelled 'degenerate art'), Bayer remained in Nazi Germany and accepted several cultural commissions from the National Socialist party until eventually fleeing to the US in 1938. In New York, he designed covers for *Fortune* and *Harper's Bazaar*, as well as instigating exhibitions for MoMA, including the 1938 'Bauhaus 1919–1928', curated by Walter Gropius and designed by Bayer. His striking exhibition catalogue design would prove an invaluable resource for US designers and educators keen to learn about the early Bauhaus.

In 1946, at the invitation of Walter Paepcke, chief executive of the Container Corporation of America (CCA), Bayer moved to Aspen, Colorado, where he worked as a consultant for the CCA, as well as for other clients, such as the Aspen Cultural Center and the Atlantic Richfield Company (ARCO). In 1953, the CCA commissioned him to design its *World Geographic Atlas*. A *tour de force* that took Bayer and fellow designers Martin Rosenzweig, Henry Gardiner and Masato Nakagawa three years to complete, this meticulously researched and beautifully illustrated volume is described by Steven Heller as 'a monument to Bayer's singular vision, a precursor to current trends in information design, and an example of how complex data can be made accessible.'

Opposite *Druck Postcard No. 11* for the Bauhaus Exhibition in Weimar, by Herbert Bayer, Entwurf Reineck & Klein, summer 1923.

Above Portrait of Bayer.

Poster for Olivetti, 1959.

Herbert Bayer

- **1900** Born in Haag am Hausruck, Austria.
- 1910
- **1921** Studies at the Bauhaus School, Weimar, Germany.
- **1925** Teaches at the Bauhaus in Dessau, Germany.
- 1930
- **1937** Flees to Italy to escape Nazi Germany.
- **1938** Moves to New York and arranges 'Bauhaus 1919–1928' at MoMA.
- 1940
- **1946** Moves to Aspen, Colorado, US.
- 1950
- **1953** Designs the *World Geographic Atlas*.
- 1960
- 1970
- 1980
- **1985** Dies in California, US.

abcdefghi
jklmnopqr
stuvwxyz

d

HERBERT BAYER: Abb.1. Alfabet
„9" und „k" sind noch als
unfertig zu betrachten

Beispiel eines Zeichens
in größerem Maßstab
Präzise optische Wirkung

sturm blond

Abb. 2. Anwendung

Above Universal Alphabet, typeface,
1925.

Below *Things to Come*, letterpress,
c. 1938.

'A poster is to be viewed on the street. It should integrate architectural groups and enrich the spreading façades. It should enliven not the individual advertisement board or building, but rather the huge blocks of stone and the vast area as a whole.'

A. M. Cassandre

1901–1968

UKRAINE

A. M. Cassandre was the consummate poster designer – his bold, geometric compositions convey a strong message while being objects of beauty in themselves. *'A good poster is a visual telegram,'* he said. Cassandre's are the perfect fusion of art and commerce.

He designed over 200 posters, and is often credited as being the first designer to create a poster that could be read from a moving vehicle. Born Adolphe Jean-Marie Mouron in Ukraine, he studied painting at the École des Beaux-Arts and the Académie Julian in Paris. It was an exciting time to be in the city, with new forms of artistic expression such as Cubism, Purism and Futurism being explored by pioneering artists including Picasso, Léger and Braque. Influenced by this, as well as the nascent Art Deco aesthetic that was beginning to emerge, Cassandre's first poster was for the furniture shop Au Bûcheron. It earned him first prize at the 1925 Exposition Internationale des Arts Décoratifs et Industriels Modernes.

Cassandre found himself in great demand, and in 1927 formed the advertising company Alliance Graphique with Charles Loupot and Maurice Moyrand. Clients included international railway companies and shipping lines such as the Compagnie des Wagons-Lits, Nord Express and Normandie. Cassandre's striking airbrushed posters evoked the glamour of travel perfectly and, in contrast to most travel posters, suggested to the viewer that the journey was as important as the destination. Cassandre's use of type in his posters was

bold and assured, and he was commissioned by the type foundry Deberny & Peignot to create several of his own display typefaces, including the geometric Bifur (1929), Acier Noir (1936) and Peignot (1937).

International recognition soon came, and in 1936 Cassandre was the first graphic designer to be given a solo exhibition at MoMA in New York. This led to commissions from *Harper's Bazaar* and *Fortune* magazine, as well as the Container Corporation of America. Cassandre moved to New York, but returned to Paris, where he worked on set designs for theatre and opera.

Throughout the 1920s and 30s Cassandre created posters for many well-known brands, including Bugatti, Pernod and Pathé, and his masterful designs were used to promote everything from restaurants to radios, cigarettes to chocolate. One of his most famous designs was a poster for Dubonnet, which (like stills from an animation) effortlessly conveys in three consecutive drawings the feeling of drinking a glass of the aperitif. Like all of the best advertising, it was an idea that had been cleverly distilled to its very essence; it was clearly defined, easily understood and had an immediate impact.

Opposite *Dubonnet, Vin Tonique au Quinquina*, 1932

Above Portrait of Cassandre.

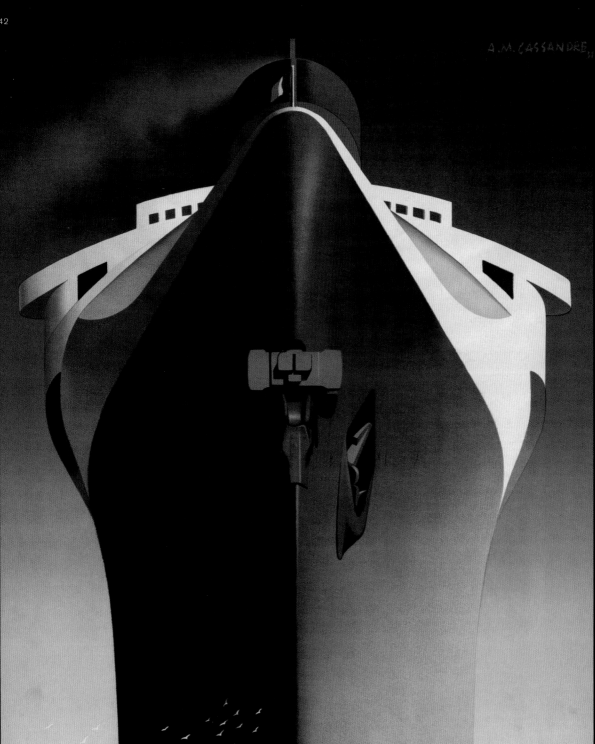

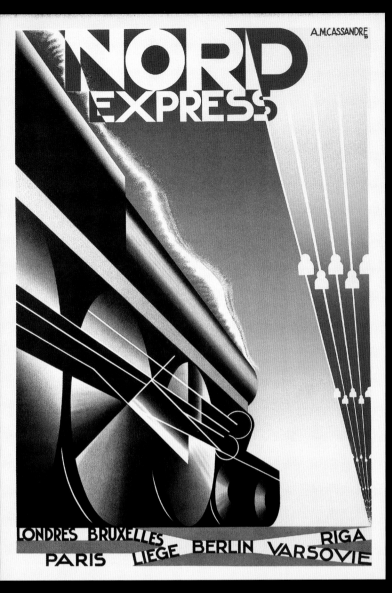

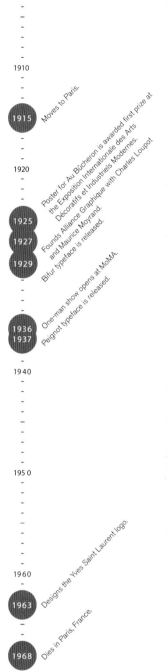

A. M. Cassandre

- **1901** Born in Kharkiv, Ukraine.
- 1910
- **1915** Moves to Paris.
- 1920
- **1925** Poster for Au Bûcheron is awarded first prize at the Exposition Internationale des Arts Décoratifs et Industriels Modernes.
- **1927** Founds Alliance Graphique with Charles Loupot and Maurice Moyrand.
- **1929** Bifur typeface is released.
- **1936** One-man show opens at MoMA.
- **1937** Peignot typeface is released.
- 1940
- 1950
- 1960
- **1963** Designs the Yves Saint Laurent logo.
- **1968** Dies in Paris, France.

Opposite *Normandie, NY*, poster, 1935.

Above *Nord Express Paris Varsovie*, poster, 1927.

Left *Pivolo Aperitif*, poster, 1924.

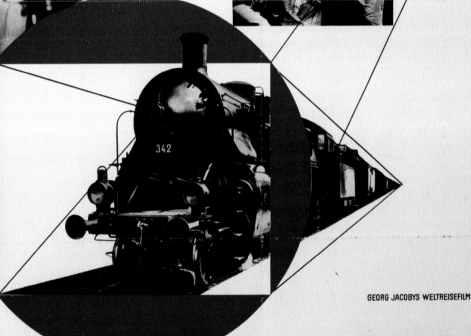

Poster for the film *Die Frau ohne Namen,*
Zweiter Teil (The Woman without a Name,
Part II), offset lithograph, 1927.

'Perfect typography is certainly the most elusive of all arts. Sculpture in stone alone comes near it in obstinacy.'

Jan Tschichold

1902–1974

GERMANY

Although Jan Tschichold is best known for his era-defining 1928 work, *Die Neue Typographie*, in which he delivers an uncompromising set of typographic rules, in later years he rejected this dogmatic approach and took a more moderate stance, particularly towards editorial design. This was an area in which he excelled, working for numerous publishers – including Penguin Books, for whom he developed an exacting set of guidelines and a logo that remained unchanged for nearly 50 years.

With a passion for typography more than likely inherited from his sign painter father, Tschichold studied calligraphy at the Leipzig Academy for Graphic Arts under Walter Tiemann. In 1923, the 21-year-old Tschichold visited the first exhibition held at the Bauhaus in Weimar. It made a huge impression on him, and (in conjunction with his growing interest in the Constructivist movement), informed his vision for a radical new approach to design and typography. The interest Tschichold received for his 1925 *Elementare Typographie* insert paved the way for his masterwork. Completed in 1928, *Die Neue Typographie* (*The New Typography*) advocated asymmetrical layouts, a grid system and dynamic type with the emphasis on clarity and hierarchy.

In 1933, Tschichold and his wife were arrested (due to his 'un-German' typography) and subsequently held under house arrest by the Nazis for six weeks. They escaped and fled to Switzerland, where Tschichold worked as a book designer. He began to see parallels between *Die Neue Typographie's* dogmatic approach and that of the Third Reich, claiming that his book's 'impatient

attitude conforms to the German bent for the absolute, and its military will to regulate and its claim to absolute power reflect those fearful components of the German character [that] set loose Hitler's power and the Second World War'.

He subsequently advocated a flexible, humanist approach that had more in common with neoclassicism, which was evident in the book design work he created later in London – first for Lund Humphries in 1935, and then between 1947 and 1949 as art director for Penguin Books. Tschichold set to work rationalizing the design of Penguin's various series, introducing a standard template for all books, drafting a set of Composition Rules for its compositors and printers, and redesigning Edward Young's original penguin symbol.

Despite being one of the instigators of what he called 'the new traditionalism', Tschichold did not reject the philosophy of *Die Neue Typographie* outright. He came to consider that the subject matter might determine the typographic treatment, making it a suitable approach for promoting subjects such as modern architecture or industrial design. It did not have any place in book design though – Tschichold himself described the experience of reading page upon page of sans-serif text as akin to 'genuine torture'.

Above Portrait of Tschichold.

gewerbemuseum basel   ausstellung

der berufsphotograph

sein werkzeug — seine arbeiten

8. mai —— 6. juni

werktags	14-19	
mittwochs	14-19	19-21
sonntags	10-12	14-19
eintritt frei		

JAN TSCHICHOLD

DIE NEUE TYPOGRAPHIE

EIN HANDBUCH FÜR ZEITGEMÄSS SCHAFFENDE

BERLIN 1928

VERLAG DES BILDUNGSVERBANDES DER DEUTSCHEN BUCHDRUCKER

Schema der bisherigen Anordnung von Klischees in Zeitschriften.
Schematische, zweilos geordnete Mittelachsengruppierung.
„Dekorativ", unpraktisch und unökonomisch (= unschön).

Auf Mitte geschlossene lebende Kolumnentitel sollten vermieden werden. Sie würden neben den asymmetrischen Abschnittteln unharmonisch wirken. Am besten stellt man sie — besser ohne irgendwelche Linien darunter! — nach außen und zeichnet sie durch Grotesk aus. Wenn schon eine Linie verwendet werden soll, vermeide man fettfeine und Doppellinien. Einfache stumpffeine bis sechspunktfette sind dann am besten.

Ein vernünfig denkender Mensch kann sich nur wundern, zu welchen unmöglichen Folgen die Starrheit des Mittelachsenprinzips hinsichtlich der Klischeeanordnung geführt hat. An den zwei hier abgebildeten Schemen habe ich versucht, den Unterschied zwischen der alten Zwangsjacke und einer vernünftigen Anordnung der Klischees darzulegen. Ich habe dabei absichtlich Klischees von verschiedenen, zum Teil zufälligen Breiten fingiert, weil man mit solchen wohl immer (in Zukunft infolge der Normung allerdings in geringerem Maße) wird rechnen müssen. Normbreite Klischees würden, wozu es keines Beweises bedarf, das Problem noch sehr vereinfachen. Auf welch kompliziertem Wege man es bisher zu lösen versuchte, geht aus der linken Abbildung deutlich hervor. Krampfhaft sind die Abbildungen auf Mitte gestellt worden, wodurch das teure und umständliche Verschmälern des Spaltensatzes notwendig wurde. Das neue Schema rechts spricht für

214

Schema für eine richtige Einordnung derselben Klischees in denselben Satzspiegel.
Konstruktiv, sinngemäß und ökonomisch (= schön).

sich selbst; es ist offenbar, um wieviel einfacher und dabei schöner diese neue Form ist. Als Kontrastform zu den meist dunklen Klischees und dem Grau der Schrift wirken die, neben den nicht die volle Spalten- oder Spiegelbreite erreichenden Klischees verbleibenden weißen Flächen erfreulich, während der frühere um die Klischees herumgeführte Satz, oft von nur Konkordanzbreite, geradezu den Eindruck von Geiz erweckt.

Nach Möglichkeit müssen die Klischees in engster Nähe des zugehörigen Textes stehen.

Ebenso wie die Abschnittitel, sollten auch die Unterschriften der Abbildungen (wie in diesem Buch) nicht mehr auf Mitte gestellt werden, sondern, wenn sie darunter stehen, im allgemeinen links beginnen. Eine Auszeichnung durch fette oder halbfette Grotesk intensiviert den Gesamteindruck der Seite. Daß man sie vielfach auch seitwärts stellen kann, geht ebenfalls aus dem Schema der neuen Klischeegruppierung hervor.

Bei den Klischees selbst sollte man das unschöne „Rändchen" unbedingt vermeiden. Das glatt abgeschnittene Klischee wirkt angenehmer und frischer. Die merkwürdigen Wolken, auf denen nicht nur kleinere Gegenstände, sondern auch schwere Maschinen zu schweben pflegen, sind aus ästhetischen Gründen und der Druckschwierigkeiten wegen bedingungslos abzulehnen.

215

Opposite Poster for *Der Berufsphotograph* exhibition, 1938.

Opposite below *Die Neue Typographie (The New Typography)*, book layout, 1928.

Below *Napoleon,* film poster, 1927.

Jan Tschichold

- 1900
- **1902** Born in Leipzig, Germany.
- 1910
- **1919** Begins studies at the Leipzig Academy for Graphic Arts.
- **1928** Publishes *Die Neue Typographie (The New Typography)*.
- 1930
- **1933** Flees from Germany to Switzerland.
- **1935** Invited to England by Lund Humphries.
- **1937** Designs the 1938 *Penrose Annual*.
- 1940
- **1947** Appointed art director at Penguin Books.
- 1950
- 1960
- **1967** Designs Sabon typeface.
- 1970
- **1974** Dies in Locarno, Switzerland.

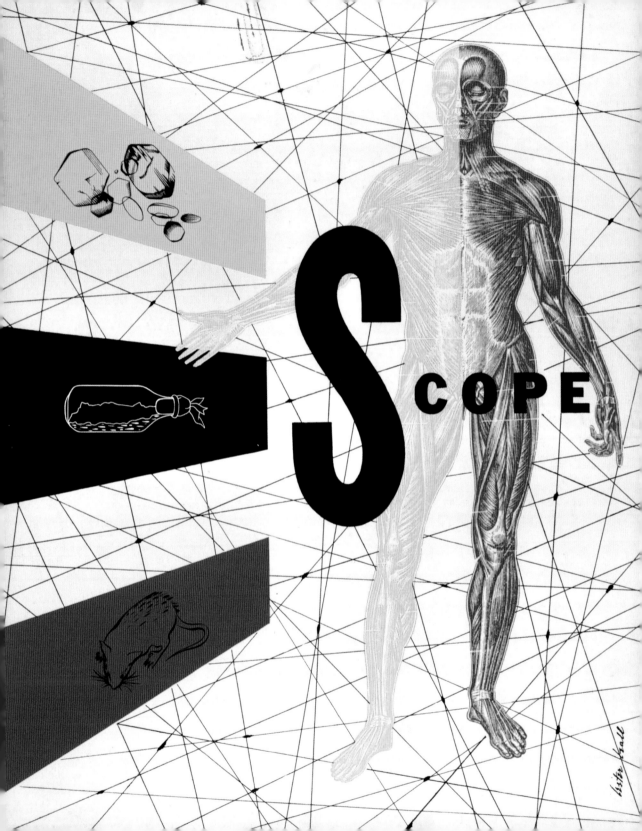

SCOPE

'The moment clients realize that revisions are not an all-you-can-eat buffet, suddenly they realize they are not hungry.'

Lester Beall

1903–1969

USA

Once described as a 'typographic surrealist', although he was heavily influenced by the European avant-garde, Lester Beall was one of the most important home-grown American designers, and in 1937 the first to be honoured with a solo show at the Museum of Modern Art in New York. He not only sold the American dream through his work in advertising, print media and corporate identity, but also lived it, working from an idyllic home and office in upstate New York for much of his career.

Moving from his native Chicago to New York in 1935, Beall continued to maintain his city-based office when he moved to Wilton, Connecticut, the following year. He worked on projects for commercial clients such as *Time* magazine and the *Chicago Tribune*, and in 1937 started the first of three poster series for the Rural Electrification Administration (REA), a federal agency created to help improve quality of life in rural areas. Beall's striking posters promoted the benefits of electricity and plumbing (running water, radio, washing machines and electric light) to farmers. Considered classic pieces of American graphic design, the posters were bold and graphic, using photomontage and primary colours to convey their message.

Beall also took on a considerable amount of editorial work throughout his career, redesigning 20 magazines for the publisher McGraw-Hill, and designing two covers for *Fortune* magazine. In 1944, he became art director of *Scope*, the magazine published by

pharmaceutical company Upjohn, a position he would hold until 1951 (see also p. 64).

In 1950 Beall moved into the property that would become known as Dumbarton Farm, Brookfield, where he converted outbuildings into office and studio space. He took on more staff and subsequently worked on bigger projects for various high-profile clients, including Merrill Lynch, Caterpillar Tractor and the New York Hilton. His 1960 identity for the International Paper Company was his most comprehensive and an early example of the new trend for creating a complete corporate identity – as well as the logo (still in use), Beall created a graphics standard manual that is still considered one of the most rigorous examples of its kind.

Beall very much saw design as a vocation, and was acutely aware of the effect his environment had on his creativity: 'By living and working in the country I felt I could enjoy a more integrated life, and although I still need the periodic stimulation of New York City, the opportunity and creative activity in an area of both beauty and tranquillity seemed to me to far exceed anything that a studio and residence in New York might offer – the way a man lives is essential to the work he produces. The two cannot be separated.'

Above Portrait of Beall.

RADIO

RURAL ELECTRIFICATION ADMINISTRATION

Below *Running Water*, poster for the Rural Electrification Administration, 1937.

Bottom *Don't Let Him Down!*, photolithograph, 1941.

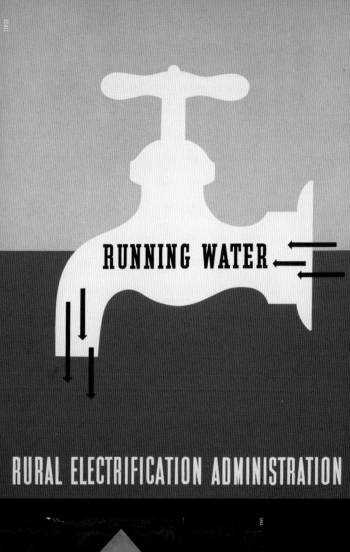

1900

1903 — Born in Missouri, US.

1910

1920

1930

1935 — Moves to New York, US.

1937 — Solo exhibition at MoMA.

1940

1950 — Moves to Dumbarton Farm and sets up his studio.

1960

1962 — 'The Graphic Work of Lester Beall' opens at the American Institute of Graphic Arts in New York.

1969 — Dies in upstate New York.

1973 — Inducted into the Art Directors Club of New York Hall of Fame.

PONTRESINA

Engadin

'Herbert's background is fascinating and enviable. He was surrounded by good graphics and learned from the best.'
– Paul Rand

Herbert Matter

1907–1984

SWITZERLAND

Photography was central to Herbert Matter's work – both in its own right and through techniques such as collage and photomontage, which formed an intrinsic part of his superlative graphic design work. The posters he created for the Swiss National Tourist Office between 1935 and 1936 are a perfect example of his ability to handle type and image with equal aplomb, creating exciting pieces that still resonate today. In 1984 Pentagram's Paula Scher (p. 236) created an affectionate homage to the iconic posters for her client, the Swiss watch manufacturer Swatch.

Matter trained at Geneva's School of Fine Arts in 1927, before heading to Paris to study under Fernand Léger at the Académie Moderne. Influenced by the likes of Man Ray, Matter was already experimenting with darkroom techniques and photomontage. He secured a position at the prestigious Deberny & Peignot type foundry, where he honed his typographic skills, and worked on architecture and poster design under the guidance of both Le Corbusier and A. M. Cassandre (p. 40).

It was on his enforced return to Switzerland (he had not renewed his foreign student visa) that Matter received a commission from the Swiss National Tourist Office to create a series of posters to promote tourism in the region. Matter's vibrant designs, cleverly combining photomontage and typography, gained him international recognition. When he visited Alexey Brodovitch in New York in 1936, Matter saw two of his posters on the wall

in Brodovitch's studio. Brodovitch subsequently commissioned him to work on *Harper's Bazaar*, and Matter decided to stay in New York, working with Studio Associates on photography and shooting covers and spreads for *Vogue* magazine.

In the post-war period Matter worked for a number of high-profile graphic design clients, including the Container Corporation of America, the New Haven Railroad and the Guggenheim Museum. Another long-standing client was the design-led furniture manufacturer Knoll, for whom Matter worked for 12 years, creating its elegant corporate identity and publicity materials.

Matter also had a long association with Yale University, becoming Professor of Photography and Graphic Design in 1952. A retrospective of Matter's work was held in 1977, with an introduction to the catalogue written in poem format by Paul Rand. Rand described Matter as 'a magician' for the way that he combined the creative with the commercial, and highlighted the apparently timeless quality of his designs: 'His work of '32 could have been done in '72 or even '82.'

Opposite *Pontresina Engadin*, poster, 1935.

Above Portrait of Matter by Mercedes Matter, 1939.

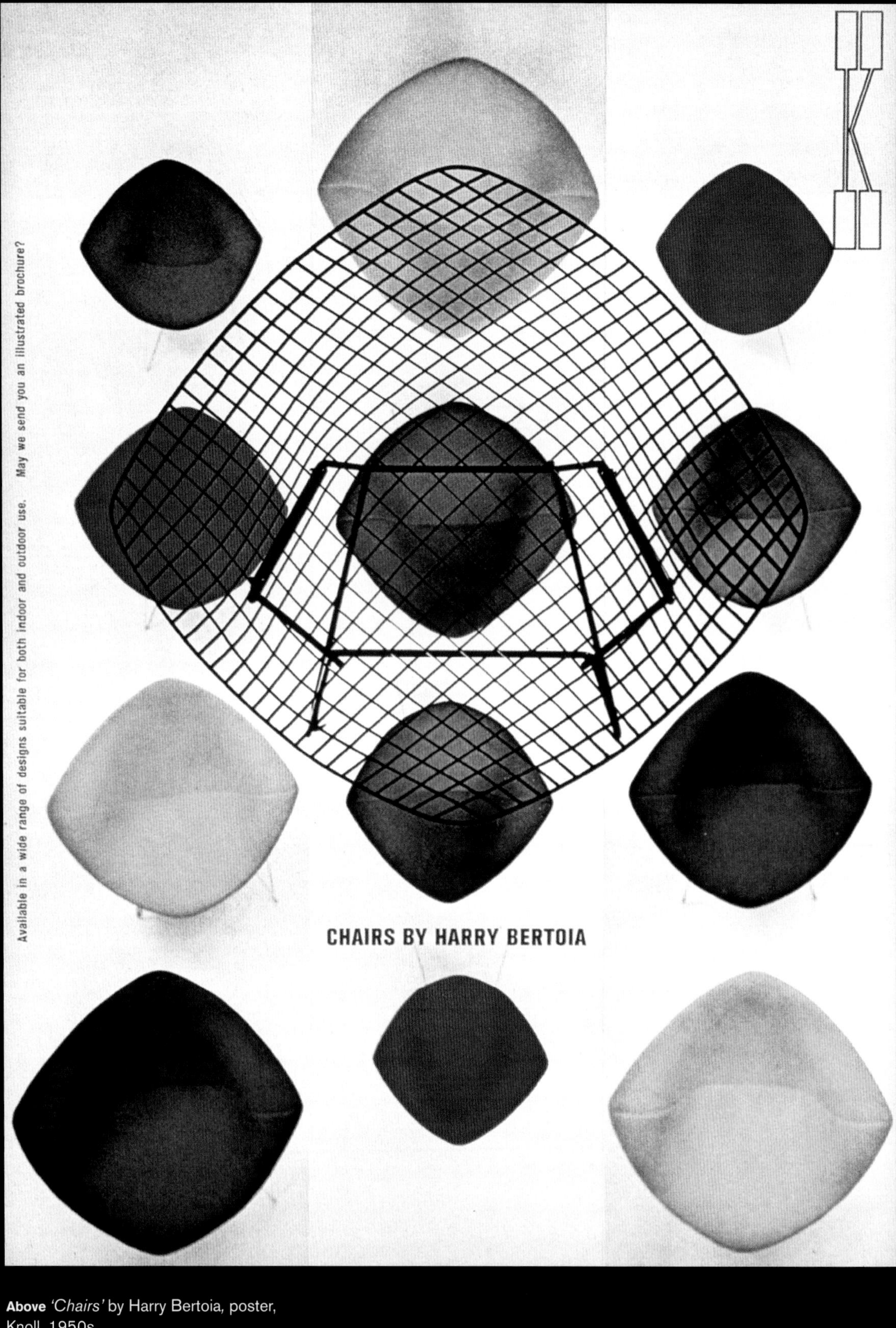

Available in a wide range of designs suitable for both indoor and outdoor use. May we send you an illustrated brochure?

CHAIRS BY HARRY BERTOIA

Above *'Chairs'* by Harry Bertoia, poster,
Knoll, 1950s.

Opposite top *America Calling, Take your
Place in Civilian Defense*, poster, 1941.

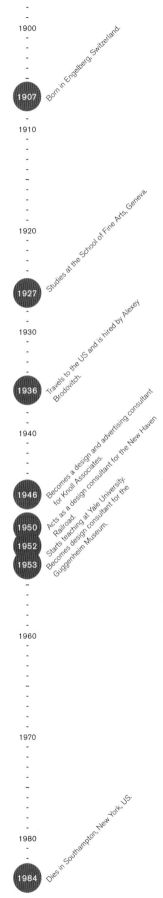

1900

1907   Born in Engelberg, Switzerland.

1910

1920

1927   Studies at the School of Fine Arts, Geneva.

1930

1936   Travels to the US and is hired by Alexey Brodovitch.

1940

1946   Becomes a design and advertising consultant for Knoll Associates.

1950   Acts as a design consultant for the New Haven Railroad.

1952   Starts teaching at Yale University.

1953   Becomes design consultant for the Guggenheim Museum.

1960

1970

1980

1984   Dies in Southampton, New York, US.

Campari, offset lithograph, 1965.

'There should be no such thing as art divorced from life, with beautiful things to look at and hideous things to use.'

Bruno Munari

1907–1998

ITALY

Bruno Munari was a true polymath, moving seamlessly from art to design and everything in between. An accomplished graphic designer, he was also a successful artist and sculptor, an award-winning industrial designer, and the author of numerous books on art and design. Passionate about encouraging children's creativity, he set up a laboratory to explore and encourage it in an art gallery in Milan, and authored many popular children's books, some of which are still in print today.

Despite his many talents, Munari was essentially self-taught. Influenced at an early age by the Italian Futurist movement, his abstract paintings soon caught the eye of its leader, Filippo Marinetti. Encouraged by Marinetti, Munari exhibited widely in Milan, developing a playful approach that many of his more serious contemporaries lacked. This was evident in pieces such as his inventive series of drawings and kinetic sculptures entitled *Useless Machines*.

In 1930 he set up a graphic design studio with Riccardo Castagnedi (known as Ricas) to work on commercial projects, including editorial design for the magazines *La Lettura*, *Natura* and *Il Tempo*, and advertisements for Campari and Shell. Throughout his career, Munari would balance his art with work for commercial clients, spending some time with Studio Boggeri, and working for Pirelli, Olivetti and IBM.

Eventually his fascination with the Futurist movement waned as it became associated with the rise of Fascism, and he became interested instead in Concrete Art, setting up the Concrete Art Movement (Movimento Arte Concreta, MAC) with Gillo Dorfles and Gianni Monnet. Munari felt strongly that it was now design (rather than art) that had the potential to be the most powerful cultural force: 'Culture today is becoming a mass affair, and the artist must step down from his pedestal and be prepared to make a sign for a butcher's shop (if he knows how to do it).' The idea that the public could be involved with, and even create, art was very exciting to Munari. Seeing the potential for this in the new Xerox technology, he installed photocopiers at the various exhibitions he was involved with, including in the Central Pavilion at the 35th Venice Biennale in 1970.

Throughout his long and varied career, Munari wrote extensively on design – in the design magazine *Campo Grafico*, and in his column in the daily newspaper, *Il Giorno*. These columns were later collected and published as the book *Arte Come Mestiere* (*Design as Art*, published in the UK in 1971). Munari was concerned with form, but believed that good design should not just be the prerogative of those who could afford it: 'When the objects we use every day and the surroundings we live in have become in themselves a work of art, then we shall be able to say that we have achieved a balanced life.'

Above Portrait of Munari by Mario De Biasi, 1998.

Below Double-page spread from
Bruno Munari's ABC, 1960.

Opposite above *Design as Art*, cover
design by YES, cover icons by Bruno
Munari, published 1966 (English edition
published by Penguin Books, 1971).

Opposite below Cover of
Drawing the Sun, published
by Edizioni Corraini.

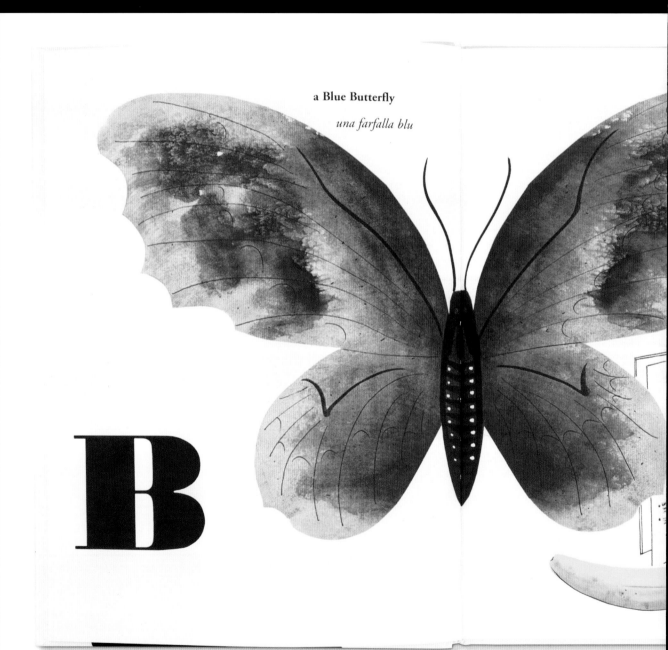

a Blue Butterfly

una farfalla blu

B

una banana
e un libro

a Banana

and a Book

Design as Art
Bruno Munari

Bruno Munari
drawing the sun

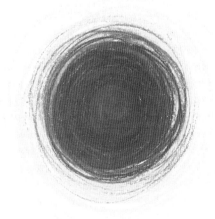

Edizioni Corraini

1907   Born in Milan, Italy.

1910

1920

1930   Founds R+M design studio with Riccardo Castagnedi.

1933   *Macchine Inutili* (*Useless Machines*) series begins.

1940

1948   Cofounds the Movimento Arte Concreta (Concrete Art Movement).

1950

1960   *Bruno Munari's ABC* published.

1966   *Arte Come Mestiere* (UK, *Design as Art*, 1971) is published.

1970

1980

1990

1998   Dies in Milan, Italy.

Konkrete Kunst, poster for the
Kunsthalle Basel, 1944.

'It is becoming apparent that "designers"… have very little imagination, and only rarely go beyond the everyday – indeed, even then, they're not able to acquit themselves honourably. The activity of the designer, as it is practised, taught and invoked, is not unlike that of the hairdresser.'

Max Bill

1908–1994

SWITZERLAND

In addition to his skills as a graphic designer and typographer, Max Bill was also an accomplished painter, architect and product designer. Together with Otl Aicher (p. 140) and Aicher's wife Inge Scholl (1917–98) in 1953 he established the Ulm School of Design, Germany.

Bill trained as a silversmith at the Zurich School of Arts and Crafts, before enrolling at the Bauhaus School in Dessau, with the intention of becoming an architect. He studied for two years under the tutorage of masters including László Moholy-Nagy, Josef Albers, Paul Klee and Wassily Kandinsky. After graduating, he moved to Zurich and established the graphic design studio Bill Reklame, working for cultural institutions, avant-garde architects and commercial clients, such as the furniture company Wohnbedarf.

His rational, Modernist approach had a direct influence on his design, which featured single-case typography and bold layouts. His interest in Concrete Art, led to him being a key member of the Allianz group of artists, formed in 1937.

As part of his multifaceted practice, Bill also wrote and lectured extensively on design. The ideas that were explored in his exhibition 'Die Gute Form' (held at the Swiss Industries Fair in 1949) and in his many writings (including his 1952 book *Form*), led to his hypothesis that the perfect combination of form, function and beauty would result in the magical quality known as 'Gestalt'.

In 1951 Bill returned to Germany, where along with Otl Aicher and Inge Aicher-Scholl, he sketched out the blueprint for a new school of graphic design. Based in Ulm, the School of Design (Hochschule für Gestaltung, HfG) played an important part in the cultural reconstruction of post-war Germany. Comprising departments for visual communication, industrial design, building, information, and later film, the school's progressive four-year curriculum was based on the assimilation of art and science, an awareness of semiotics, and expert knowledge of process and materials, with the emphasis on communication and problem solving.

Bill designed the school's celebrated buildings and became its first rector in 1953. Instantly gaining international recognition, HfG's stellar list of visiting lecturers included Charles and Ray Eames, Buckminster Fuller and Josef Müller-Brockmann (p. 100). The school also developed close links with the manufacturer Braun, collaborating in the mid-1950s with its designer Dieter Rams on a new 'honest' approach to product design. The school eventually closed in 1968 when its government funding was withdrawn.

Above Portrait of Bill by Franz Hubmann, 1955.

kunstgewerbemuseum zürich ausstellung

die farbe

23.januar – 5.märz 1944   geöffnet 10–12 und 14–17 h   montag geschlossen   eintritt 1 fr.   samstag und sonntag frei

Moderne Kunst

aus der Sammlung Peggy Guggenheim

Kunsthaus Zürich

15. April – Mitte Mai 1951   Täglich 10–12 und 14–17 Uhr   Montag geschlossen

Poster for the Munich Olympics, 1972.

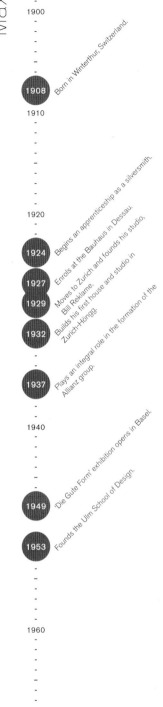

1900

1908 · Born in Winterthur, Switzerland.

1910

1920

1924 · Begins an apprenticeship as a silversmith.

1927 · Enrols at the Bauhaus in Dessau.

1929 · Moves to Zurich and founds his studio, Bill Reklame.

1932 · Builds his first house and studio in Zurich-Höngg.

1937 · Plays an integral role in the formation of the Allianz group.

1940

1949 · 'Die Gute Form' exhibition opens in Basel.

1953 · Founds the Ulm School of Design.

1960

1970

1980

1990 · Dies in Berlin, Germany.

1994

A photograph of the Upjohn Brain
exhibit, 1960.

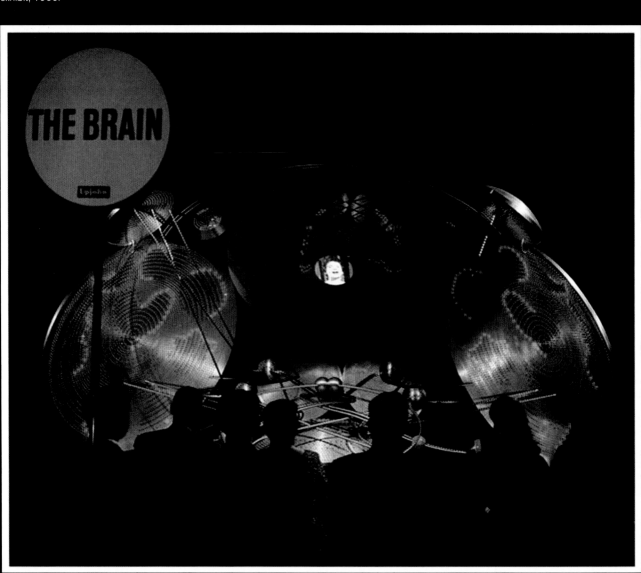

'The creative person who can find himself or herself in this expanding universe is not only fortunate but indispensible.'

Will Burtin

1908–1972

GERMANY

One of the most significant but least celebrated US designers, Will Burtin's commitment to using design to simplify and enhance our understanding of complex, often scientific, ideas means that he is considered by many as the father of 'data visualization'.

Burtin ran a design studio in his native Cologne in the 1930s, but after refusing invitations first from Josef Goebbels, then Adolf Hitler, to join the Nazi Ministry of Propaganda, he emigrated to New York, where he began to forge a successful career, working for the US Federal Works Agency and the pharmaceutical giant Upjohn.

He was drafted into the US Army in 1943, and his skills were put to good use designing training manuals for aerial gunners, which could be easily interpreted regardless of reading ability. *Fortune* magazine then secured his release from the army to become their art editor, a position he held from 1945 to 1949. *Fortune* was a *tour de force* of graphs, charts and graphic devices, aimed at helping the reader understand complex issues.

Will Burtin, Inc. was established in 1949, and work for clients such as IBM, Herman Miller and Eastman Kodak followed. However, it was Burtin's long-standing relationship with Upjohn that produced some of his most memorable work. Burtin art-directed the company's magazine *Scope* (see also p. 48), he redesigned its original marque, and went on to apply his design to all of its drug packaging.

Burtin did not restrict himself to working solely in two dimensions. In 1957, he suggested to Upjohn that he build a giant model of a human cell. After visiting various scientific institutions in the US and Europe to research and gather data, he created a walk-through cell, a million times bigger than real life and with pulsing lights. It was the first time something so complex had been built using plastic, and it was eventually seen by over a million people while on display in New York, Chicago and San Francisco.

The Cell was deemed a huge success by Upjohn, and Burtin went on to create *The Brain* (1960), *Metabolism* (1963), *Genes in Action* (1966) and *Defense of Life* (1969), all with the Director of Special Projects at Upjohn, Dr Bruce McLeod, and a team of model-makers, photographers, lighting designers and electricians.

Passionate about the role and responsibility of design in society, Burtin was a founding member of the International Design Conference at Aspen in 1949, an event that featured speakers from several different disciplines. He also chaired the groundbreaking Vision '65 and Vision '67 conferences, a summit for new ideas and new thinking, which were attended by a wide range of practitioners, including the likes of Richard Buckminster Fuller, Umberto Eco, Max Bill and Jean Tinguely.

Above Portrait of Burtin by Charles Bonnay, 1966.

THINK

December 1958

POSITION FIRING

SECTION OF THE GUNNER'S INFORMATION FILE
AIR FORCES MANUAL No. 20 · MAY 1944 ·

RESTRICTED

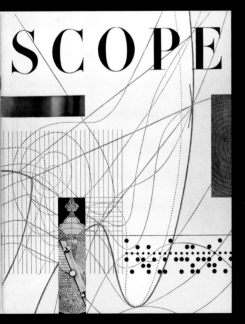

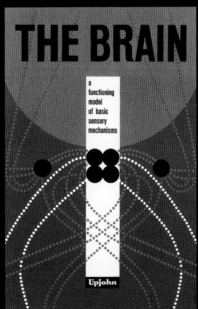

a
functioning
model
of basic
sensory
mechanisms

Upjohn

Top *Position Firing*, WWII gunnery
manual, cover, May 1944.

Above *Scope* magazine cover,
spring 1953.

Above right *The Brain*, silkscreen
poster, 1960.

1900

1908   Born in Cologne, Germany.

1910

1920

1927   Establishes a design studio in Cologne.

1930

1939   Emigrates to the US.

1945   Becomes the art director of *Fortune* magazine.

1949   Establishes Will Burtin, Inc. in New York.

1960

1970

1971   Receives the AIGA Medal.
1972   Dies in New York City, US.

Pubblicità in Italia, poster, 1957–58.

'I have tried to widen the range of my own activity, applying myself to experimental work that often overlaps scientific fields such as psychology and physics. It is from just such a fusion of elements, as well as through decanting and contamination, that graphic design can find its own evolution in new ways of expression.'

Franco Grignani

1908–1999

ITALY

Experimentation runs through all of Franco Grignani's work. His strong graphic sensibility, combined with distorted text and monochrome optical patterns, perfectly encapsulated the futuristic mood of the 1960s, whether applied to posters, advertisements, magazine covers or logos. The design that Grignani's name will always be associated with, however, is the Woolmark logo, which he may or may not have designed.

Grignani originally trained as an architect in Turin and practised there for several years before studying graphic design and starting to experiment with photography and Op Art. In 1950 he started working with the printer Alfieri & Lacroix, which would prove to be the start of a long-lasting and prolific relationship. Grignani was given free rein in the various campaigns he created for the firm, resulting in a stunning series of advertisements that frequently feature his signature monochrome Op Art experiments and distorted type. The ads were abstract representations that just hinted at the idea of print rather than describing it literally. Grignani also wrote the copy.

Many other commissions followed from the likes of Pirelli, Penguin Books, Linea Grafica and Graphis. In 1958, the first of nearly 50 solo exhibitions of his work was held in Italy, followed by shows in the UK, US, Germany, Switzerland and Venezuela.

In 1964, the International Wool Secretariat (IWS) held a competition to create its new Woolmark logo.

Despite looking remarkably like Grignani's handiwork, the geometric symbol (which is still in use today) is credited to another Italian designer, Francesco Saroglia. No trace of Saroglia can be found, and there are a couple of theories as to what happened. One is that Grignani's original design was appropriated and submitted by a Milan advertising agency under Saroglia's name. The other is that, being on the IWS jury, Grignani entered the competition under a pseudonym. Some time afterwards Grignani started to take credit for the design, but without offering an explanation for its history. Much later, at an exhibition of his work in 1995, a page taken from his 1964 diary was exhibited, showing nine possible design solutions for the IWS competition – including the design in question, clearly singled out.

Above Self portrait of Grignani, 1964.

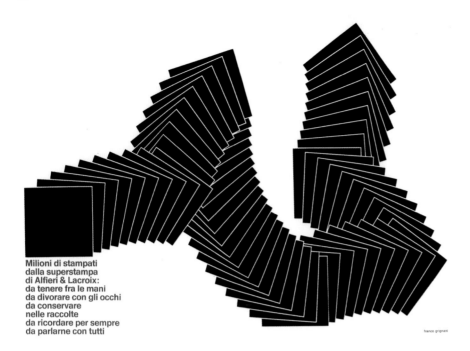

Milioni di stampati
dalla superstampa
di Alfieri & Lacroix:
da tenere fra le mani
da divorare con gli occhi
da conservare
nelle raccolte
da ricordare per sempre
da parlarne con tutti

franco grignani

Above Advertisement for
Alfieri & Lacroix, 1967.

Below Cover for *Pirelli* magazine,
May/June 1967.

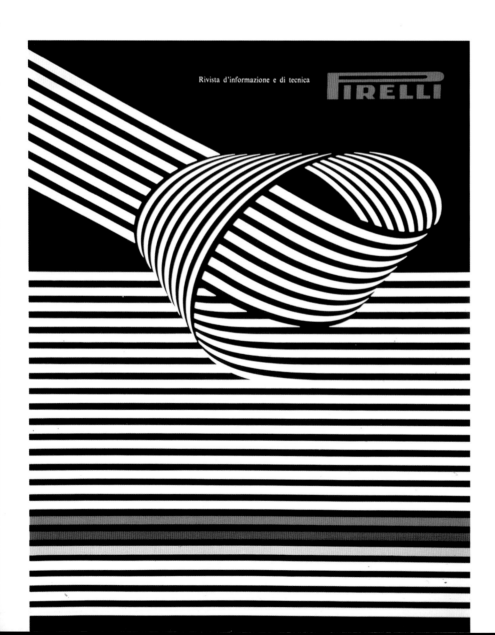

Left Woolmark, logo for the International Wool Secretariat, 1964.

Below Advertisement for Alfieri & Lacroix, 1966.

1908 Born in Pieve Porto Morone, Italy.
1910
1920
1930
1940
1950 Becomes a member of the AGI.
1952 Works on the graphic design section of the Milan Triennale.
1957 First solo exhibition is held in Italy.
1958
1960 International Wool Secretariat logo competition is held.
1964 Wins an award at the Warsaw Poster Biennale.
1966
1970
1980
1990
1999 Dies in Milan, Italy.

l'evoluzione della grafica accompagna la dimensione quotidiana della vita umana Alfieri & Lacroix tipolitozinco grafia in Milano

franco grignani

Above *Exploring the Universe,* General Dynamics poster, 1958.

Opposite Gebrauchsgraphik, cover, 1956.

'I would hate to have to apologize for a design, to have people puzzle and ask, "What is it?"'

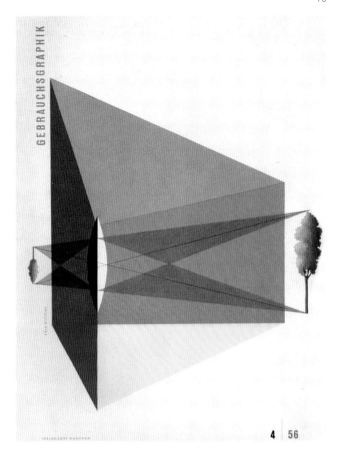

Erik Nitsche

1908–1998

SWITZERLAND

Erik Nitsche may not be as well known as many of his compatriots. However, the work created over his prolific 60-year career demonstrates that his lower profile is not related to the quality of his work, but rather to his reportedly very modest disposition. When confronted by Nitsche's work, László Moholy-Nagy famously asked: 'Who is this guy doing the Bauhaus in New York?' Although the artist (and Bauhaus tutor) Paul Klee was a family friend, Nitsche studied at the Collège Classique in Lausanne, and then the School of Applied Arts in Munich. While his work contains a nod towards Modernism, it is much less dogmatic and more expressive.

Throughout his career, Nitsche was something of a nomad, working in Cologne, Hollywood, New York, Paris, Connecticut, Geneva and Munich. In 1934, after a few years working in Europe, he moved to the US. His career then took off when, after a brief spell in Hollywood, he moved to New York and began working for publications including *Vanity Fair, Fortune, Life* and *Harper's Bazaar*. Nitsche also turned his hand to advertising campaigns for department stores, record covers for Decca, posters for the New York Transit Authority, and various film and theatre campaigns.

In 1950, Nitsche set up a studio in Connecticut. He began working for the Gotham Agency, which at that time held the General Dynamics account – a move that would prove extremely fortuitous. In 1953 General Dynamics became part of a huge conglomerate

supplying the US Department of Defense with everything from atomic submarines to jet bombers. Nitsche was commissioned to create a series of ads to promote nuclear power as a symbol of peace. It impressed General Dynamics' president, John Jay Hopkins, so much that he offered him a job.

It was to prove a very fruitful partnership. Over the next ten years, Nitsche oversaw the company's complete corporate identity, producing advertisements, brochures, annual reports and posters. Much of Nitsche's imagery was taken from scientific sources, as the nature of his subject matter (atomic energy and top-secret nuclear submarines) demanded a more abstract approach. These restrictions actually proved to be advantageous. Nitsche produced a stunning body of work, culminating in a 420-page book on the history of the company – *Dynamic America*, published in 1960.

Nitsche then returned to Switzerland, setting up his own studio in Geneva, where he produced a series of 12 beautifully illustrated books on science and technology, followed by a second series – 20 volumes visualizing the history of music. Spells in Paris and Hamburg followed, as did numerous children's books, and a set of over 200 philatelic first-day covers for the Unicover Corporation, a company for whom Nitsche continued to work into his eighties.

Opposite *Atoms for Peace*, poster for General Dynamics, 1955.

Above General Dynamics, annual report, 1959.

Below *Convair 880*, poster for General Dynamics, 1958.

GENERAL DYNAMICS

CONVAIR

ERIK NITSCHE

- 1908 Born in Lausanne, Switzerland.
- 1910
- 1920
- 1930
- 1934 Moves to the US.
- 1940
- 1947 Becomes art director and vice-president in charge of design at Dorland International.
- 1950
- 1960 Moves to Geneva and founds Erik Nitsche International.
- 1965 Moves to Paris.
- 1970
- 1980
- 1990
- 1996 Returns to the US.
- 1998 Dies in New York City, US.

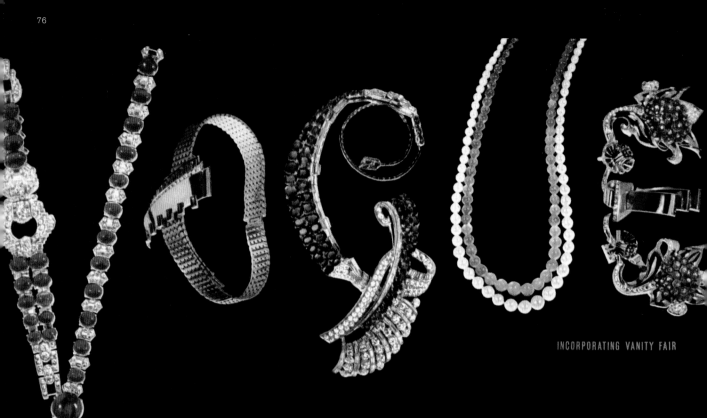

VOGUE

INCORPORATING VANITY FAIR

CHRISTMAS GIFTS

NORTH AND SOUTH
FASHIONS

DECEMBER 1, 1939
PRICE 35 CENTS

'We tried to make the prosaic attractive without using the tired clichés of false glamour. You might say we tried to convey the attractiveness of reality, as opposed to the glitter of a never-never land.'

Cipe Pineles

1908–1991

AUSTRIA

It is unfortunate that the designer Cipe Pineles will never be remembered for her work alone. While she was a talented illustrator and art director, who worked on several groundbreaking magazines, the fact that (after ten years of being proposed) she was the first female designer to become a member of Art Directors Club (ADC) of New York in 1943, and then the first female designer to be inducted into its Hall of Fame in 1975, is never far away.

Born in Vienna but raised in Poland, Pineles and her family emigrated to New York in 1923. After graduating from the Pratt Institute and experiencing discrimination from potential employers who seemed impressed by her portfolio but not in person, she eventually found work with the multidisciplinary design agency Contempora. Her project for the fabric company Everlast so impressed Condé Nast's wife, Leslie, that Pineles was offered a job as assistant to the art director for *Vogue*, *House and Garden* and *Vanity Fair*, M. F. Agha.

Despite being the only woman in the design department, Pineles flourished under Agha's strict guidance. In 1942 she was appointed art director for the fashion magazine *Glamour*, applying her witty and distinctive style to what was considered a fairly conservative, mid-market publication.

After a short spell working on a publication for servicewomen in Paris, Pineles was appointed art director of *Seventeen*, a magazine created to satisfy the emerging post-war teenage market. Edited by Helen Valentine, it represented a new breed of publication, taking an intelligent, unpatronizing approach to its readers and treating them as independent young women, and not simply brides-in-waiting or mothers-to-be. Under Pineles' assured direction, *Seventeen*'s design was as arresting visually as its content.

In 1950 Pineles became art editor of *Charm*, a magazine aimed at her own demographic – professional women. Dealing with the challenges of presenting well-worn subjects in a fresh and engaging way, she commissioned a raft of exciting artists and photographers, including Ladislav Sutnar, André Kertész, Herbert Matter and a young Seymour Chwast. In 1962, after a brief spell as art director of *Mademoiselle*, Pineles' career took a new direction and she started teaching editorial design at Parsons School of Design, where she was also the Head of Publications. She remained there for over 20 years.

Married to two behemoths of American graphic design, Bill Golden (p. 121) and Will Burtin (p. 64), Pineles' accomplishments were eventually recognized by her male peers. It took ten years of being proposed by M. F. Agha (and a nudge from Golden) for the ADC to accept her as a member. More than 30 years later in 1975 she was inducted into the ADC's Hall of Fame.

Opposite *Vogue* cover, December 1939.

Above Portrait of Pineles.

CHARM

the magazine for women who work

BLUEPRINT FOR
SPRING IN THIS ISSUE - PART II

WHAT TO WEAR:
under a coat
over a dress
with a suit
to a wedding

MARCH 1952 • 25 CENTS

Below *Seventeen* magazine cover,
July 1948.

Bottom *Seventeen* magazine cover,
July 1949.

Cipe Pineles

1900

1908 Born in Vienna, Austria.

1910

1920

1923 Emigrates with family to New York.

1930

1932 Joins Condé Nast.

1940

1943 Becomes first female member of the Art
Directors Club of New York.

1947 Becomes art director of *Seventeen*.

1950 Joins *Charm*.

1961 Appointed art director at *Mademoiselle*.

1970

1975 Becomes the first female to be inducted into
the Art Directors Club of New York Hall
of Fame.

1980

1991 Dies in Suffern, New York, US.

'Design is form. Sometimes it is decorative form, and has no other function than to give pleasure to the eye. It is always abstract; but like a gesture or a tone of voice it has the power to command and hold attention, to create symbols, to clarify ideas.'

Leo Lionni

1910–1999

THE NETHERLANDS

A true polymath, Leo Lionni was a Futurist painter, a critic and a dedicated teacher, as well as a talented illustrator and designer. Despite creating memorable work for commercial clients such as *Fortune* magazine, Olivetti and Ford Motors, it is for his dozens of engaging children's books that he is best remembered.

The product of a creative and cultured family, as a child Lionni spent many hours drawing from casts at the Rijksmuseum in Amsterdam. A move to Genoa in Italy (via Philadelphia) followed, where Lionni met his future wife, whose father was the head of the Italian Communist Party. Moving to Milan, Lionni was influenced by the growing Futurist movement, his abstract paintings catching the attention of its founder, Filippo Marinetti. As well as designing advertisements for Domus and Campari, Lionni also started writing architecture criticism for the magazine *Casabella,* edited and designed by Eduardo Persico.

In 1939, Lionni left Italy for Philadelphia to work for the ad agency N. W. Ayer, where he won a last-minute pitch to create artwork for a Ford Motors campaign. This represented a major promotion for Lionni, who then became the director of one of the largest advertising accounts in the country. He seized the opportunity to commission the likes of Fernand Léger, Alexander Calder and Willem de Kooning, as well as commercial artists such as Saul Steinberg and a young Andy Warhol.

In 1948, Lionni moved to New York, set up a studio and took on the art direction of *Fortune* magazine (after

Will Burtin's departure), a position that he would hold for 14 years. His approach was to make the design more accessible, with the use of the typeface Century Schoolbook, and by commissioning talented artists and illustrators, many of whom were sent on far-flung assignments. Speaking later about his time under the directorship of Time-Life's Henry Luce, Lionni recalled Luce asking him, '"Why can't *Fortune* be as good looking as *Harper's Bazaar*?" My answer was obvious: "Because businessmen are not as good looking as fashion models".'

Lionni's other clients included Olivetti (for whom he was art director) and MoMA, and he created a controversial design for the American pavilion for the Brussels World's Fair in 1958. He also spent a period as the art director and co-editor of *Print* magazine, widening its remit and encouraging debate within the graphic design community.

In 1959, Lionni decided to leave the US for a simpler life in Italy. Shortly prior to his departure, he was on a train with his grandchildren, and to keep them amused he assembled a story using torn pieces of paper from a copy of *Life* magazine. This inspired *Little Blue and Little Yellow*, the first of over 40 books which Lionni designed for children.

Above Portrait of Lionni.

which way out?

for family counseling call

AFFILIATED WITH FAMILY SERVICE ASSOCIATION OF AMERICA

little blue and little yellow

by Leo Lionni

Opposite *Which Way Out*, offset lithograph, 1954.

Above *Little Blue and Little Yellow*, book cover, Knopf, 1959.

Below left *Cancer is Curable if Treated Early*, silkscreen, 1954.

Below right *Keep 'Em Rolling*, offset lithograph, 1941.

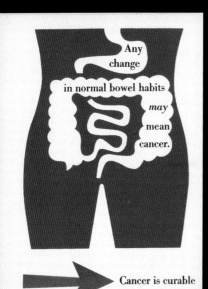

Leo Lionni

1910 — Born in Amsterdam, the Netherlands.

1920

1925 — Moves to Genoa, Italy.

1930

1940

1948 — Moves to New York and becomes art director of *Fortune* magazine.

1950

1959 — First children's book published.
1960 — Moves back to Italy.

1970

1980

1984 — Receives AIGA Gold Medal.

1990

1999 — Dies in Rome, Italy.

'Design is a question of substance, not just form. It's a tool a company uses… as a tangible reflection of a way of being and operating.'
—Adriano Olivetti

Giovanni Pintori

1912–1999

ITALY

Giovanni Pintori's name might not be as well known as some of his contemporaries, because for over 30 years he worked in-house for the Italian typewriter manufacturer, Olivetti. The company became hugely successful during the 1950s and '60s and Pintori played a crucial role in defining the Olivetti brand, creating a wealth of exciting publicity material, which helped transform what was a well-designed but very practical piece of office equipment into an object of desire.

Pintori's talent was recognized from an early age. At 18 he won a scholarship to the Higher Institute for Industrial Arts in Monza, near Milan. His first encounter with Adriano Olivetti was in 1936, when the latter commissioned him to draw up some plans for a proposed development. This lead to Pintori joining Olivetti, working in the company's advertising and publicity department – first under Renato Zveteremich, and then Leonardo Sinisgalli. In 1950, Pintori became Olivetti's artistic director.

The next 20 years were a very prosperous time for Olivetti, and Pintori created some of his most stunning works during this period. Olivetti was at the forefront of design and technology, with designers including Marcello Nizzoli, Mario Bellini and Ettore Sottsass creating new products such as portable typewriters, calculators and computers.

Pintori was responsible for designing everything from adverts and posters to the company's promotional calendar. As art director he was also responsible for commissioning a wide range of talented artists and illustrators. His posters were striking compositions, and if the typewriter featured at all in the design, it was always in a minor way. The emphasis was instead on bold, abstract graphics, often taken from parts of the typewriter, such as the keys or the ribbon. Self-assured and playful in its approach, Pintori's art direction defined Olivetti as a company committed to good design, setting it firmly apart from its more conservative rivals.

In 1952 Pintori made his first trip to New York, and was surprised to receive an enthusiastic welcome from designers such as Paul Rand and Leo Lionni. A cover for *Fortune* magazine followed, and in the same year the Museum of Modern Art held an exhibition entitled 'Olivetti: Design in Industry', the majority of which consisted of Pintori's output. This exhibition attracted much attention and visited London, Lausanne, and Paris, where it showed at the Louvre. After three decades, Pintori finally left Olivetti in 1967 to set up his own studio in Milan.

Above Portrait of Pintori, photographer unknown, 1950s.

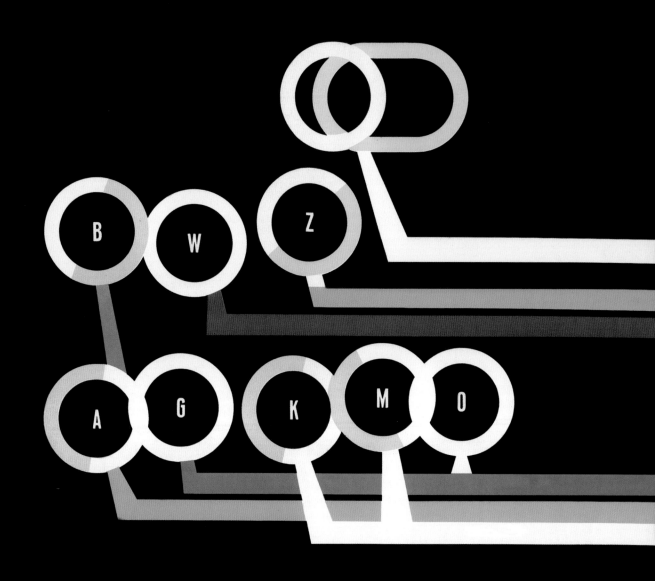

Olivetti Graphika

Olivetti Graphika, poster, 1959.

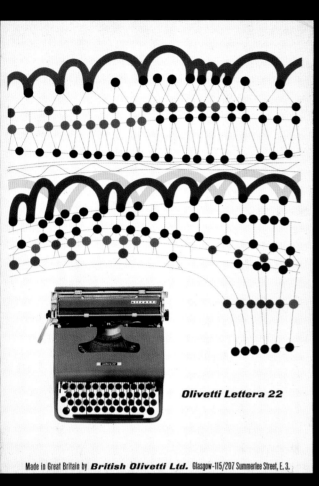

Olivetti Lettera 22

Made in Great Britain by **British Olivetti Ltd.** Glasgow-115/207 Summerlee Street, E.3.

Olivetti Elettrosumma 22

Top British poster for Olivetti Lettera 22, 1956.

Above Olivetti Elettrosumma 22, poster, 1962.

Giovanni Pintori

- 1910
- **1912** Born in Sardinia, Italy.
- 1920
- **1930** Enrols at the Higher Institute for Industrial Arts, Monza.
- **1936** Starts working for Olivetti.
- 1940
- 1950
- **1952** Makes his first trip to New York.
- **1955** Olivetti exhibition is held at the Louvre.
- 1960
- **1967** Sets up his own studio in Milan.
- 1970
- 1980
- 1990
- **1999** Dies in Milan, Italy.

Please Stand on the Right, poster for
London Transport, 1949.

'I look back and my figures, well, they are all smiling, I can't bear it now. But we had to make posters then to cheer people up. Always smiling.'

Tom Eckersley

1914–1997

UK

As well as being the most celebrated British-born poster artist (he was granted an OBE for services to poster design in 1948), through his long-standing association with the London College of Printing (now the London College of Communication), Tom Eckersley was also one of the country's most influential graphic design educators.

Eckersley's artistic talents were recognized early on in his career. He studied at Salford School of Art, and was awarded the Heywood Medal for best student in 1930. A move to London with his friend and fellow designer Eric Lombers in 1934 saw them set up in partnership as poster designers Eckersley-Lombers. The pair created striking posters for prestigious clients such as the BBC, Austin Reed, London Transport, Shell and the GPO. During this time both designers also became visiting lecturers at the Westminster School of Art.

The outbreak of war saw the partnership dissolve. Lombers joined the army and Eckersley joined the RAF, where his design skills were utilized as a cartographer. During this period he designed his remarkable series of public-information posters for the Royal Society for the Prevention of Accidents. The educational campaign was aimed at the influx of workers to factories supporting the war effort, who it was believed were taking up valuable hospital resources, due to having mainly preventable accidents. Eckersley designed 22 striking instructional posters in total, usually squeezing them into the 24 hours' leave he had from his regular RAF duties.

After World War II, his elegant work was still very much in demand. He picked up numerous poster commissions from clients including London Transport, the GPO and Gillette, and illustrated several children's books (including one by his wife Daisy). In addition to recognition at home, Eckersley was internationally renowned for his designs, and in 1950 was one of the first British designers invited to join the prestigious members organization, Alliance Graphique Internationale.

Still passionate about education, Eckersley joined the London College of Printing in 1954, shortly afterwards becoming head of Graphic Design (a post he held for 20 years). Always putting the welfare of his students above his own needs, Eckersley made a significant and lasting contribution to this field of education, establishing the first undergraduate graphic design courses in the UK.

Eckersley continued to practise throughout his time at the LCP, thus ensuring that both his educational approach and commercial work remained current. His later commissions included work for UNICEF and WWF, and murals for the London Underground – his duelling pistols and Concorde tail sections can still be seen on the station platforms at Finsbury Park and Heathrow Terminals 1, 2, 3 respectively.

Above Portrait of Eckersley.

Above *Boat Race*, poster for London
Transport, 1951.

Right *Aluminium Reduces Fuel
Consumption*, poster for British
Aluminium Co Ltd, 1957.

Be First, Not Last – Post Early,
poster, 1955.

1910

1914 Born in Lancashire, UK.

1920

1930

1934 Moves to London from his native Lancashire.

1937 Teaches poster art at the Westminster School of Art.

1940

1950 Elected member of the Alliance Graphique Internationale.

1954 Joins the London College of Printing.

1957 Appointed head of Graphic Design at the London College of Printing.

1960

1970

1980

1990

1997 Dies in London, UK.

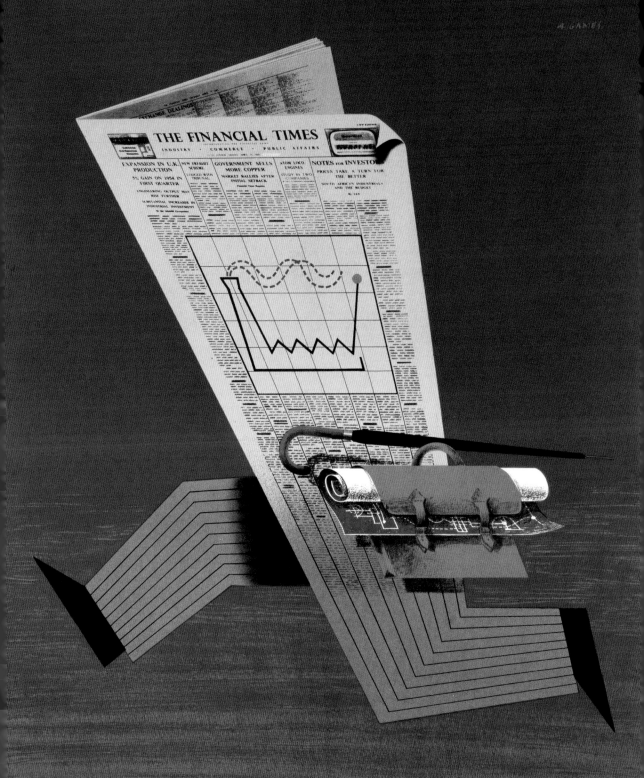

men leaping ahead in industry read

THE FINANCIAL TIMES

every day

'Maximum meaning,
minimum means.'

Abram Games

1914–1996

UK

The name Abram Games is rarely mentioned without his well-known mantra 'Maximum meaning, minimum means' being uttered in the same breath. This phrase sums up one of the prolific poster designer's talents perfectly – the ability to convey a message elegantly, with clarity, impact and, above all, economy.

Nowhere was this more important than in the numerous posters Games designed in his capacity as Official War Poster Artist. Although he was denied the chance to fight on the front line, it could be argued that these forthright posters played an equally important role in fighting the war on the home front.

Games was born to Eastern European parents in Whitechapel, East London. After a brief spell at St Martin's School of Art, he cut his teeth at the commercial art studio Askew-Younge, before eventually being fired in 1936. By this time Games had won first prize in a London City Council competition in 1935, and he worked as a successful poster artist in his own right until 1940, at which point he was conscripted. Despite opting to join the infantry, he was posted to the 54th Division as a draughtsman; a transferral then saw him go on to design over 100 posters for the War Office.

The poster was seen as a powerful weapon in the war effort, a tool to inspire a feeling of shared responsibility in the fight for victory. Soldiers were encouraged to keep their feet clean, and ventilate ammunition, while the public were urged to grow their own food, knit socks and refrain from gossip. Games was also responsible for designing recruitment posters; one

of his most famous was the glamorous *Join the ATS* ('Blonde Bombshell') poster of 1941, which was later replaced with a more 'suitable-looking' brunette.

Although primarily known for his posters, Games also designed a moving TV emblem for the BBC in 1953, as well as symbols for the Ind Coope brewery, British Aluminium and the Queen's Award to Industry, which was used from 1966 to 1999.

As rationing ended and disposable incomes increased, so did Games's poster commissions. He worked for several commercial clients, including the *Financial Times*, BOAC, BEA and P&O. Like many of his contemporaries, he also enjoyed a long-standing relationship with London Transport, for whom he designed 18 posters, as well as a beautiful swan mosaic on the Victoria Line at Stockwell, representing the not quite so beautiful public house opposite the station.

Opposite *Men Leaping Ahead in Industry Read the Financial Times Every Day*, poster, 1955.

Above Portrait of Abram Games with ATS poster, 1941.

Above Festival of Britain guide, 1951.

Below *London Zoo*, poster for London Underground, 1976.

Abram Games

1910

1914 Born in London, UK.

1920

1930

1935 Wins first prize for his entry in a London City Council poster competition.

1941 Designs the *Join The ATS* poster.
1942 Becomes the Official War Poster Artist.

1948 Wins competition to design the 1951 Festival of Britain emblem.

1950

1957 Awarded an OBE for services to graphic design.

1960

1970

1980

1990

1996 Dies in London.

B·O·A·C
FLIES TO ALL SIX CONTINENTS

A. GAMES

BRITISH OVERSEAS AIRWAYS CORPORATION IN ASSOCIATION WITH QANTAS EMPIRE AIRWAYS LIMITED · SOUTH AFRICAN AIRWAYS · TASMAN EMPIRE AIRWAYS LIMITED

BOAC Flies to All Six Continents,

STOP NUCLEAR SUICIDE CAMPAIGN FOR NUCLEAR DISARMAMENT 2 CARTHUSIAN ST LONDON EC1

Stop Nuclear Suicide, poster, 1963.

'In 1942 and 1943 I worked 15 hours a day at the Ministry of Information. In the afternoon I'd go over to the US Office of War Information, Grosvenor Square. There, graphic designers at the rank of colonel put together magazines for the American armed forces.'

FHK Henrion

1914–1990

GERMANY

Henrion's significant contribution to the war effort with his work for the Ministry of Information, his masterful corporate identity work with Studio H (later Henrion Design Associates) and his leadership of several significant design associations made him a key figure in shaping the graphic design landscape in post-war Britain.

Originally from Nuremberg in Germany, Henrion emigrated to Paris in 1933, first to study textile design, then to study poster and graphic design at the École Paul Colin. He left for England in 1936, working as a graphic designer, and creating a variety of exhibitions, packaging and posters until the outbreak of World War II, when he was interned as an enemy alien. After six months he was released and ironically given the job of designing forthright posters for the Ministry of Information, urging the public to grow its own food and eat its greens, and creating hard-hitting images such as the swastika being pulled apart by the Allied Forces. Henrion's talent for communication was also exploited by the London-based office of the United States Office of War Information.

Henrion established Studio H in 1948, a multidisciplinary consultancy that worked on a variety of graphic design, product and exhibition projects, including the Festival of Britain's Countryside and Agricultural pavilions, and the British pavilion at Montreal's Expo 67. As the post-war economy grew, Studio H's clients came to include several of the newly formed electrical goods companies of the time, such as Philips and Murphy. The studio also produced a detailed identity scheme for the Bowater paper company that is considered one of the first examples of what we now call corporate identity. Work for Tate & Lyle, BEA and the London Electricity Board followed, but Henrion's most noteworthy corporate identity scheme was for the Dutch airline KLM, which he oversaw from 1959 to 1984. His 1967 book, *Design Coordination and Corporate Image* (written with Alan Parkin), was the first publication to comprehensively cover this emerging discipline.

Despite his passion for the corporate world, one of Henrion's most striking pieces was not for a commercial client. In 1963 he created a poster for the Campaign for Nuclear Disarmament. Depicting a skull superimposed with a mushroom cloud, the poster was a stark yet brilliantly simple depiction of what for many people at the time was a very real fear.

As well as teaching at the Royal College of Art and the London College of Printing, Henrion was president of the Society of Industrial Artists and Designers, the Alliance Graphique Internationale and the International Council of Graphic Design Associations, for which he set up a hugely popular series of student seminars.

Above Portrait of Henrion, 1950s.

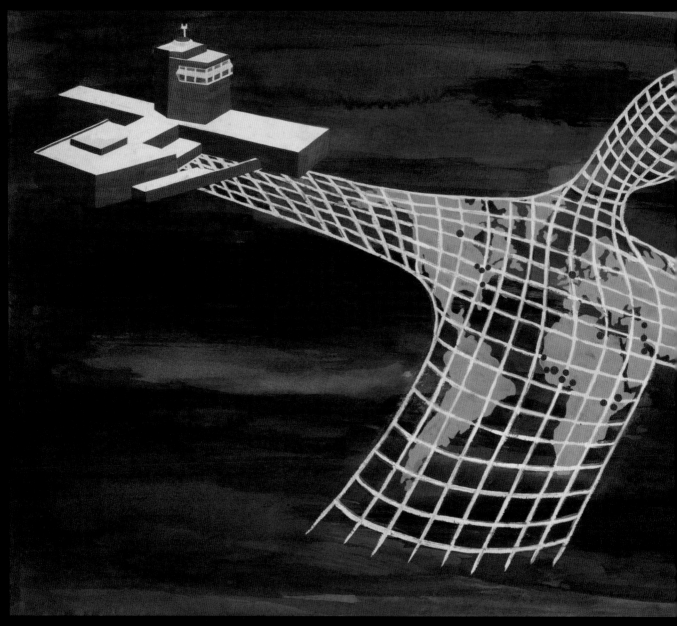

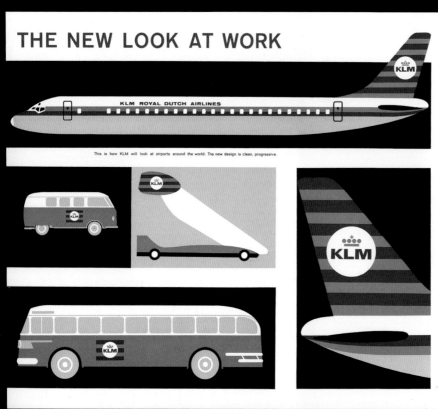

Above *Taylor Woodrow Built this Airport*, poster, 1955.

Left KLM identity, 1963.

Right *Four Hands*, D-Day poster, 1944.

FHK Henrion

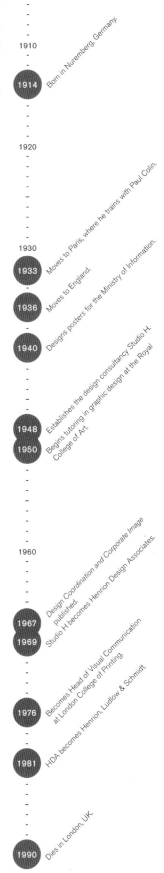

1910

1914 — Born in Nuremberg, Germany.

1920

1930

1933 — Moves to Paris, where he trains with Paul Colin.

1936 — Moves to England.

1940 — Designs posters for the Ministry of Information.

1948 — Establishes the design consultancy Studio H.
1950 — Begins tutoring in graphic design at the Royal College of Art.

1960

Design Coordination and Corporate Image published.
1967 — Studio H becomes Henrion Design Associates.
1969

Becomes Head of Visual Communication at London College of Printing.
1976 — HDA becomes Henrion, Ludlow & Schmidt.

1981

1990 — Dies in London, UK.

carl schuricht leitung

erica morini violine

beethoven brahms strauss

tonhalle grosser saal
donnerstag, 10. november 1955, 20.15 uhr
wiederholung des 3. abonnementskonzertes
der tonhalle-gesellschaft zürich
beethoven vierte sinfonie in b-dur, op. 60
brahms violinkonzert in d-dur, op. 77
strauss till eulenspiegels lustige streiche, op. 28
karten zu fr. 3.50–9.50
vorverkauf tonhallekasse, hug, jecklin, kuoni

Carl Schuricht Leitung – Erica Morini
Violine – Beethoven – Brahms –
Strauss, poster for the Tonhalle-
Gesellschaft, Zurich, 1955.

'The grid system is an aid,
not a guarantee.'

Josef Müller-Brockmann

1914–1996

SWITZERLAND

While Wim Crouwel was assigned the moniker of Mr Gridnik, it was perhaps the Swiss designer Müller-Brockmann (a personal hero and huge influence on Crouwel) who really deserved the title. Müller-Brockmann will forever be associated with the grid system he passionately promoted, and his 1961 book *The Graphic Artist and His Design Problems* is still considered essential reading for any self-respecting graphic designer.

Müller-Brockmann was a key figure (along with Max Bill, Emil Ruder and Armin Hofmann) in the movement that became known as the International Typographic Style – arguably the most significant influence on graphic design in the post-war period (and far beyond). Taking up where Modernism left off, the Swiss Style, as it became widely known, eschewed decoration, used asymmetric layouts and sans-serif typefaces, and represented order and clarity.

While Müller-Brockmann promoted the grid as a way of instilling order, he was well aware of the constraints that it imposed. He urged designers not to be bound by its limitations, to respect its function and to accept that 'one must learn how to use the grid; it is an art that requires practice'. While this approach to design might sound dull, when used intelligently it simply provides a solid framework for the typographic expression that is visible in so many of Müller-Brockmann's own posters.

Nowhere is this expression more apparent than in his stunning series of posters for the Zurich Tonhalle (concert hall), created between 1950 and 1985. Heavily influenced by Concrete Artists, his approach was to combine type with abstract imagery: 'I tried to interpret

musical themes such as rhythm, transparency, weightlessness, and so on with concrete, abstract forms, which I brought together into logical relationships. I had to unify only the geometrical elements – in terms of form and proportion – and the typography.'

The influence of the Swiss Style spread across Europe and the United States. This was helped enormously by *Neue Grafik,* a groundbreaking quarterly publication set up by Müller-Brockmann together with Richard Paul Lohse, Hans Neuburg and Carlo Vivarelli. Published between 1958 and 1965, and printed in English, German and French, it had a distinctive square format and, unsurprisingly, was based on a rigid grid system. While it professed to feature the best graphic design from around the world, the rigorous (or some might say partisan) selection procedure of its editors led to its content being almost exclusively of Swiss origin.

Müller-Brockmann was also a committed educator, and published several books on design: *The Graphic Artist and His Design Problems* (1961), *History of the Poster* (with his wife, Shizuko, 1971), *A History of Visual Communication* (1971), and *Grid Systems in Graphic Design* (1981), all of which were reissued after his death.

Above Portrait of Müller-Brockmann, 1960s.

Strawinsky – Berg – Fortner – Tonhalle
Grosser Saal, poster, 1955.

beethoven

tonhalle grosser saal
dienstag, den 22. februar 1955,
20.15 uhr
4. extrakonzert
der tonhalle-gesellschaft

leitung carl schuricht
solist wolfgang schneiderhan

beethoven ouverture zu «coriolan», op. 62
violinkonzert in d-dur, op. 61
siebente sinfonie in a-dur, op. 92

vorverkauf tonhalle-kasse, hug, jecklin,
kuoni
karten zu fr. 3.50 bis 9.50

Above *Beethoven – Tonhalle – Grosser Saal*, poster, 1955.

Left *Charles Dutoit – Jürg von Vintschger – Tonhalle-Orchester*, poster, 1968.

tonhalle- gesellschaft
zürich
freitag den 5. januar 1968
20.15 uhr
grosser tonhallesaal

karten zu fr. 1.– bis 5.–
vorverkauf tonhallekasse, hug, jecklin
kuoni und
filiale oerlikon kreditanstalt

charles dutoit
jürg von vintschger
tonhalle- orchester

igor strawinsky
musica viva variations in
memoriam
aldous huxley
1963/64
albert moeschinger
klavier konzert op. 96
1965
uraufführung rudolf kelterborn
sinfonie 1966
uraufführung
alban berg
drei orchesterstücke
op. 6

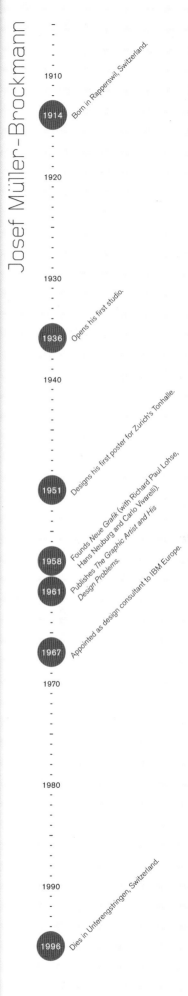

Josef Müller-Brockmann

1910

1914 Born in Rapperswil, Switzerland.

1920

1930

1936 Opens his first studio.

1940

1951 Designs his first poster for Zurich's Tonhalle.

1958 Founds *Neue Grafik* (with Richard Paul Lohse, Hans Neuburg and Carlo Vivarelli).

1961 Publishes *The Graphic Artist and His Design Problems*.

1967 Appointed as design consultant to IBM Europe.

1970

1980

1990

1996 Dies in Unterengstringen, Switzerland.

'A logo cannot survive unless it is designed with the utmost simplicity and restraint.'

Paul Rand

1914–1996

USA

Shortly before Paul Rand died, he was described by Apple's founder, Steve Jobs, as 'the greatest living graphic designer'. As well as the logo for Jobs's NeXT computers, Rand created identities for business giants such as IBM, UPS, ABC television, Westinghouse and Enron, all of which are well and truly engrained into the American psyche.

It was Rand's understanding of the relationship between art and commerce that was key to his success. László Moholy-Nagy called Rand 'an idealist and a realist, using the language of the poet and the businessman. He thinks in terms of need and function. He is able to analyse his problems, but his fantasy is boundless.'

While he will always be associated with the iconic logos he created, Rand had established himself as a successful graphic designer many years before. Graphic design had not been considered a suitable career by his grocery-store-owning parents. In 1936, he was asked to design an anniversary issue of *Apparel Arts* magazine. This led to a full-time job and, shortly afterwards, the opportunity to art-direct the fashion pages of *Esquire*. Rand also designed a series of notable covers for *Direction*, and was art director at the William Weintraub agency for 11 years, up to 1955.

Rand was hired as a consultant by IBM's Eliot Noyes in 1956, and his work there spanned three decades. Rand was responsible for all aspects of the IBM identity, including its packaging and marketing materials. He introduced the striped version of the logo, as well as the playful *Eye-Bee-M* poster.

He taught extensively and was a professor of graphic design at the Yale School of Art for many years. He published a number of books on graphic design, the best-known being *Thoughts on Design*, first published in 1947. Subsequent titles were published by Yale University Press, which employed its Rand-designed logo from 1985 until 2009. Rand also illustrated four children's books written by his second wife, Ann.

One of Rand's key skills was his ability to sell his ideas to his clients. According to the graphic designer Louis Danziger, 'He almost singlehandedly convinced business that design was an effective tool… Anyone designing in the 1950s and 1960s owed much to Rand, who largely made it possible for us to work. He more than anyone else made the profession reputable. We went from being commercial artists to being graphic designers largely on his merits.'

Opposite *Eye-Bee-M*, poster for IBM, 1981.

Above Portrait of Rand.

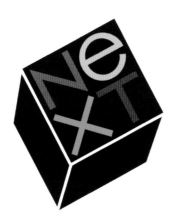

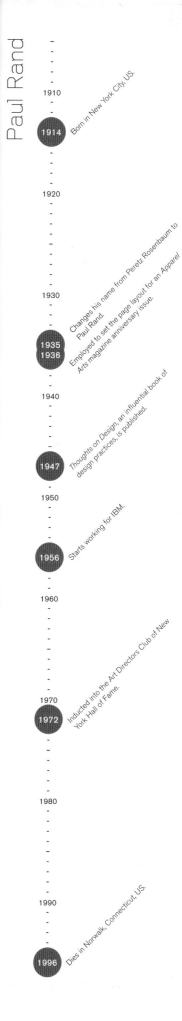

Born in New York City, US. · 1914

Changes his name from Peretz Rosenbaum to Paul Rand. · 1935

Employed to set the page layout for an *Apparel Arts* magazine anniversary issue. · 1936

Thoughts on Design, an influential book of design practices, is published. · 1947

Starts working for IBM. · 1956

Inducted into the Art Directors Club of New York Hall of Fame. · 1972

Dies in Norwalk, Connecticut, US. · 1996

Opposite *Skull and Olive Branch.* Fogg Art Museum Harvard University, colour lithograph on heavy white wove paper. 91.1 x 61.0 cm (35⅞ x 24in.). Gift of Tamar Cohen, 1999-6-2, *1969*.

Top Enron logo, 1996.

Middle NeXT computers logo, 1986.

Bottom UPS logo, 1961.

die gute Form

Gewerbemuseum Winterthur am Kirchplatz
17. Mai bis 29. Juni 1958
Werktags 14-18 Uhr, Mittwoch u. Freitag auch 19-21 Uhr
Sonntag 10-12 und 14-17 Uhr

Entwurf Ruder
Druck Gewerbeschule Basel

'Typography has one plain duty before it and that is to convey information in writing. No argument or consideration can absolve typography from this duty.'

Emil Ruder

1914–1970

SWITZERLAND

Along with Armin Hofmann, Emil Ruder was a key figure in the development of the teaching programme at the Basel School of Design, and a keen advocate for what eventually became known as the International Typographic Style. Ruder firmly believed in the power of typography to communicate ideas and wrote extensively on the subject – including the classic work, *Typography: A Manual for Design,* which is still considered essential reading for typographers today.

Ruder had a very hands-on introduction to the craft of typography, training as a typesetter in his native Basel. He went on to study in Paris, before returning to Switzerland, where he was exposed to the philosophy of Jan Tschichold (p. 44) and the teachings of the Bauhaus. In 1942 he began to teach the professional typography class at the Basel School of Design and five years later was joined there by Armin Hofmann. Ruder and Hofmann worked closely on the school's teaching programme, with Hofmann concentrating on graphic design and Ruder on typography. Under their direction, the Basel School soon gained a reputation for its rigorous curriculum, and Ruder's typography class attracted long waiting lists. He eventually became the director of the school in 1965.

Ruder continued his practice during his time in education, creating a series of memorable posters and designing covers for the professional journal *Typografische Monatsblätter,* to which he contributed extensively. Four related articles that appeared in the publication between 1957 and 1959 ('The Plane', 'The Line', 'The Word' and 'Rhythm') formed the basis of his

seminal 1967 *Typography: A Manual for Design.* His previous publication *Die Farbe* (billed as a short course in colour for letterpress printers), which he both wrote and designed, had received an equally positive reception when it was published in 1948. As historian Richard Hollis notes, 'No other designer since Jan Tschichold was as committed as Ruder to the discipline of letterpress typography or wrote about it with such conviction.'

Like his contemporaries, Ruder favoured sans-serif type, and was particularly enamoured with a new typeface created by the young Adrian Frutiger: 'Emil Ruder saw my first specimens of Univers and was so delighted with them that he designed and published many works with this type in association with his Basel students.' Univers was to become Ruder's typeface of choice, and it would feature heavily in his work from the mid-1950s onwards.

Ruder was a staunch proponent of the grid system, advocating asymmetry and thus rejecting many of Tschichold's doctrines. He saw the typographer as having certain responsibilities, with communication at the very centre of those: 'It is our job to give language form, to give it durability and to ensure that it has a future life.'

Opposite *Die Gute Form*, poster, 1958.

Above Portrait of Ruder, 1950s.

Joan Miró

Kunsthalle Basel   24.März bis 29.April

Joan Miró, poster, 1956.

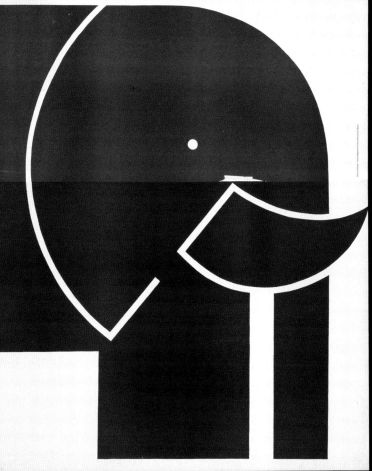

14. November 1959
bis
20. Januar 1960

Ausstellung
Gewerbemuseum
Basel

Täglich
10-12 und 14-17 Uhr
Eintritt frei

das Kinderbilderbuch

Above *Das Kinderbilderbuch*, exhibition
poster, 1959.

Below *10 Zürcher Maler* exhibition
poster, 1957.

10 zürcher maler

carigiet
früh
graeser
herbst
jacob
leuppi
lobeck
lohse
moser
varlin

kunsthalle basel
15.5.bis 24.6.

Emil Ruder

1910

1914 — Born in Zurich, Switzerland.

1920

1929 — Begins training as a typesetter in Basel.

1940

1942 — Teaches at the Basel School of Design.

1948 — *Die Farbe* is published.

1950

1960

1962 — Helps found the International Center for the Typographic Arts (ICTA), New York.

1965 — Becomes director of the Basel School of Design.

1967 — *Typography: A Manual for Design* is published.

1970 — Dies in Basel, Switzerland.

Hiroshima Appeals, poster, 1983.

'I simply cannot get inspiration to do work that does not seem worthwhile and of interest to me. My work is only valid if I am involved in creating the image for the entire company in terms of logos and poster designs and so forth.'

Yusaku Kamekura

1915–1997

JAPAN

Often described as one of the godfathers of Japanese design, Yusaku Kamekura played an important part in shaping the country's emerging graphic design industry in the post-war recovery period. One of the founders of the Nippon Design Centre, Kamekura also played a key role in establishing the organizations that brought together the design community, such as the Japan Advertising Artists Club (JAAC), the Tokyo Art Directors Club, the Japan Design Committee and the Japan Graphic Designers Association (JAGDA).

Kamekura was educated at the Institute of New Architecture and Industrial Arts in Tokyo. Privately run by Renshichiro Kawakita, the curriculum was unusual as it was based on the teachings of the Bauhaus. After graduating, Kamekura worked at the Nippon Kobo studio as an art director for various Japanese magazines, including *NIPPON* and *Commerce Japan.* He embraced the Modernist approach and, along with other designers including Paul Rand (p. 104) had a selection of his posters included in the 'Graphic '55' exhibition, at the Takashimaya department store.

Prime Minister Hayato Ikeda's Income-Doubling Plan saw Japan undergo a huge period of growth through exports in the 1960s. The journalist Matsuo Suzuki foresaw the key role that advertising and design would play in this surge and, along with fellow journalist Masataka Ogawa, persuaded Kamekura to join their newly formed design organization. Kamekura then enlisted fellow designers Ryuichi Yamashiro and Hiromu Hara, and the Nippon Design Centre was born.

The NDC was funded by eight commercial companies (who were also its clients), as well as its three founding members, and expanded rapidly, creating work for brands such as Toyota, Nikon and Asahi. In addition to achieving commercial success it sought to drive standards up within the Japanese advertising and design industry.

Kamekura's work effortlessly blended Eastern and Western sensibilities. Throughout his lengthy career, Kamekura tirelessly promoted Japanese graphic design, both through the various organizations that he founded and led, and through *Creation,* a limited-edition magazine that ran to 20 issues, all of which he edited and art-directed.

Above Portrait of Kamekura.

原子エネルギーを平和産業に！

国際原子力平和利用会議

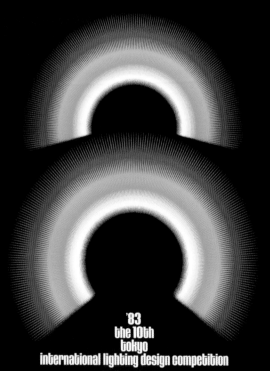

Above *Atomic Energy for Peaceful Industry*, poster, 1956.

Opposite *Tokyo 1964*, poster, 1964.

Below 10th Tokyo International Lighting Design Competition, poster, 1983.

'83
the 10th
tokyo
international lighting design competition
Theme: Lighting as Communication

Yusaku Kamekura

- 1910
- 1915 — Born in Niigata Prefecture, Japan.
- 1920
- 1930
- 1935 — Graduates from the Institute of New Architecture and Industrial Arts, Tokyo.
- 1938 — Joins the Nippon Kobo design studio.
- 1940
- 1950
- 1953 — Exhibits at MoMA, New York. Organizes and takes part in the 'Graphic '55' poster exhibition.
- 1955 — Cofounds the Nippon Design Centre.
- 1960 — Designs poster for the 1964 Tokyo Olympic Games.
- 1964
- 1970
- 1978 — JAGDA is founded, with Kamekura as its first president.
- 1980
- 1989 — Founds *Creation* magazine.
- 1997 — Dies in Tokyo, Japan.

Above Scale model of roundabout sign. Transport lettering and overall design of signing system: Jock Kinneir and Margaret Calvert, Ministry of Transport, 1957–63.

Below Cover of ICI's *Plastics Today* magazine featuring signs designed by Kinneir and Calvert, cover designed by Fletcher/Forbes/Gill 1965.

'We started from scratch, with a specification for the ideal letterform, having looked at other possibilities, including adapting the typeface Akzidenz Grotesk, a major influence.' (MC)

Jock Kinneir and Margaret Calvert

1917–1994 (Kinneir) / b. 1936 (Calvert)

UK

Although responsible for designing many successful signage systems around the world, it is the signs that revolutionized Britain's road system that have become Jock Kinneir and Margaret Calvert's lasting legacy. Implemented between 1957 and 1967, the signs have become as much a part of the fabric of the British landscape as the red pillar box or the black cab.

Kinneir had worked as a designer at the Design Research Unit (p. 228) before setting up his own practice in 1956. When he was invited by one of the architects to design the signage system for the redevelopment of Gatwick Airport in 1957, he enlisted Calvert, one of his students at the Chelsea School of Art. It was an ambitious project and a steep learning curve for both – Kinneir had never worked on such a comprehensive signage project before; it was Calvert's first job.

When Colin Anderson became chairman of the government committee appointed to look at the country's motorway signs he called on Kinneir again. Increased wealth and car production had led to an explosion in the number of motorists in the UK, and the government planned to expand the road network with miles of new motorway. Existing signage had grown organically and was clearly not up to the job, so Kinneir and Calvert (who was made an associate designer in 1966) set about creating a comprehensive system that was clear and easy to read at high speeds. Transport, a new

letterform, influenced by the typeface Akzidenz Grotesk with regard to proportion and overall appearance, was designed specifically for use in 'upper- and lower-case' letters, to aid word recognition of place names. Great attention was paid to appropriate word spacing; the arrangement of information, and the size and colour of each specific group of signs relating to specific routes, relative to the UK network.

The signs were tested in an underground car park in Knightsbridge, in Hyde Park and then on the Preston bypass in Lancashire. They were a resounding success, and Kinneir was tasked with redesigning the signage for all British roads. It was a huge undertaking. Using the European protocol of triangular signs for warnings, circular signs for instructions and rectangular signs for information, the system was strictly colour-coded and based on a set of pictograms, mostly drawn by Calvert.

In 2012 the digital font New Transport, based on Calvert's drawings, was produced in close collaboration with Calvert by Henrik Kubel of A2-TYPE, in six weights, for general release. Two of these weights were adapted for the award-winning Gov.uk website.

Above Portrait of Kinneir and Calvert in Old Barrack Yard, by Ian Middleton, c. 1972.

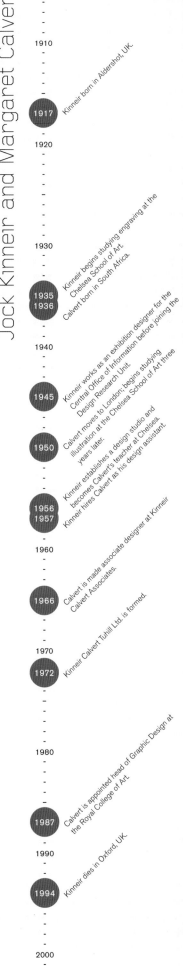

Jock Kinneir and Margaret Calvert

Above Jesmond Station, platform sign, Tyne and Wear metro, 1981.

Bottom New Rail Alphabet, produced in collaboration with Henrik Kubel. Digital update of the British Rail Alphabet designed in the 1960s, 2009.

Below Cabin baggage labels, P&O Orient Line, *c.* early 1960s.

New Rail Alphabet

Off White — *Off White Italic*
White — *White Italic*
Light — *Light Italic*
Medium — *Medium Italic*
Bold — ***Bold Italic***
Black — ***Black Italic***

- 1917 Kinneir born in Aldershot, UK.
- 1935 Kinneir begins studying engraving at the Chelsea School of Art.
- 1936 Calvert born in South Africa.
- 1945 Kinneir works as an exhibition designer for the Central Office of Information before joining the Design Research Unit.
- 1950 Calvert moves to London; begins studying illustration at the Chelsea School of Art three years later.
- 1956 Kinneir establishes a design studio and becomes Calvert's teacher at Chelsea.
- 1957 Kinneir hires Calvert as his design assistant.
- 1960 Calvert is made associate designer at Kinneir Calvert Associates.
- 1966 Kinneir Calvert Tuhill Ltd. is formed.
- 1972
- 1987 Calvert is appointed head of Graphic Design at the Royal College of Art.
- 1994 Kinneir dies in Oxford, UK.

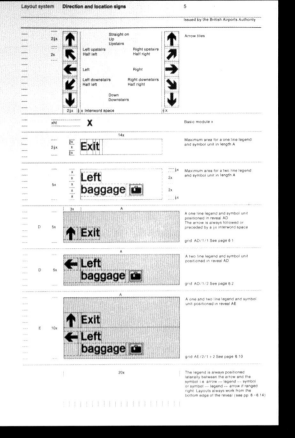

Above Airport signing system, British Airports Authority, manual, 1972.

Left Drawing of letters for the GDS Transport typeface, 2012.

Left below GDS Transport typeface, light and bold weights, 2012.

ABCDEFGHIJKLMNOPQRSTUVWXYZ
([{&}])?!:.,0123456789%
abcdefghijklmnopqrstuvwxyz
GDS Transport

**ABCDEFGHIJKLMNOPQRSTUVWXYZ
([{&}])?!:.,0123456789%
abcdefghijklmnopqrstuvwxyz
GDS Transport**

Worth Repeating

The Columbia Broadcasting System turned in a superb journalistic beat last night, running away with the major honors in reporting President Johnson's election victory. In clarity of presentation the network led all the way... In a medium where time is of the essence the performance of CBS was of landslide proportions. The difference...lay in the CBS sampling process called Vote Profile Analysis...the CBS staff called the outcome in state after state before its rivals. JACK GOULD, The New York Times (11/4)

CBS News

'There's no such thing as boring design projects, just boring designers.'

Lou Dorfsman

1918–2008

USA

Lou Dorfsman's name will forever be associated with one company – broadcasting giant, Columbia Broadcasting System. Dorfsman joined CBS in 1946, working his way up to become the creative director and vice-president. He was responsible for shaping the look of the entire CBS output, from its sophisticated advertising to the legendary mural in the cafeteria.

Apparently attracted by its 'high graphic standards', Dorfsman joined CBS after he left the army in 1946, starting as an assistant to Bill Golden (creator of the iconic 'eye' logo). In 1951 Dorfsman became the art director for the radio arm of CBS, shaping the department's strategy as well as its look, and turning around what was seen as a dying medium. In 1959, when Golden died unexpectedly, Dorfsman was made Art Director for Television. A promotion to Director of Design for the entire network came in 1964.

Dorfsman believed passionately in the value of design, and he worked hard to retain creative control – no mean feat, given the scale of CBS's operation. He oversaw everything, from the set for Walter Cronkite's newsroom to the paper cups in the cafeteria. He also designed annual reports, and a number of stunning promotional pieces, including *10:56:20 PM, 7/20/69* a hardback book featuring a dust jacket blind-embossed with a moon crater, celebrating CBS's coverage of the 1969 moon landing. It associated CBS with a truly historic event and became an instant collector's item.

In 1965 CBS moved into an impressive new building on Sixth Avenue, designed by Eero Saarinen. Nicknamed the 'Black Rock', Dorfsman took the opportunity to design everything from the stationery to the hoardings outside. He commissioned two typefaces from the designer Freeman Craw (CBS Didot and CBS Sans), and these featured throughout the building, even

on the fire-exit signs; 80 clocks were also dismantled and put back together with new faces.

Dorfsman's *tour de force* was the enormous food-themed *Gastrotypographicalassemblage*, which he created with the help of long-time friend Herb Lubalin (p. 124) and partner Tom Carnase. Comprised of nine panels, 10.6m (35ft) long, 2.6m (8ft 6in) high, and covered with 1,650 individually hand-turned wooden letterforms, the typographic mural remained on the wall of the CBS canteen for 25 years. It is currently being restored to its former glory by the designer Nick Fasciano.

Dorfsman finally left CBS in 1987, later becoming the art director for the Museum of Broadcasting, run by former CBS chief, William S. Paley. Dorfsman was a key figure in the development of corporate identity, respected by all for his no-compromise approach. According to fellow art director, George Lois, 'He was the kingpin of the New York School of Design, a pluperfect, fearless, uncompromising perfectionist, and a father of corporate image in the world.'

Opposite *Worth Repeating*, CBS advertisement, 5 November 1964.

Above Portrait of Dorfsman.

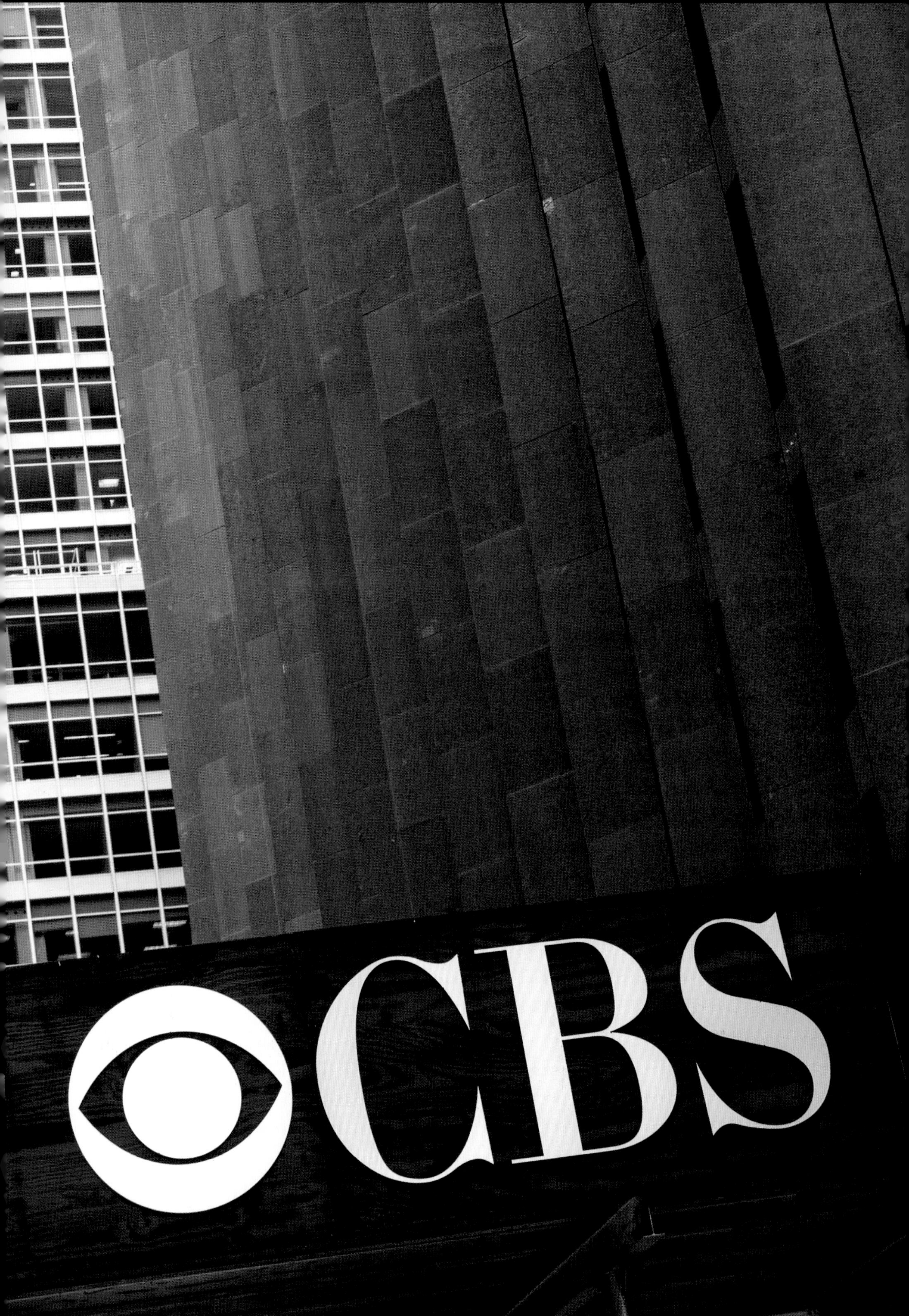
CBS

CBS1981

ANNUAL REPORT

Top: A microscopic diamond stylus for videodisc mastering is prepared at the CBS Technology Center. Bottom: Rock superstar Billy Joel has sold more than 25 million albums in his eight-year career with CBS Records.

CBS News Correspondent Dan Rather (top) anchors television's most-watched news broadcast, the CBS Evening News. Bottom: Millions of children learn the basics of reading, mathematics and science with textbooks by Holt, Rinehart & Winston.

Top: CBS Sports' 26th consecutive year of broadcasting NFL football was highlighted by a substantial audience increase. Bottom: Family Weekly, CBS's Sunday newspaper magazine, is read by more than 27 million adults.

Actor, writer and director Alan Alda stars in M*A*S*H, which returned for its tenth season on the CBS Television Network in 1981.

Top: The Gabriel Industries Division's Pretty Cut & Grow,™ one of the nation's most popular dolls in 1981. Bottom: Rock group REO Speedwagon reached superstar status in 1981 with their phenomenal album, Hi Infidelity. More than six million copies had been sold at the year's end.

Gemeinhardt flutes (top) are manufactured to exacting specifications for music students and performing artists around the world. Bottom: The Challenge, the CBS Theatrical Films Group's second feature film, will be released in 1982.

Opposite CBS lettering on the CBS building, New York City.

Above CBS Annual Report, 1981.

Below The Inside Track logo, designed by Peter Katz, art direction Lou Dorfsman, 1977.

Lou Dorfsman

- 1918 Born in New York City.
- 1920
- 1930
- 1939 Makes displays for the New York World's Fair.
- 1943 Serves in the US Army.
- 1946 Starts working for the CBS Radio Network.
- 1950
- 1960
- 1964 Becomes Director of Design at CBS.
- 1966 Designs the Gastrotypographicalassemblage mural with Herb Lubalin and Tom Carnase.
- 1970
- 1980
- 1987 Establishes his own studio.
- 1990
- 2000
- 2008 Dies in Roslyn, New York, US.

The Sweden/Norway Tour. Nu kommer Alan Peckolick och Tom Carnase till Sverige och Norge. Ni känner säkert igen mycket av det dom har gjort. Men varför har dom gjort det och hur har dom gjort det. Det blir spännande eftermiddagar med massor av diabilder och film. **Turnéplan:** Malmö 20 maj. Lokal: Klubbrummet, Hotell S:t Jörgen, Nygatan 35. Tid: kl. 13—17.00 med kaffepaus kl. 14.30. Boka plats senast onsdag d. 14.5. Göteborg 22 maj. Lokal: Rum A-B, Hotell Park Avenue, Kungsportsavenyn 36—38. Tid: kl. 12—16.00 med kaffepaus kl. 14.00. Boka plats senast onsdag d. 14.5. Stockholm 26 maj. Lokal: Filmhuset Gärdet Tid: kl. 13.00—17.00 med kaffepaus kl. 14.30. Boka plats senast torsdag d. 22.5. Bergen Norge 28 maj. Fyll i bifogade. **ABCD konferensen 1975.**

'Typography can be as exciting as illustration and photography. Sometimes you sacrifice legibility to increase impact.'

Herb Lubalin

1918–1981

USA

Herb Lubalin will forever be associated with the name Avant Garde, both for the typeface and the magazine masthead where it originated. His playful approach to designing with words and images, treating type as image (and vice versa) was the antithesis of the regimented approach of the Swiss School that had dominated graphic design in the post-war era.

Lubalin spent the early part of his career in advertising as an art director, but it was for his editorial work that he became most famous (or infamous). In 1962 he collaborated with publisher Ralph Ginzburg on a quarterly magazine called *Eros*. A 96-page hardback publication with no adverts, it provided Lubalin with an amazing platform for expression and experimentation. Billed as 'the magazine of love', its daring subject matter proved highly controversial, and eventually led to Ginzburg being jailed for eight months for sending obscene material through the post. Lubalin was not penalized, but later said that he felt he should have gone to prison too.

Undeterred by this, *Fact* magazine was the pair's next collaboration, a low-budget whistle-blowing magazine, with each issue illustrated entirely by one illustrator. After this came *Avant Garde*, a more elaborate fiction- and reportage-based publication, with a square format and Lubalin's most expressive layouts to date. One of the key factors was his use of phototypesetting (exposing negatives of letterforms on to photographic paper); Lubalin was one of the first graphic designers to really explore the technique's many possibilities.

Offering freedom from the constraints of traditional metal type, phototypesetting revolutionized the world of graphic design in the 1960s. Its affordability suddenly led to hundreds of new typefaces being created, and the reissue of traditional ones, particularly many decorative Victorian fonts. Two key features were the ability to backslant and overlap characters, and nowhere was this more apparent than in Lubalin's typeface, Avant Garde. Originally created as the masthead for the eponymous magazine, Avant Garde featured a regular set of characters, plus an extra set of special characters and ligatures with 45-degree angles. These gave the user the chance to play around with the letters as they set them, and it was well known that Lubalin was not particularly impressed by many of these home-grown typographic experiments. Lubalin also designed the popular typefaces Lubalin Graph, Ronda and ITC Serif Gothic.

In 1970 the International Typeface Corporation (ITC) was established, and Lubalin became its design director. One of his roles was to edit and design *U&lc* (*Upper & Lower Case*), the ITC's bi-annual, tabloid-format promotional magazine. Relishing the chance to finally 'be his own client', Lubalin created some truly exciting issues. Under his editorship (until his death in 1981), *U&lc* proved to be hugely influential, at the height of its popularity it had over 170,000 subscribers.

Above Portrait of Lubalin, 1975.

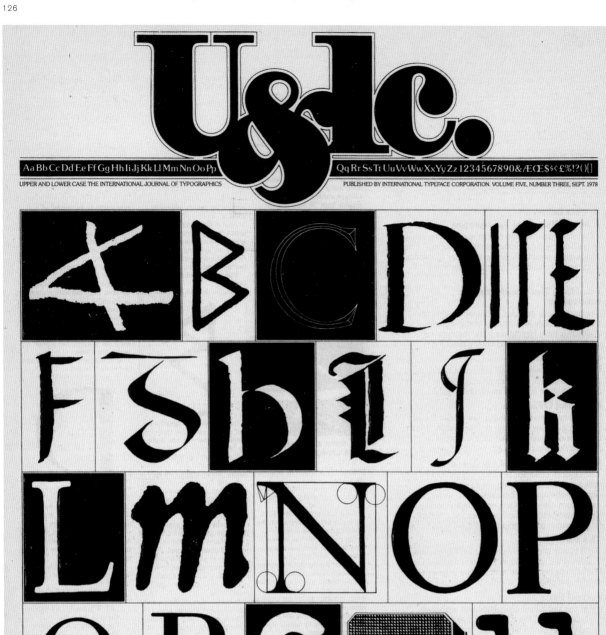

Aa Bb Cc Dd Ee Ff Gg Hh Ii Jj Kk Ll Mm Nn Oo Pp   Qq Rr Ss Tt Uu Vv Ww Xx Yy Zz 1234567890 & ÆŒ $¢ £ %!? () []

UPPER AND LOWER CASE THE INTERNATIONAL JOURNAL OF TYPOGRAPHICS   PUBLISHED BY INTERNATIONAL TYPEFACE CORPORATION. VOLUME FIVE, NUMBER THREE, SEPT. 1978

U&lc Volume 5, issue #3
cover, 1978.

1918 Born in New York City, US.

1920

1930 Graduates from the Cooper Union.

1940

1945 Joins Sudler & Hennessey in New York.

1950

1960
1962 First issue of *Eros* is published.
1964 Founds Herb Lubalin Inc.

1968 First issue of *Avant Garde* is published.
1970 ITC Avant Garde typeface is released.

1973 First issue of *U&lc* is published.

1981 Dies in New York City, US.

Top '72 holiday card design, lettering by Tom Carnase, 1971.

Above Herb Lubalin Inc. logo, lettering by John Pistilli, 1964.

Above *Avant Garde* magazine, issue 13, cover, 1971.

Gran premio dell' Autodromo di Monza,
poster, 1948.

'The visual punctuations
that brought Huber fame
unambiguously reverberate with
Marinetti's rabble-rousing *parole
in libertà* (words in freedom).'
– Stanislaus von Moos

Max Huber

1919–1992

SWITZERLAND

A Swiss-born designer who brought his unique take on Modernism to Milan, Max Huber's exuberant designs feature bright colours, bold shapes and abstract patterns, combining Swiss sophistication and Italian flair to great effect. Many of his designs employ the technique of overprinting, and nowhere is this more effective than in those he created for the Autodromo Nazionale di Monza racetrack, epitomizing the speed and glamour of Italian motor racing in the late 1940s.

After graduating from the Zurich School of Applied Arts, and a spell working at the publishing house Conzett & Huber, Huber moved to Milan in 1940. Despite not speaking a word of Italian, he went to work for Antonio Boggeri at Studio Boggeri. The onset of war meant a return to Zurich the following year, but his love affair with Italy was far from over; he returned at the end of the war, and remained there for many years.

While in Switzerland, Huber worked on a series of exhibition projects with Max Bill. He also joined the Allianz group of Swiss Concrete Artists (which included Bill and Richard Paul Lohse) and exhibited with them at the Galerie des Eaux Vives. Huber had also obviously made a big impact in Milan – while he was in Zurich during the war, the journal *Typographische Monatsblätter* published an issue dedicated to Italian graphic design, which acknowledged its profound influence on Swiss design, and featured an homage to Huber.

Despite his long association with Studio Boggeri, Huber always worked as an independent designer, and

on his return to Milan in 1946 he worked on projects for publisher Einaudi and for the 8th Milan Triennale. Shortly after this, he started to produce posters for the Monza racetrack, one of the most famous being for the 1948 Grand Prix. Deceptively simple, its combination of overprinted arrows and elongated typography managed to convey the idea of both speed and excitement without showing a car or a racetrack. Huber designed a number of equally memorable posters for motorsport events at Monza up until the early 1970s.

Huber's real passion was music. A massive jazz fan, in the early 1950s he designed record sleeves for Parlophone and covers for *Ritmo* and *Jazztime* magazines. His record boxes, individually decorated to match their contents, are works of art in themselves.

Huber also worked for corporate clients across many different industries, from fashion to home furnishings, publishing, textiles and food. Some of his finest work was for the landmark Milan department store la Rinascente, which first employed him in 1950. Huber oversaw the design of everything from the wrapping paper to the visual identity for the store's bicycle race; his artistic vision helped to turn the store from a shop into a lifestyle brand.

Above Portrait of Huber.

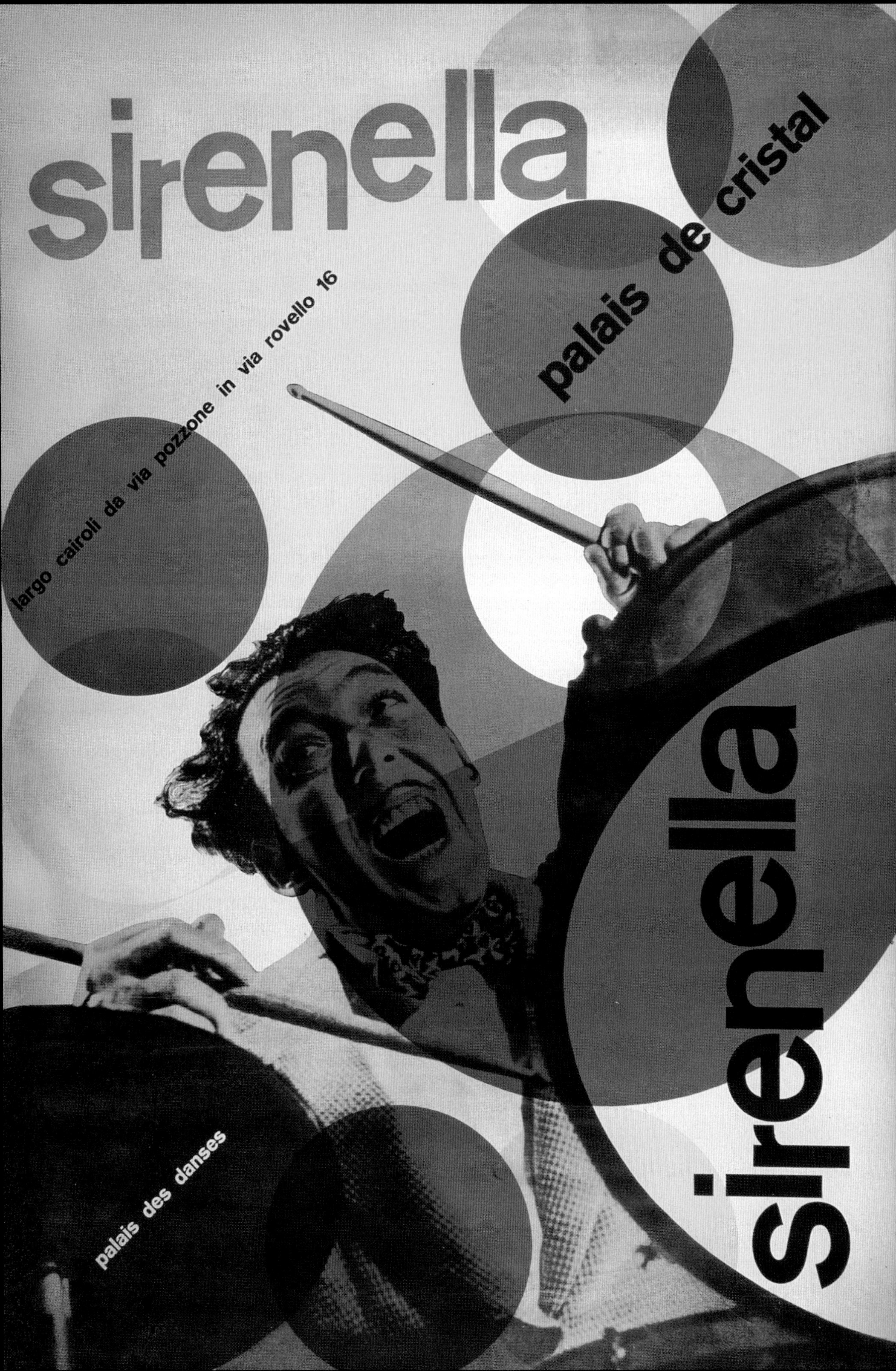
sirenella
palais de cristal
largo cairoli da via pozzone in via rovello 16
sirenella
palais des danses

- 1919 Born in Baar, Switzerland.
- 1930
- 1935 Studies at the Zurich School of Applied Arts.
- 1940 Travels to Milan to work for Studio Boggeri.
- 1941 Returns to Zurich.
- 1942 Member of the Allianz group.
- 1946 Returns to Milan.
- 1950
- 1958 Speaks at the ADC's First International Seminar on Typography in New York.
- 1960
- 1965 Work is exhibited at the Matsuya Design Gallery in Tokyo.
- 1970
- 1980
- 1990 Dies in Sagno, Switzerland.
- 1992

Opposite *Sirenella – Palais de Cristal – palais des danses*, poster, 1946.

Above *Italia URSS*, poster, 1966.

Left *Borsalino*, poster, 1949.

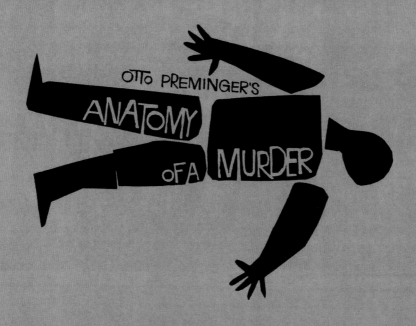

STARRING
JAMES STEWART
LEE REMICK
BEN GAZZARA
ARTHUR O'CONNELL
EVE ARDEN
KATHRYN GRANT

and JOSEPH N. WELCH as Judge Weaver

'Sometimes when an idea flashes, you distrust it because it seems too easy. You qualify it with all kinds of evasive phrases because you're timid about it. But often, this turns out to be the best idea of all.'

Saul Bass

1920–1996

USA

Widely considered to be the master of film-title design, through his collaborations with directors such as Otto Preminger, Alfred Hitchcock and Martin Scorsese, Saul Bass is credited with transforming the two- or three-minute opening credits of a film into an art form. His clever use of type, bold graphics and animation held the viewer's attention in a way that was completely new.

Bass worked as a freelance designer in his native New York before moving to Los Angeles in 1946. After seeing his poster for the film *Carmen Jones*, director Otto Preminger asked Bass to design the film's title sequence. This led to him being commissioned to create titles for Robert Aldrich's *The Big Knife* (1955) and Billy Wilder's *The Seven Year Itch* (1955). His next Preminger project was the highly controversial *The Man with the Golden Arm* (1955), starring Frank Sinatra as a recovering heroin addict. Bass's stark black-and-white treatment, with its accompanying poster featuring the jagged silhouette of an arm, was instantly recognizable. The film caused a huge stir and Bass found himself much in demand.

Bass's first collaboration with the British director Alfred Hitchcock was for his film *Vertigo* (1958). It featured a menacing close-up of a woman's eye and spinning, kinetic graphics. Bass went on to create striking titles for Hitchcock's *North by Northwest* (1959) and *Psycho* (1960), as well as numerous blockbuster films, including Preminger's *Anatomy of a Murder* (1959) and Stanley Kubrick's *Spartacus* (1960).

There followed a foray into directing with the ill-fated sci-fi film *Phase IV* (1974), then three short films:

Notes on the Popular Art (1977), *The Solar Film* (1980) and *Quest* (1983). He returned to title sequences after being approached by *Broadcast News* director James L. Brooks in 1987, and this was followed up by an ongoing collaboration with Martin Scorsese on *Goodfellas* (1990), *Cape Fear* (1991) and *The Age of Innocence* (1993). The very last titles Bass created were for Scorsese's 1995 film, *Casino*.

In addition to film titles, Bass was also responsible for many well-known corporate identities, including Continental Airlines, AT&T, United Airlines and Minolta. A 2011 survey found that logos designed by him had an average lifespan of 34 years – a huge achievement in the often fickle world of branding and corporate identity.

Bass changed the way film titles were perceived forever, turning them from a formality to be projected over closed curtains to constituting an integral part of the film-going experience. 'I had felt for some time that the audience involvement with the film should really begin with the very first frame,' he explained. 'There seemed to be a real opportunity to use titles in a new way – to actually create a climate for the story that was about to unfold.'

Opposite *Anatomy of a Murder*, poster, 1959.

Above Portrait of Bass, c. 1960.

FRANK SINATRA · ELEANOR PARKER · KIM NOVAK

THE MAN WITH THE GOLDEN ARM

A FILM BY OTTO PREMINGER · FROM THE NOVEL BY NELSON ALGREN · MUSIC BY ELMER BERNSTEIN · PRODUCED & DIRECTED BY OTTO PREMINGER

A JOHN FRANKENHEIMER FILM IN CINERAMA

STARRING
JAMES GARNER·EVA MARIE SAINT·YVES MONTAND
TOSHIRO MIFUNE·BRIAN BEDFORD·JESSICA WALTERS
ANTONIO SABATO·FRANCOISE HARDY·ADOLFO CELI
Directed by John Frankenheimer · Produced by Edward Lewis

Opposite *The Man with the Golden Arm*, poster, 1955.

Above *Grand Prix*, poster, 1966.

Left *Exodus*, poster, 1960.

EXODUS

OTTO PREMINGER PRESENTS
PAUL NEWMAN · EVA MARIE SAINT
RALPH RICHARDSON · PETER LAWFORD
LEE J. COBB · SAL MINEO · JOHN DEREK
HUGH GRIFFITH · GREGORY RATOFF
JILL HAWORTH IN "EXODUS"

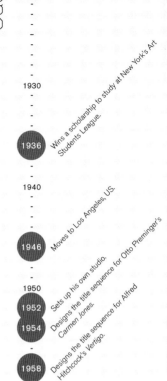

Saul Bass

- 1920 Born in New York City, US.
-
-
-
1930
-
- 1936 Wins a scholarship to study at New York's Art Students League.
-
1940
-
- 1946 Moves to Los Angeles, US.
-
1950
- 1952 Sets up his own studio.
- 1954 Designs the title sequence for Otto Preminger's *Carmen Jones*.
-
- 1958 Designs the title sequence for Alfred Hitchcock's *Vertigo*.
1960
-
-
-
-
-
1970
-
-
-
-
-
1980
-
-
-
-
1990
-
-
- 1996 Dies in Los Angeles.

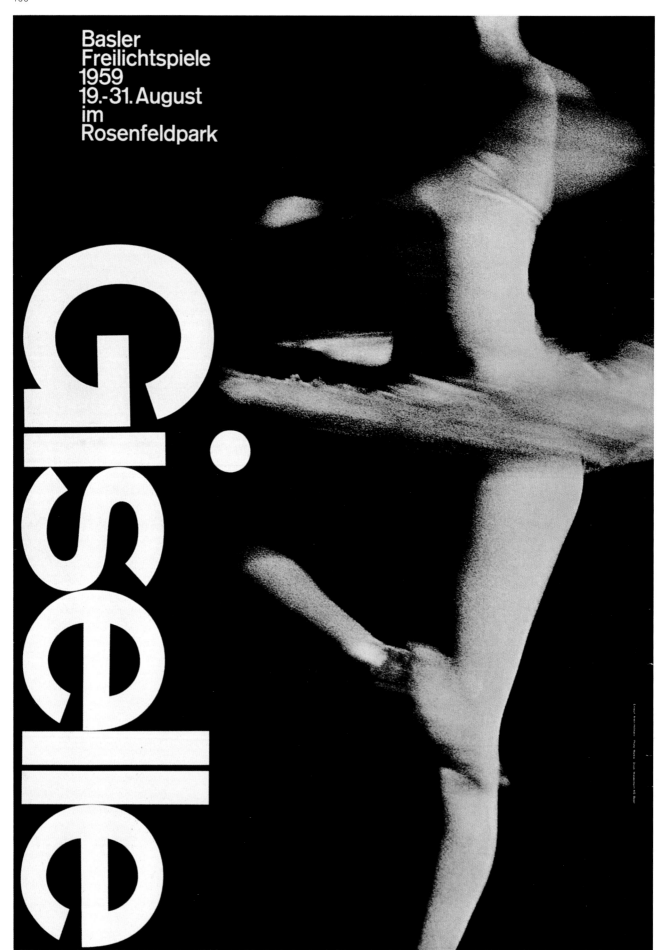

Basler
Freilichtspiele
1959
19.-31. August
im
Rosenfeldpark

Giselle

Giselle, poster for Basler
Freilichtspiele, 1959.

> 'There should be no separation between spontaneous work with an emotional tone and work directed by the intellect. Both are supplementary to each other and must be regarded as intimately connected. Discipline and freedom are thus to be seen as elements of equal weight, each partaking of the other.'

Armin Hofmann

b. 1920

SWITZERLAND

By the time he retired in 1991, Armin Hofmann's teaching career had spanned nearly 45 years. During his time at Basel he mentored thousands of students, many of whom went on to become successful designers, including April Greiman (p. 232), Dan Friedman and Steff Geissbuhler. A charismatic teacher, Hofmann was also an accomplished designer; his designs for the Stadt Theater Basel and the Kunsthalle Basel are stunning examples of poster design – restrained, elegant, yet massively impactful and as inspirational now as they were over 50 years ago.

After studying at the School of Arts and Crafts in Zurich, Hofmann went to work as a lithographer, before opening his own studio in Basel. Hofmann was to remain at Basel for more than 40 years; in 1968 he established the Advanced Course in Graphic Design, and in 1973 he became head of Graphic Design. There were only 12 students per year on the four-year course, and Hofmann's classes were rigorous exercises in form and composition. He often worked in black and white, or two colours, recognizing the value that this restriction brought: 'When reduced to black and white, the processes of contrast and confrontation become clearer, more understandable, and easier to learn – as much for the designer as for the audience.' Hofmann insisted on hand-drawn rather than typeset lettering, which distinguished his teaching from other more regimented courses such as that taught by Müller-Brockmann

(p. 100) at Zurich. Hofman also taught in Philadelphia and at Yale, and in 1965 his book *Graphic Design Manual: Principles and Practice* was published (a revised edition of which is still in print).

Hofmann's designs for cultural institutions were manifestations of his design doctrines. His black-and-white poster for an open-air performance of *Giselle* created in 1959 – is described by designer and historian Richard Hollis as 'one of the defining moments in Swiss graphic design'. The designer Paul Rand also acknowledges the huge contribution made by Hoffman: 'Few of us have sacrificed so much time, money and comfort for the sake of their profession as has Armin Hofmann. He is one of the few exceptions to Shaw's dictum, "He who can, does; he who cannot teaches". His goals, though pragmatic, are never pecuniary. His influence has been as strong beyond the classroom as within it. Even those who are his critics are as eager about his ideas as those who sit at his feet. As a human being he is simple and unassuming. As a teacher he has few equals. As a practitioner he ranks among the best.'

Above *Die Gute Form*, poster, 1954.

Stadt Theater Basel 63/64,
poster, 1963.

63/
64

STADT
THEATER
BASEL

Armin Hofmann

1920 — Born in Winterthur, Switzerland.

1930

1940

1947 — Starts teaching at the Basel School of Design.

1950

1955 — Starts teaching at the Philadelphia College of Art.

1960

1965 — Publishes *Graphic Design Manual: Principles and Practice*.

1968 — Establishes the Advanced Course in Graphic Design.

1970 — Becomes head of Graphic Design at Basel.

1973

1980

1991 — Retires.

2000

2010

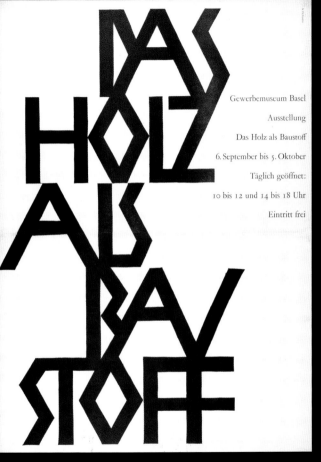

Above left *Das Holz als Baustoff,*
linocut, 1952.

Above right *Plakate aus der Sammlung
des Gewerbemuseums Basel,*
poster, 1964.

Lufthansa, corporate identity, 1969.

'Good art inspires; good design motivates.'

Otl Aicher

1922–1991

GERMANY

As design director for the 1972 Olympics, Otl Aicher created one of the most admired identities in the history of graphic design. Often credited as the first designer to create printed 'brand guidelines', his singular vision and rigorous application has left a legacy that still influences graphic designers more than 40 years later.

Aicher grew up in Nazi Germany and was involved with the White Rose resistance movement; he was arrested for refusing to join the Hitler Youth. After the war he studied sculpture at the Academy of Fine Arts in Munich before setting up his own studio in Ulm in 1947. A keen educator, in 1953 he founded the Ulm School of Design with his wife Inge Scholl and his friend Max Bill (p. 60). Housed in a building designed by Bill, the school's experimental outlook made it hugely influential in its approach to design education.

In 1966, Aicher received the commission to become design director of the 1972 Munich Olympics. His corporate identity was designed to work with architect Günther Behnisch's radical stadium design, and to reflect the motto of the so-called 'Happy Games' (unfortunately later overshadowed by the murder of 11 Israeli athletes).

Aicher chose a bright colour palette to reflect the surrounding countryside, adapted Coordt von Mannstein's winning spiral logo design ('Bright Sun') and created the first ever Olympic mascot – the multicoloured dachshund, Waldi. He oversaw every piece of collateral, from the posters for individual sports to medals, badges, tickets, timetables, uniforms, and a raft of souvenirs, including crockery, umbrellas and inflatables. This meticulous attention to detail led to an accomplished (and flawless) identity project, which many would say has yet to be surpassed.

One of Aicher's most enduring designs for the Games was a set of elegant grid-based pictograms, which was also used four years later in Montreal. Often cited as being almost impossible to improve on, the pictograms live on via German lighting company ERCO, which licensed, developed and expanded the range for commercial use.

Aicher also undertook many other significant projects, including the identities for Lufthansa, Munich Airport, TV channel ZDF and Dresdner Bank. As a consultant for electronics firm Braun, he was responsible for overseeing its new Modernist aesthetic and for hiring the designer Dieter Rams.

In 1972 Aicher set up a studio in Rotis, in southern Germany, where he wrote several books on design and set up the Rotis Institute for Analogue Studies. It was here, too, that he designed the typeface Rotis in 1988, a distinctive yet extremely legible typeface family that was used extensively in the 1990s by global corporations such as Nokia and Accenture, and some years later by Peter Saville (p. 128) for Factory Records impresario Tony Wilson's gravestone.

Above Portrait of Aicher by Sisi von Schweinitz, 1954.

München ⬯⬯⬯ 1972

Above *Women's Floor*, duotone poster, 1972 Munich Olympic Games.

Right Pictograms created for the 1972 Munich Olympic Games.

Below *Waldi*, design for the first Olympic mascot, 1972.

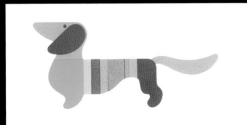

Wrestling, duotone poster, 1972 Munich
Olympic Games.

1972

1920
1922 Born in Ulm, Germany.

1930

1940

1947 Opens his studio in Ulm.
1950 Founds the Ulm School of Design with Max Bill
1953 and Inge Scholl.

1960

1966 Commissioned to create identity for the 1972
Munich Olympics.
1969 Creates corporate identity for Lufthansa.
1972 Moves to Rotis and sets up his studio.

1980

1988 Designs the Rotis typeface family.

1991 Dies in Günzburg, Germany.

144

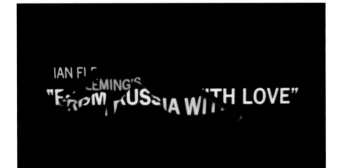

'For some reason (probably clear to a psychiatrist) four design projects in which I have been recently involved have all had a strong emphasis on sex in the form of the female anatomy.'

Robert Brownjohn

1925–1970

USA

Now something of a cult figure, Robert Brownjohn was the consummate 1960s graphic designer, blurring the boundaries between work and life, and between graphic design and conceptual art. Moving with ease from the New York to the London design scene, he lived fast and died young, leaving a modest but significant body of work that ensured a place in the canon of graphic design history.

Born in New Jersey to British parents, Brownjohn studied at the Institute of Design in Chicago under the famous Bauhaus émigré, László Moholy-Nagy. Brownjohn embraced his teacher's experimental methods, exploring how new technology could influence graphic design, and using light and film to embrace these ideas.

Brownjohn moved to New York, and in 1957 set up Brownjohn, Chermayeff & Geismar (with Ivan Chermayeff and Tom Geismar, p. 252). The agency worked on projects such as the US pavilion at the 1958 Brussels World's Fair, and for corporate clients such as Pirelli, Columbia Records and Pepsi. Friends with musicians like Miles Davis, Charlie Parker and Stan Getz, Brownjohn partied on the New York jazz scene and developed the requisite heroin habit. A move to London (for a fresh start) in 1960 saw Brownjohn arrive just in time to embrace the Swinging Sixties. He was introduced to the emerging London graphic design scene by Alan Fletcher (p. 184) and fellow American Bob Gill, and worked as an art director for J. Walter Thompson and McCann Erickson. 'He liked his ideas to seem off the cuff,' Fletcher recalled.

'He liked to seem lazy, but he could work hard at it.'

Brownjohn's work was sophisticated but edgy, and retained a sense of spontaneity. His famous poster promoting the 'Obsession and Fantasy' exhibition at the Robert Fraser Gallery featured Brownjohn's topless girlfriend with his hand-drawn type spread across her chest. It encapsulated his twin obsessions – sex and typography – and caused quite a stir.

Brownjohn might have remained an underground figure had it not been for a commission to create the film titles for the second James Bond film, *From Russia With Love* (1963). Allegedly inspired by seeing people walk in front of the projector at a lecture, the sequence featured type projected on to the body of a belly-dancing model, to great effect and widespread acclaim. An equally striking sequence for *Goldfinger* (1964) used a similar technique with a model clad in a gold bikini.

One of Brownjohn's last commissions was the design of the Rolling Stones LP *Let It Bleed* (1969). Commissioned by his friend Keith Richards, and based on an automatic record changer, the striking 'before' and 'after' images also feature a gaudy cake created by a little-known chef called Delia Smith.

Opposite Title sequence for *From Russia with Love*, Robert Brownjohn (director) and Trevor Bond (animator), 1963.

Above Portrait of Brownjohn, 1968.

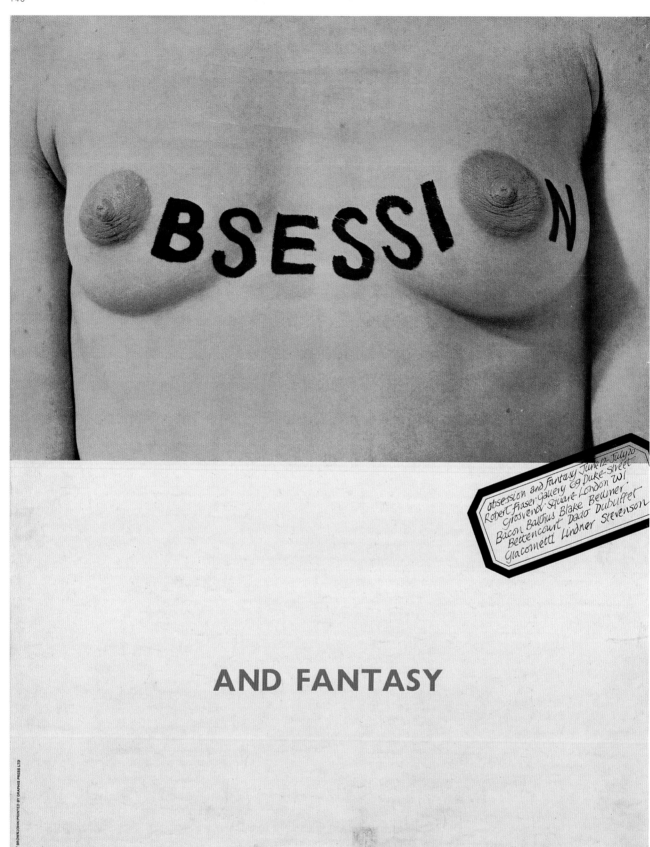

Obsession and Fantasy, exhibition
poster, 1963.

Above and below *Let It Bleed*, Rolling
Stones LP cover, front (above) and back
(below), 1969.

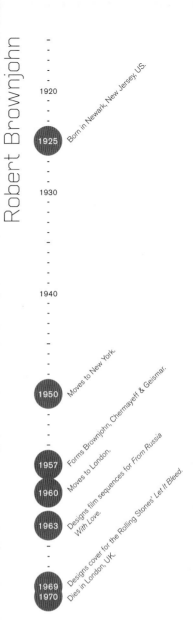

Robert Brownjohn

1920

1925 — Born in Newark, New Jersey, US.

1930

1940

1950 — Moves to New York.

1957 — Forms Brownjohn, Chermayeff & Geismar.

1960 — Moves to London.

1963 — Designs film sequences for *From Russia With Love*.

1969
1970 — Designs cover for the Rolling Stones' *Let It Bleed*.
       Dies in London, UK.

BOUR
LIN
GUER

Blaise Cendrars

le Club du meilleur livre

'There is no real difference between a poster and a book cover: they both have to be seen as you move past them, and they have to impress you quickly and convincingly.'

Robert Massin

b. 1925

FRANCE

Robert Massin is a designer for whom words have always been as significant as images. A book designer par excellence, he was art director of the Gallimard publishing house for over 20 years. He is known for groundbreaking pieces of expressive book design – editions of Raymond Queneau's *Exercices de style*, *La lettre et l'image* and *La Cantatrice Chauve* – and has also published his own writing, although much of it under a pseudonym.

Massin (as he became known in the 1950s) served an apprenticeship with the book designer, Pierre Faucheux, at the Club Français du Livre – one of the book clubs set up in France after World War II to satisfy the growing demand for books after the Nazi occupation. It was Massin's first introduction to layout, typesetting and printing, and very much a hands-on education.

From 1952 to 1960, Massin was the art director for another club – Le Club du Meilleur Livre. Members chose one book a month, from an eclectic mix of novels, classics and out-of-print works. With no commercial constraints on the covers, the book was treated as more of an object in its own right. It was, according to Massin, 'No longer this rectangular parallelepiped as thick and inert as a brick, but something living; while printing was usually thought of as existing on the flat surface, we made a point of the book's being three-dimensional.' This allowed experimentation with a range of binding materials, including wallpaper, wood and velvet.

Massin's move to Gallimard in 1960 saw him fully immersed in the world of commercial book publishing.

He was responsible for a catalogue of over 10,000 titles, and introducing a standardized format for paperbacks – the Folio series was a perfect example, with pristine white covers and text beautifully set in Baskerville.

While Gallimard required a more classical approach to typography, Massin's personal work was infinitely more expressive. His playful 1948 version of *Exercices de style* is a short story represented typographically in 100 different ways, demonstrating the power of typography to add meaning.

His 1964 interpretation of an avant-garde Ionesco play, *La Cantatrice Chauve*, is considered by many to be his masterwork. Each actor's words are painstakingly set by hand in different typefaces, and there is no punctuation apart from exclamation and quotation marks. Type is set at many different angles and sizes, and is overlaid to convey heated exchanges in the play. Images are in black and white, and one two-minute scene takes up 48 pages. The play reaches a dramatic conclusion, as Massin describes: 'At the end of the piece, the rhythm speeds up, images and words jostle and shove one another in a sort of verbal frenzy which finishes in language being demolished: as if it were returning to its roots, reduced to onomatopoeia or single consonants and vowels.'

Above Portrait of Massin by Sophie Bassouls, 1989.

le Club du meilleur livre

Left *Les Vrais Mystères de Paris* by Eugène François Vidocq, front and back cover, 1950.

Left above *Le Club du Meilleur Livre*, wrapping, 1954.

Left below *La Cantatrice Chauve* by Eugène Ionesco, cover, 1964.

ionesco
LA CANTATRICE CHAUVE
suivie d'une scène inédite. Interprétations *typographique* de Massin et *photo-graphique* d'Henry Cohen d'après la mise en scène de Nicolas Bataille   Éditions Gallimard

Robert Massin

1920

1925 — Born in Bourdinière-Saint-Loup, France.

1930

1940

1948 — Starts working with Pierre Faucheux.

1950

1952 — Starts working for the book club Le Club du Meilleur Livre.

1960 — Appointed art director at Gallimard.

1964 — *La Cantatrice Chauve* (*The Bald Prima Donna*) is published.

1970

1980

1990

2000

2010

milioni
di
ciclisti
scelgono

velo

'Don't bore the public
with mysterious designs.'

Bob Noorda

1927–2010

THE NETHERLANDS

Despite originating from Amsterdam and spending the majority of his career in Milan (where he designed for clients including Pirelli and Olivetti), it is the city of New York that Bob Noorda's name will always be linked to. It was Noorda who, along with Massimo Vignelli, was responsible for creating the signage system for the New York subway system, much of which is still in place today.

Noorda's rigorous Bauhaus-influenced education at the School of Applied Arts (now the Gerrit Rietveld Academie) gave him a grounding in design that would prove invaluable in his later projects. He moved from his native Amsterdam to Milan in 1954, and it was here that he met the Milanese designer Massimo Vignelli (p. 188).

Pirelli had a tradition of commissioning the very best design talent for its publicity material; designers included Max Huber (p. 128), Bruno Munari (p. 56), Lora Lamm (p. 160) and Walter Ballmer. Noorda's playful designs for the tyre manufacturer gained him widespread attention, and in 1961 he became the company's art director.

Noorda was subsequently commissioned to work on the complete graphic system (which included signage, maps and posters) for the new Metropolitana Milanese underground railway, which opened in 1964. Noorda's meticulously researched designs brought him much acclaim (including the prestigious Golden Compass award), and this experience was proved invaluable when, in 1966, he and Vignelli (then working under the umbrella of Unimark International) were commissioned by the New York City Transit Authority (NYCTA) to create a new signage system for the city's subway network.

Noorda's expertise led to further commissions for subway systems in Naples and Italy, and after Unimark was disbanded in 1972, he kept the Milan office open until 2000, working for a range of corporate clients including Total, Agip and Alfa Romeo.

Vignelli recalls Noorda's methodical approach: 'I remember when Bob came to New York and spent everyday underground in the Subway to record the traffic flow in order to determine the points of decision where the signs should be placed. I also remember how we decided all details, from typeface to type spacing, from colour coding to implementation. Bob Noorda had a very systematic mind.'

Above Portrait of Noorda.

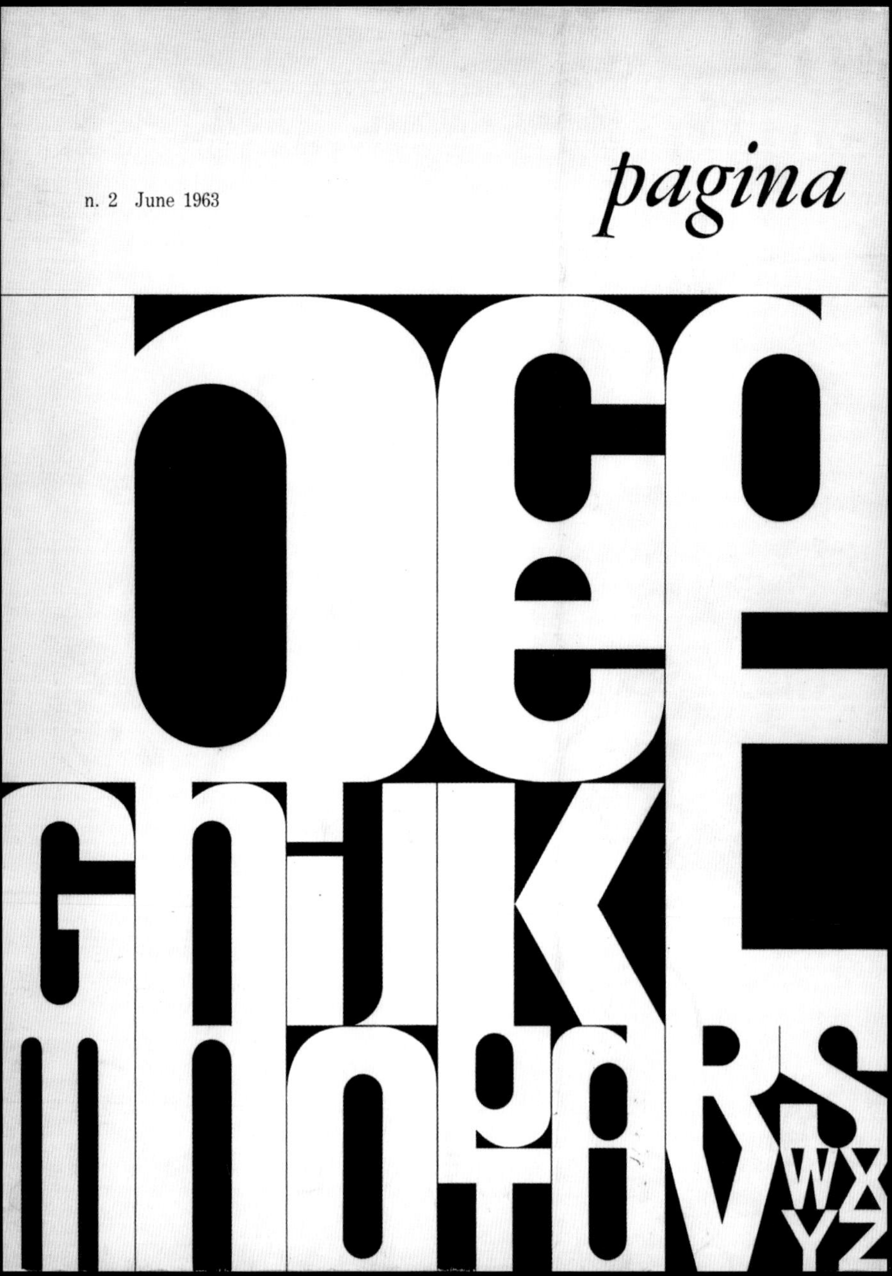

n. 2   June 1963

pagina

ABCDEFGHIJKLMNOPQRSTUVWXYZ

Above Cover of *Pagina* magazine, no. 2, June 1963.

Left Lanco advertisement, 1956.

LANCO

Swiss made

Bob Noorda

- 1920
- **1927** Born in Amsterdam, the Netherlands.
- 1930
- 1940
- **1950** Graduates from the Gerrit Rietveld Academie.
- **1954** Leaves Amsterdam for Milan.
- **1961** Becomes art director for Pirelli. Becomes art director for La Rinascente department store.
- **1963** Cofounds Unimark International.
- **1965** Unimark awarded contract by the NYCTA.
- **1966** Unimark's Milan office becomes independent.
- 1970
- **1972**
- 1980
- 1990
- 2000
- **2010** Dies in Milan, Italy.

Above New York Subway signage.

Below Advertisement for Pirelli Rolle
tyres, 1959.

Right Advertisement for Pirelli Cinturato
tyres, 1960.

'I am an engineer,
troubled by aesthetics.'

Wim Crouwel

b. 1928

THE NETHERLANDS

Almost by default, it could be argued that with the design of the New Alphabet, Wim Crouwel was responsible for the creation of one of the twentieth century's most important pieces of typeface design. It was Crouwel's response to seeing the first ever computerized typesetting and composing machine at a printing fair in Germany, and its very poor reproduction of the typeface Garamond. Instead of trying to shoehorn existing fonts, Crouwel had the idea of creating a typeface specifically for use with the new technology and its limitations.

He created an experimental, abstract font with no differentiation between upper and lower case, and 90- and 45-degree angles based on a squared grid system. This very cleverly allowed the characters to be scaled up or down without any distortion. Crouwel's father helped him cut the original letterforms, and a brochure was printed that showcased the typeface and the methodology behind it. It proved very controversial (in part, down to the font being almost unreadable) and Crouwel lectured widely on it over the following years.

Crouwel's hugely successful Gridnik typeface (named after Crouwel's nickname, Mr Gridnik, and digitized and developed by The Foundry) was developed as a response to restrictions created by technology. It began life as Politene, a font commissioned by Olivetti in 1974 for use with its electric typewriters. The typeface was never used, but Crouwel put this elegant grid-based monoline typeface to good use on a series of numerical

stamps he designed for the Dutch Post Office (PTT), which were in circulation from 1976 to 2002.

During his time working for the Stedelijk Museum Crouwel created many other grid-based display typefaces. His approach, pioneered in his earlier work for the Van Abbemuseum, was to promote exhibitions by representing them typographically with a series of striking screen-printed posters and catalogues, designed using a strict grid system. Crouwel's relationship with the Stedelijk lasted for 20 years. He subsequently swapped from being designer to client in his new post as director of the Museum Boijmans Van Beuningen – between 1985 and 1993, he commissioned 8vo (p. 292) to design over 40 catalogues and around 25 posters for the museum.

A version of New Alphabet was used by Brett Wickens on Peter Saville's artwork for the Joy Division LP *Substance* in 1988, and versions of it began to appear in various music magazines. In 1996 The Foundry worked with Crouwel to develop four of his fonts for use on the Mac, including the first digitized version of the New Alphabet, which was released in 1997. A full typeface family was later developed from Crouwel's original designs for Gridnik, meaning that as well as discovering his work, a new generation of designers could also design using his typefaces.

Opposite *Vormgevers*, poster, 1968.

Above Double portrait of Crouwel by Vincent Mantzel, 2011.

Above Postage stamp for the PTT, 1976.

Below *Neu Alphabet*, cover, 1967.

Left *Luchtkunst*, poster, 1971.

Below *Visuele Communicatie Nederland*, poster, 1969.

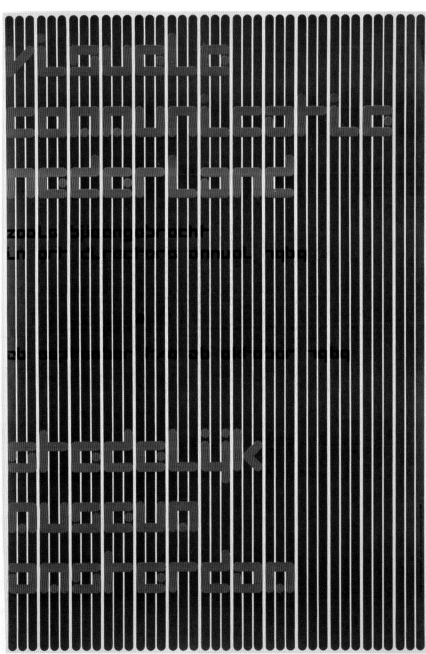

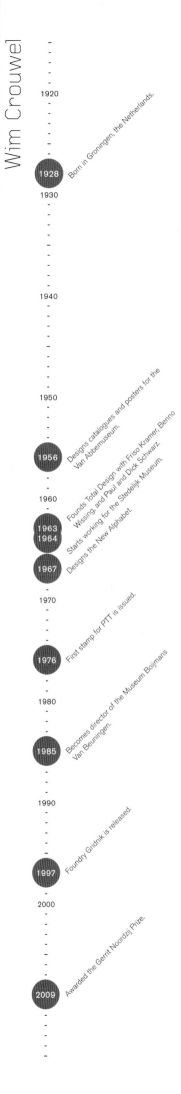

1920

1928 Born in Groningen, the Netherlands.

1930

1940

1950

1956 Designs catalogues and posters for the Van Abbemuseum.

1960

1963 Founds Total Design with Friso Kramer, Benno Wissing, and Paul and Dick Schwarz.
1964 Starts working for the Stedelijk Museum.

1967 Designs the New Alphabet.

1970

1976 First stamp for PTT is issued.

1980

1985 Becomes director of the Museum Boijmans Van Beuningen.

1990

1997 Foundry Gridnik is released.

2000

2009 Awarded the Gerrit Noordzij Prize.

La Moda si Diffonde con la Rinascente,
poster, 1959.

'Precise, lucid, immediate, democratic and full of *joie de vivre.*' – Emilio de Maddalena

Lora Lamm

b. 1928

SWITZERLAND

Lora Lamm was one of a number of Swiss designers to flock to Milan in the post-war period, but unlike such contemporaries as Max Huber (p. 128), Walter Ballmer and Carlo Vivarelli, Lamm was somehow written out of the canon of design history, which is surprising given the quality of her designs – particularly the impressive body of work she created for the prestigious Milan department store La Rinascente in the late 1950s and early 1960s. According to designer Italo Lupi, who worked there as an intern under Lamm, 'the graphic output of Lora Lamm did a great deal to create an extraordinary corporate image at la Rinascente'.

Like many Swiss designers, Lamm attended the Zurich School of Arts and Crafts, where she studied for four years under the directorship of Bauhaus master Johannes Itten and professors Ernst Keller and Ernst Gubler. On graduating, and on the advice of advertising agency director Frank Thiessing, who had introduced her to Antonio Boggeri, Lamm moved to Milan to work at Studio Boggeri. The following year Lamm started working for la Rinascente. So impressive was Max Huber's reference that Lamm was not required to attend an interview; soon afterwards, Huber joined Rinascente's design studio himself as creative director. Lamm's energetic style was used to promote everything from fashion to homeware; her posters combined exuberant illustrations with exciting layouts and bold typography.

Lamm's work was very well received and, in 1958, as the store began to focus on attracting more female customers, she became a consultant. This allowed Lamm to continue her work for la Rinascente while also designing for a number of other companies, including Elizabeth Arden, Niggi Profumerie and Pirelli, for whom she designed a series of memorable posters in the early 1960s, promoting bicycle tyres, scooters and hot-water bottles, among other things.

Like Cipe Pineles in the US, Lamm was something of a trailblazer at a time when women graphic designers were rarely recognized for their achievements. In 1960 Lamm was put forward for membership of the Alliance Graphique Internationale (AGI) by two fellow Swiss designers. She was rejected – not on the grounds of her work, but simply because the constitution did not allow for female members. Perhaps if she had been accepted, she might have secured her place in graphic design history.

In 1963 Lamm made the decision to leave Milan. Unable to obtain a visa for the US, she settled back in Zurich, where she forged a successful career, becoming a partner at Frank Thiessing's agency, BCR.

Above Portrait of Lamm, 1963.

apertura di stagione

/R

Apertura di Stagione, la Rinascente,
poster, 1957.

CYNAR

Aperitivo CYNAR

CYNAR

Apéritif CYNAR

CYNAR

Apéritif CYNAR

Cynar, poster, 1962.

1920

1928   Born in Arosa, Switzerland.

1930

1940

1946   Enters the Zurich School of Arts and Crafts.

1950

1952   Starts working at the Romain Sager office.
1953   Moves to Milan and starts working for Studio Boggeri.
1954   Begins working for la Rinascente.

1960

1963   Returns to Switzerland.

1970

1980

1990

2000

2010

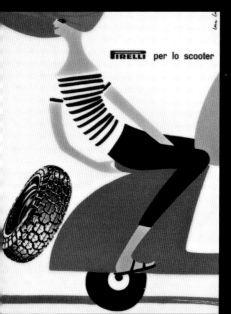

Above left *Pirelli per lo Scooter*, window decal, 1959.

Above right *Pneumatici Pirelli per Biciclette*, poster/offset print, 1959.

Design

Council of Industrial Design   171   March 1963   3s 6d

Kenneth Garland

a special issue

> 'Don't be fooled into thinking you will have great power when you have become a graphic designer; your greatest power will always be through your ability (as a voter at the very least) to contribute to political change.'

Ken Garland

b. 1929

UK

Perhaps as much known for his forthright views as his design work (his 1964 'First Things First' manifesto, rarely off the agenda, was redrafted in 1999 and again in 2014 for a new generation of designers), Ken Garland is that all too rare thing – a designer with principles, who designs for causes he believes in, which in his case have included the Labour Party and the Campaign for Nuclear Disarmament (CND).

Garland studied at the Central School of Arts and Crafts in London. A first job at *Furnishing* magazine was followed by the art editorship of *Design*, the in-house magazine of the Council of Industrial Design (now the Design Council). A high-profile job for an inexperienced designer, Garland felt 'alarmingly exposed', but stayed for six years before setting up his own consultancy in 1962.

Ken Garland & Associates was always a close-knit group, consisting of Garland and no more than three other designers, working across many different sectors. Galt Toys remained a client for over 20 years, commissioning everything from the identity for its first shop in 1961, to wooden toys and card-based games including Anymals, Fizzog and the best-selling Connect.

In 1963, while at a meeting of the Society of Industrial Designers at London's ICA, Garland drafted what was to become known as the 'First Things First' manifesto. A call to arms against the increasingly consumerist focus of the design industry, it was signed by 21 other like-minded creatives. Originally self-published, it gained much attention when it was later published in *The Guardian* by the MP Tony Benn and picked up on by the

BBC. It was subsequently reproduced around the world.

Garland's work for political and social causes was carried out independently of his studio. In 1962 he designed a poster for the CND's Easter march from Aldermaston to London. He was not paid for the work, but describes CND's organizing secretary Peggy Duff as his 'most inspiring and endearing client'.

A keen writer and educator, Garland's 1966 *Graphics Handbook* was a best-seller, and in 1994 a collection of his writing entitled *A Word in Your Eye* was published to accompany an exhibition at the University of Reading. Garland established his own photography-based imprint, Pudkin Books, in 2008.

The 'First Things First' manifesto was in the news again in 1998, when it was resurrected by *Adbusters*. Tibor Kalman (p. 240) suggested a twenty-first-century update, and (with Garland's approval) a revised text was drafted, signed by 33 luminaries from the design world and published jointly by *Adbusters*, *AIGA Journal*, *Blueprint*, *Emigre*, *Eye*, *Form* and *Items*. Again, it was the source of much debate within the industry, although Garland remains resolutely modest: 'Written and proclaimed at the Institute of Contemporary Arts on an evening in December 1963, the manifesto was published in January 1964. Inexplicably, to me, reverberations are still being felt.'

Above Portrait of Garland.

Below CND poster, 1962.

ALDERMASTON TO LONDON EASTER 6:

Aldermaston Good Friday 12noon	Reading Easter Saturday 9am	Slough Easter Sunday 9.30am	Acton Green Easter Monday 9.30am	Hammersmith	Kensingt

RALLY HYDE PARK [near Hyde Pk Corner] 12.30-3PM

FINAL MARCH :

Hyde Pk Corner	Sloane St	Victoria St	Whiteha

Below Connect, game for Galt Toys, 1968.

Bottom 'First Things First', manifesto, 1964.

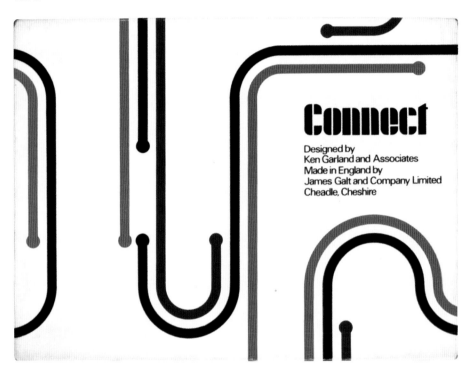

Connect

Designed by
Ken Garland and Associates
Made in England by
James Galt and Company Limited
Cheadle, Cheshire

first things first

A manifesto

We, the undersigned, are graphic designers, photographers and students who have been brought up in a world in which the techniques and apparatus of advertising have persistently been presented to us as the most lucrative, effective and desirable means of using our talents. We have been bombarded with publications devoted to this belief, applauding the work of those who have flogged their skill and imagination to sell such things as:

cat food, stomach powders, detergent, hair restorer, striped toothpaste, aftershave lotion, beforeshave lotion, slimming diets, fattening diets, deodorants, fizzy water, cigarettes, roll-ons, pull-ons and slip-ons.

By far the greatest time and effort of those working in the advertising industry are wasted on these trivial purposes, which contribute little or nothing to our national prosperity.

In common with an increasing number of the general public, we have reached a saturation point at which the high pitched scream of consumer selling is no more than sheer noise. We think that there are other things more worth using our skill and experience on. There are signs for streets and buildings, books and periodicals, catalogues, instructional manuals, industrial photography, educational aids, films, television features, scientific and industrial publications and all the other media through which we promote our trade, our education, our culture and our greater awareness of the world.

We do not advocate the abolition of high pressure consumer advertising: this is not feasible. Nor do we want to take any of the fun out of life. But we are proposing a reversal of priorities in favour of the more useful and more lasting forms of communication. We hope that our

society will tire of gimmick merchants, status salesmen and hidden persuaders, and that the prior call on our skills will be for worthwhile purposes. With this in mind, we propose to share our experience and opinions, and to make them available to colleagues, students and others who may be interested.

Edward Wright
Geoffrey White
William Slack
Caroline Rawlence
Ian McLaren
Sam Lambert
Ivor Kamlish
Gerald Jones
Bernard Higton
Brian Grimbly
John Garner
Ken Garland
Anthony Froshaug
Robin Fior
Germano Facetti
Ivan Dodd
Harriet Crowder
Anthony Clift
Gerry Cinamon
Robert Chapman
Ray Carpenter
Ken Briggs

Published by Ken Garland
Printed by Goodwin Press Ltd, London N4

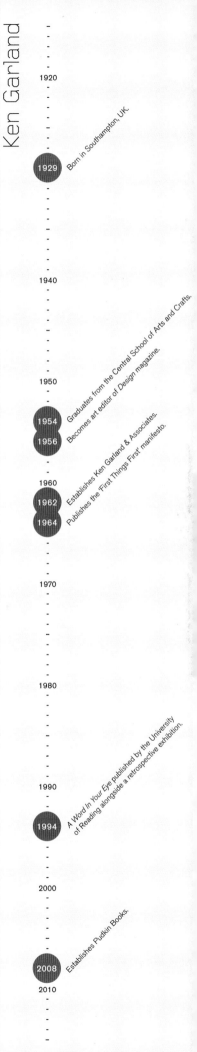

Ken Garland

1920

1929 — Born in Southampton, UK.

1940

1950 — Graduates from the Central School of Arts and Crafts.

1954 — Becomes art editor of *Design* magazine.
1956 — Establishes Ken Garland & Associates.

1960
1962 — Publishes the 'First Things First' manifesto.
1964

1970

1980

1990

1994 — *A Word In Your Eye* published by the University of Reading alongside a retrospective exhibition.

2000

— Establishes Pudkin Books.
2008

2010

'We are all born with genius. It's like our fairy godmother. But what happens in life is that we stop listening to our inner voices, and we no longer have access to this extraordinary ability to create poetry.'

Milton Glaser

b. 1929

USA

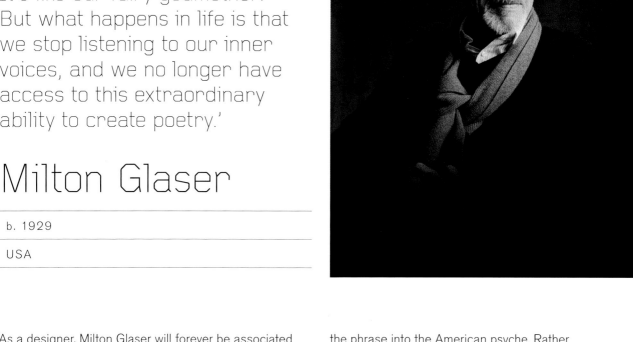

As a designer, Milton Glaser will forever be associated with New York. As well as cofounding the city's eponymous magazine, he was responsible for creating its much copied 'I ♥ New York' logo – still used to promote the city today, having been first launched in 1977.

A native New Yorker, Glaser studied at the Cooper Union and (via a Fulbright Scholarship) with the painter Giorgio Morandi at the Academy of Fine Arts in Bologna, Italy. In 1954 he set up Push Pin Studios in New York with Reynold Ruffins, Seymour Chwast and Edward Sorel. Push Pin's playful approach was the antithesis of the all-pervasive Modernist aesthetic of the period, and Glaser's iconic 1967 psychedelic-influenced poster of Bob Dylan for his *Greatest Hits* LP made a major impact. Hugely influential in both the US and Europe, Glaser ran the studio with Chwast for 20 years, going on to form Milton Glaser, Inc. in 1974.

Milton Glaser, Inc. designed a huge number of posters, publications, identities and interiors for a range of high-profile clients. Publishing was an area close to Glaser's heart, and in 1968 he co-founded *New York* magazine with Clay Felker, which he art-directed until 1977. In 1983 Glaser set up WBMG with Walter Bernard, which designed over 50 magazines and periodicals.

In 1976 Glaser was asked to work on a campaign to encourage tourism in New York State with the agency Wells Rich Greene. On the verge of bankruptcy, and with rising levels of crime, the city had reached its lowest point. The agency had come up with a slogan, but it was Glaser's masterful graphic interpretation that cemented

the phrase into the American psyche. Rather appropriately designed in the back of a New York taxi, it is thought that Glaser's substitution of a heart for the word 'love' inspired the inclusion of this symbol as a special character in most modern typefaces. The logo was a huge success, embraced by New Yorkers and copied the world over.

Glaser revisited the logo in 2001, in response to the 11 September terrorist attacks: 'I ♥ NY More Than Ever' featured a black dot on the heart representing the World Trade Center, and became a symbol of defiance for a city under siege.

The State of New York earns royalties from the yearly sales of official merchandise; Glaser, however, receives nothing and was not even paid for the job, which he did purely for altruistic reasons: 'At the beginning, it was not even copyrighted, because for the first ten years the idea was to let everyone use it, so that it would proliferate and enter into the culture. I agreed to do it as a pro bono job because it was of benefit to the state.'

Opposite Dylan poster, from *Bob Dylan's Greatest Hits*, 1967.

Above Portrait of Glaser by Michael Somoroff.

Doors.

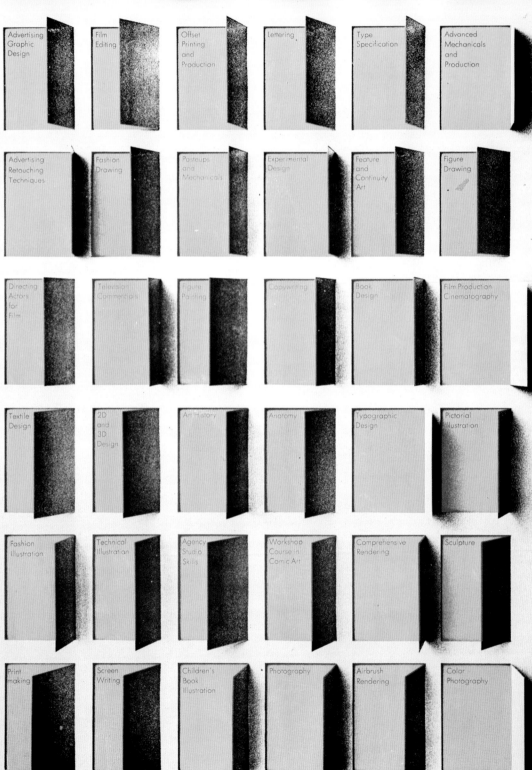

School of Visual Arts, 209 East 23 Street, New York City, OR 9-7350

Opposite *Doors*, School of Visual Arts, poster, 1967.

Above I ♥ NY *(I Love New York)* concept layout, 1976.

Below Baby Teeth typeface, 1968.

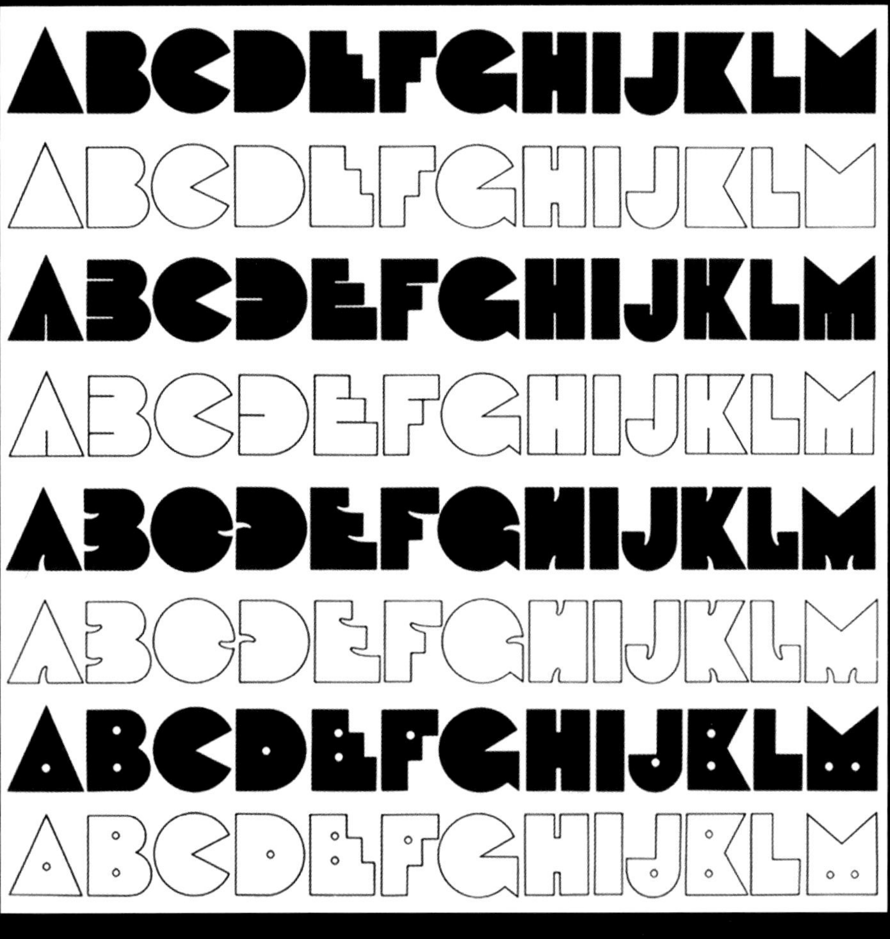

1920

1929 — Born in New York City, US.

1940

1950

1954 — Cofounds the revolutionary Push Pin Studios.

1960

1968 — Founds *New York* magazine with Clay Felker.

1970

1974 — Establishes Milton Glaser, Inc.

1980

1983 — Forms the publication design firm WBMG with Walter Bernard.

1990

2000

2004 — Awarded the Cooper-Hewitt Lifetime Achievement Award.

2009 — Becomes the first graphic designer to be awarded America's National Medal of Arts.

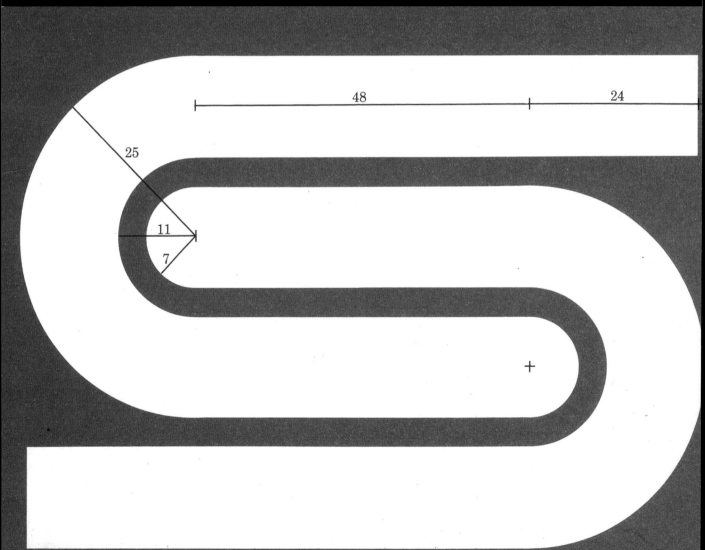

Above *Bliar*, poster for Stop the War
Coalition poster, 2006.

Below British Steel Corporation
logo, 1970.

'What I know about design,
as opposed to wood engravings
or illustrating, I really learnt
from stamps.'

David Gentleman

b. 1930

UK

David Gentleman literally changed the face of British stamps. With over 103 of his designs issued so far, and many more that were never used, he rightly deserves the accolade of 'most prolific and acclaimed stamp designer in Britain'.

His first stamps were issued in 1962. However, it was in 1965, as part of an experimental project commissioned by then Postmaster General Tony Benn, that Gentleman first proposed representing the Queen's head with a simple cameo. This and other suggestions were included in what became known as *The Gentleman Album*, a work that outlined new themes and a new format for an exciting collection of commemorative stamps, and left a lasting legacy for British stamp design.

Gentleman's prolific career is not defined entirely by his stamp designs, though. He has also designed numerous book covers (including the extensive New Penguin Shakespeare series), posters (including several series for the National Trust) and identities, such as his British Steel logotype, which was in use for 30 years. His 100-m (330-ft) mural at Charing Cross underground station is seen by millions of commuters every year.

Gentleman's work has always had an unashamedly popular appeal – his self-penned reportage books, including *David Gentleman's Britain* (1982), *David Gentleman's India* (1994) and *David Gentleman's Italy* (1997), were all best-sellers, and combined his love of travel with his expressive watercolour illustrations. Closer to home, his 2012 book, *London, You're Beautiful*, demonstrates his ongoing fascination with the capital in a series of drawings created over a whole year.

It is perhaps Gentleman's fierce independence that is most impressive. He has stuck to his original intention not to teach, commute to an office or work with anyone else. This might seem par for the course now, when all you need to be a designer is a laptop and internet access, but in Gentleman's early career, such a stance was very unusual.

Gentleman has also never shied away from taking a political stand. His 1987 book *A Special Relationship* is a powerful comment on the UK's somewhat sycophantic relationship with the US under the Thatcher government, but it did not make much impact due to its book format. (Gentleman regretted not creating a series of posters instead.)

His posters and placards for the Stop The War Coalition, starting in 2003, had much more impact, however, and they played an important and very visible part in its ongoing campaign against the Iraq War. His *Bliar* poster, in particular, was a great example for a new generation of the power of graphic design to both express and galvanize public opinion.

Above Portrait of Gentleman by Barry Lewis, 2000.

Petworth tyretrack, poster for the
National Trust, 1976.

David Gentleman

1920

1930 — Born in London, UK.

1940

1950 — Enters the Royal College of Art, London.

1960
1962 — Designs his first stamps for Royal Mail.

1968 — Designs the British Steel logo.
1970

1978 — Designs the mural for Charing Cross
underground station.
1980

1985 — *David Gentleman's London* is published.

1990

2000

2006 — Designs *Bliar* poster for Stop the War Coalition.

2010

Battle of Britain commemorative stamps
for the Royal Mail, 1965.

Above Mural for Charing Cross
underground station, 1978.

Above right Illustration from *A Special
Relationship*, 1987.

**les colorants qui ont
révolutionné la teinture
pour laine. Résultats
excellents en grand
teint, même sur filés
fortement tordus
et sur tissus serrés**

Irgalane

Teinture rapide, tranchage exceptionnel. Ces
deux propriétés, qui semblent contradic-
toires, sont admirablement réunies dans les
colorants Irgalane.
Autre qualité: ils donnent, en toute circons-
tance, des teintures parfaitement solides.
Seuls les meilleurs colorants au chrome leur
sont comparables.

 Produits Geigy
45, rue Spontini, Paris 16e

'I appreciate the moral imperative that no task is so insignificant that it needn't be accomplished in keeping with the highest standard.'

Karl Gerstner

b. 1930

SWITZERLAND

One of the so-called 'second wave' of Swiss graphic designers, Karl Gerstner took everything he learnt from his tutors at the Basel School of Design to a new level. He is best known for his designs for the pharmaceutical firm, Geigy, for whom he worked in the 1950s. Gerstner also wrote extensively on design throughout his career, and his 1963 book *Designing Programmes* was ahead of its time, described by the historian Richard Hollis some 40 years later as being 'what the future of graphic design is largely about'.

Gerstner studied on the foundation course at Basel under Emil Ruder (p. 108), before taking up an apprenticeship in Fritz Bühler's studio, where Max Schmid and Armin Hofmann worked at the time. Schmid left to head the design studio at Geigy, and Gerstner subsequently started designing for the pharmaceutical company in 1949. Geigy was at the forefront of both product research and graphic design in the post-war period, commissioning a raft of high-profile designers, including Hofmann and Herbert Leupin.

Gerstner created a series of striking advertisements for Geigy, but perhaps his most memorable work came in 1958, with a publication created with its advertising director Markus Kutter to celebrate the company's bicentenary. The 320-page *Geigy Heute* (*Geigy Today*), was designed in a square format, with headings and text unjustified and ranged left throughout. The groundbreaking book was a triumph of information design, and one of the first to illustrate a company's history with charts, diagrams and assorted infographics (which Gerstner referred to as 'organigrams').

In 1959 Gerstner and Kutter set up the advertising agency Gerstner + Kutter, with Gerstner as creative director and Kutter as the writer. GGK (as it became in 1962) was a 'full service' agency, offering everything from PR to print in addition to design, employing 'integral typography' – a seamless marriage of copy and graphics – to execute their ideas.

Gerstner also wrote about design throughout his career, from the 1955 issue of the architecture publication, Werk (which he both edited and designed), to his 1964 book, *Designing Programmes*. Written in the very early days of computers and programming, it hinted at the myriad creative possibilities that were to come, taking as its starting point the idea of creating these so-called 'programmes' by repeating fixed units, and using them to solve design problems.

Opposite *Irgalane/Solophényle*, Geigy advertisement for dyes, 1953.

Above Portrait of Gerstner by Angelika Platen, 1971.

Irgalane   Geigy

Ein Fortschritt in der Entwick-
lung der Wollechtfarbstoffe!

Spitzenprodukte für die Woll-
echtfärberei mit überraschend
neuer Färbeweise:
1¼ Std. Färbezeit bei neutralem
bis schwachsaurem Färben.
Ausgezeichnete Gesamtecht-
heiten. Eignen sich auch für Na-
turseide und Nylon.

Geigy

Geigy

Geigy

Die Geigy-Erzeugnisse, seien es Farbstoffe, Textilchemikalien, synthetische
Gerbstoffe, Produkte für Schädlingsbekämpfung und Pflanzenschutz oder
pharmazeutische Spezialitäten, geniessen das uneingeschränkte Vertrauen
von Millionen von Verbrauchern in der ganzen Welt. Dieser Erfolg ist das
Ergebnis einer mit den letzten Erkenntnissen von Wissenschaft und Technik
übereinstimmenden Tätigkeit in unsern Forschungs- und Produktionsstätten.
J. R. Geigy A.G., Basel

Karl Gerstner

1920

1930 Born in Basel, Switzerland.

1940

1944 Studies at the Basel School of Design.

1949 Starts working for Geigy.

1958 Designs *Geigy Heute* for Geigy's bicentenary.
1959 Establishes Gerstner + Kutter with
Markus Kutter.

1964 Publishes *Designing Programmes*.

1970

1980

1990

2000

2010

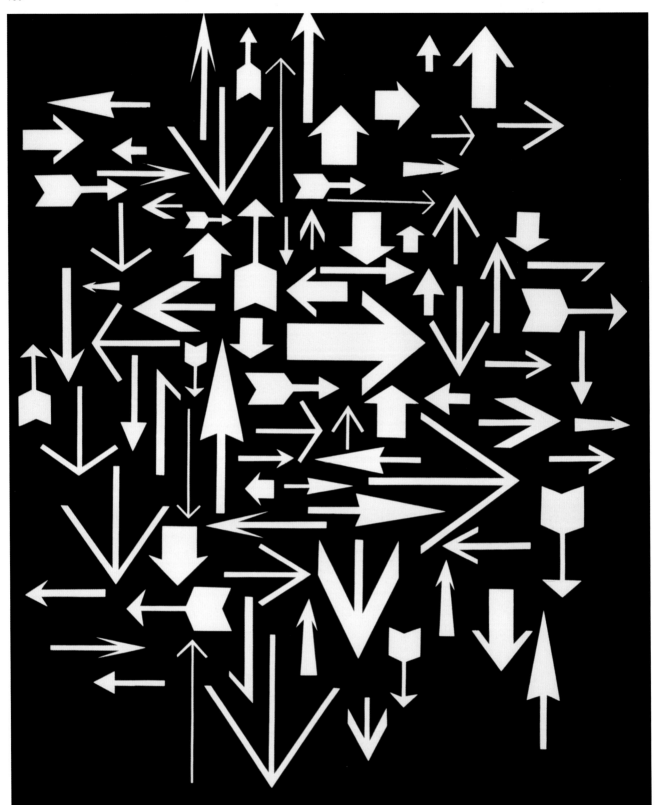

1959年 7月14日—7月19日 池袋 三越 6階ホール 主催 共同通信社
世界商業デザイン展

季刊誌 グラフィック・デザイン 9月創刊 発行所 芸美出版社

World Commercial Design Exhibition
poster, 1959.

Nihon Buyo
UCLA
Asian Performing Arts
Institute 1981
Los Angeles
Washington, D.C.
New York

'His work is completely modern yet deeply influenced by Japanese culture. He was a master of the fine art of Japanese calligraphy and an expert with Western typography, which made him unique among his colleagues.'
— Paul Davies

Ikko Tanaka

1930–2002

JAPAN

Nowhere is Ikko Tanaka's effortless blend of East and West more apparent than in his 1981 poster promoting the traditional Japanese dance nihon buyo. Featuring a striking geometric geisha, it has the timeless quality that is apparent in so much of his work. A member of the Nippon Design Centre (NDC, p. 112) and a key figure in the post-war Japanese design industry, Tanaka's vision of elegance and simplicity lives on through Muji, the brand he helped establish and which he art-directed until 2001.

Tanaka studied textiles at the Kyoto City College of Fine Arts, and after five years working as a designer for the newspaper group Sankei Shimbun Press, he became one of the founder members of the NDC, where he worked for a range of commercial clients. There was a strong Modernist influence on Japanese design at this time, strengthened further by the World Design Conference held in Tokyo in 1960, which featured speakers such as Saul Bass, Josef Müller-Brockmann, Otl Aicher and Herbert Bayer.

Inspired by a trip to New York, Tanaka set up his own studio in 1963. Prestigious commissions followed, including the poster, logotype and medals for the 1964 Tokyo Olympic Games, and then the government pavilion at Expo 70, held in Osaka.

Tanaka designed many theatre posters during his prolific career. In 1961 he designed a poster for the Kanze Noh theatre in Osaka, forming a relationship that lasted over 30 years. He also designed posters for the National Theatre for Traditional Performing Arts and the Seibu Theatre in Tokyo (owned by the Seibu department store group for which he was creative director at the time). Another long-standing client was Tokyo's New National Theatre; Tanaka received his first commission in 1996 and went on to create 38 posters for them.

Tanaka also collaborated with several Japanese fashion designers, including Kenzo Takada, Issey Miyake and Hanae Mori, and in 1980 was invited to participate in, and create the graphics for, the V&A's 'Japan Style' exhibition.

In the same year, along with the interior designer Takashi Sugimoto and marketing consultant Kazuko Koike, he formed Mujirushi Ryohin ('no-brand quality goods'). The brand became Muji; Tanaka was its art director for over 20 years, until he was succeeded by Kenya Hara in 2001. The products were functional and elegant, and the packaging and graphics were minimal — although many were designed by high-profile designers, they remained anonymous.

Above *Nihon Buyo*, poster, 1981.

サンケイ観世能

主催＝サンケイ新聞社　大阪新聞社　後援＝文化庁

昭和五十八年二月二十七日（日）

サンケイホール　特設能舞台

第一部　（午前十時）

猩々乱　双之舞　　　浦田保利

文山立　狂言　　　　山本勝一郎

三輪　白式　　　　　善竹忠一郎

正尊　起請文　囃人　観正元正

　　　　　　　　　　観世元昭

第二部　（午後二時三〇分）

景清　松門之会釈　小返　観世銕之丞

福の神　狂言　　　　茂山千作

羽衣　彩色　　　　　梅若紀彰

道成寺　赤頭　中之段飜蹿　観世喜之

1988 HIROSHIMA APPEALS

art direction / design / illustration : Ikko tanaka
printing : toppan printing co., ltd.
sponsors : hiroshima international cultural foundation, inc.
japan graphic designers association, inc. (jagda)

Above *1988 Hiroshima Appeals*, poster, 1988.

Right *Sapporo '72*, poster, 1968.

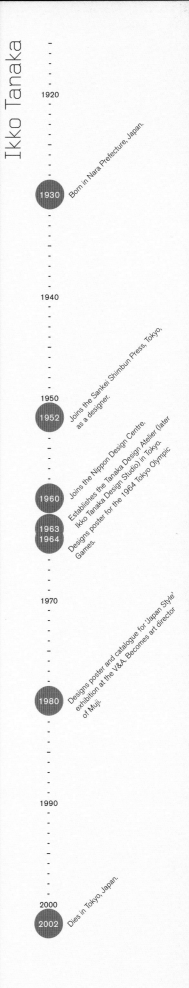

Ikko Tanaka

- 1920

- 1930 Born in Nara Prefecture, Japan.

- 1940

- 1950
- 1952 Joins the Sankei Shimbun Press, Tokyo, as a designer.

- 1960 Joins the Nippon Design Centre.
- 1963 Establishes the Tanaka Design Atelier (later Ikko Tanaka Design Studio) in Tokyo.
- 1964 Designs poster for the 1964 Tokyo Olympic Games.

- 1970

- 1980 Designs poster and catalogue for 'Japan Style' exhibition at the V&A. Becomes art director of Muji.

- 1990

- 2000
- 2002 Dies in Tokyo, Japan.

Get on board ⊖ London's Buses.

'I'm not given to self-analysis, but I am given to insatiable curiosity.'

Alan Fletcher

1931–2006

UK

Perhaps more so than any other designer, Alan Fletcher has made a lasting impact on the post-war British graphic design industry. Mixing an American sensibility with British flair, Fletcher/Forbes/Gill was arguably the first commercial graphic design agency in the UK. Pentagram (p. 284), the studio it had become by 1972, rewrote the rules about how a graphic design agency could be run. Fletcher was so much more than the companies he set up, though. A true designer's designer, he made no differentiation between his work and his life, and his playful approach and mischievous sense of humour permeated both.

While studying at Central School of Arts and Crafts, Fletcher met future partners Colin Forbes and Theo Crosby, as well as contemporaries Derek Birdsall and Ken Garland. The Royal College of Art followed, and a scholarship on graduation led to a year in America, studying at Yale (where he was taught by Paul Rand and Josef Albers, meeting such luminaries as Robert Brownjohn, Chermayeff and Geismar, and Saul Bass).

Fletcher returned to the UK via a short stint working for Pirelli in Milan, who would become a long-standing client. He began working with Forbes, and two years later, along with American designer Bob Gill, they formed Fletcher/Forbes/Gill. Operating from a mews in Mayfair they created exciting work for clients such as Penguin Books and ICI, even making an appearance in *Vogue*.

During the 1960s, the breadth of projects that the studio attracted increased, and architect Theo Crosby replaced Bob Gill. They were later joined by Mervyn Kurlansky and product designer Kenneth Grange. Fletcher realized the limitations of a name based on a list of surnames. He chose the name Pentagram, and in 1972 one of the world's most respected and successful design companies was born. Each partner was

responsible for winning and running their own projects, and the company grew, with more partners and offices in San Francisco and New York.

Fletcher worked at Pentagram for the next 20 years, creating iconic identities for clients such as the V&A and Reuters, before eventually opening his own studio in 1991–92. He worked for a variety of clients, notably the publisher Phaidon, for whom he was consultant art director and with whom he published several books, including his magnum opus, *The Art of Looking Sideways* (2001). This 1,068-page volume is a cornucopia of images, ideas, anecdotes and curiosities, all beautifully illustrated by the self-confessed 'visual jackdaw'. It was declared an instant classic and was that rare thing – a design book that could be appreciated by designers and non-designers alike.

Another of Fletcher's many legacies was to establish a membership organization solely for graphic designers. In 1963, in an attempt to professionalize the industry, he and several of his contemporaries set up a British equivalent to the Art Directors Club of New York, calling it the Design and Art Director's Association, or D&AD as it later became known.

Opposite *Parties – Get on Board London's Buses*, London Transport poster, 1993.

Above Portrait of Fletcher by Jennie Mayle, c. 1990s.

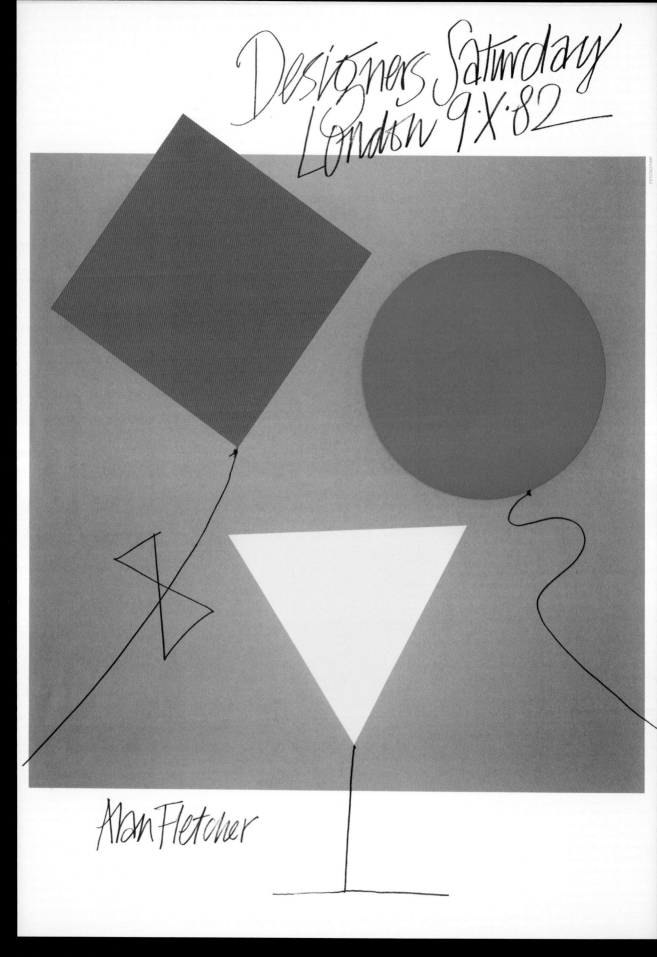

Designers Saturday, poster, 1982.

Portraits of famous British Personalities
from 1945 to the 1990's are on permanent
exhibition at the 20th Century Galleries
in the National Portrait Gallery.
Free admission. Open 10 to 5pm weekdays,
10 to 6pm Saturdays and 2 to 6pm Sundays.
Nearest ⊖ Leicester Square & Charing Cross

National Portrait Gallery poster, 1990.

Victoria and Albert Museum
logotype, 1990.

Alan Fletcher

- 1920
- 1931 — Born in Nairobi, Kenya.
- 1936 — Moves to the UK.
- 1940
- 1950
- 1953 — Enrols at the Royal College of Art.
- 1960
- 1962 — Founds design firm Fletcher/Forbes/Gill with Colin Forbes and Bob Gill.
- 1970
- 1972 — Design firm becomes Pentagram.
- 1980
- 1982 — Elected International President of the Alliance Graphique Internationale.
- 1990
- 1992 — Leaves Pentagram and sets up own studio. Becomes consultant art director at Phaidon Press. Wins the Prince Philip Designers' Prize.
- 1993
- 2001 — Publishes The Art of Looking Sideways.
- 2006 — Dies in London, UK.

188

System Map

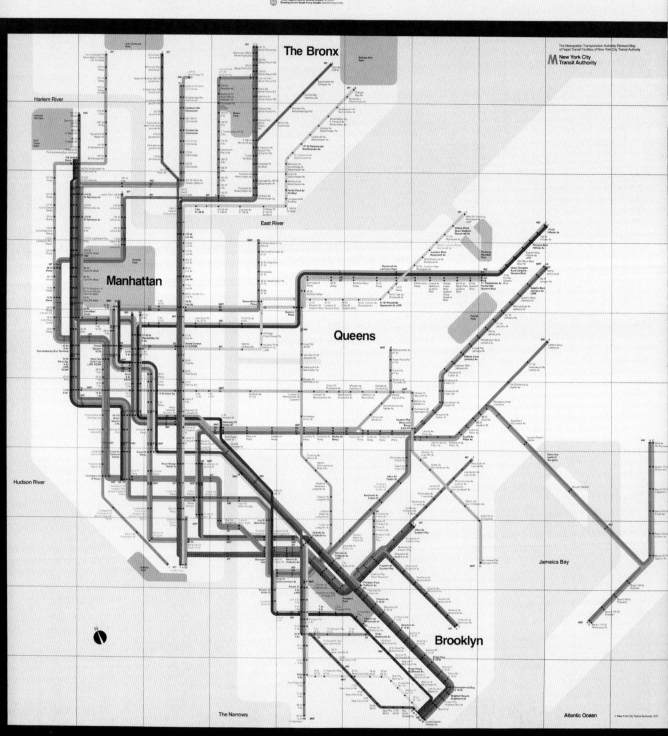

New York Subway map,
lithograph, 1970.

'If we need something and we can't find it, then we design it.'

Massimo Vignelli

1931–2014

ITALY

Often cited as one of America's greatest designers, and credited as taking Italian design to New York, in addition to numerous high-profile corporate identities for clients such as Bloomingdales and American Airlines, Massimo Vignelli's elegant, Modernist approach has been applied to everything from packaging and product design, interior and environmental design to clothing and furniture. As Vignelli Associates, he worked in partnership with his architect wife, Lella, for over 40 years.

Architecture was always a strong influence on Vignelli – he studied it in Milan and Venice and later taught it at Chicago's Institute of Design. He was also influenced by – and became good friends with – Max Huber (p. 128), who is credited with introducing him to the rigours of Swiss typography and grid systems. In 1960, when Vignelli returned to Italy from his first stay in the United States, he set up the Vignelli Office of Design and Architecture in Milan.

In 1965, along with fellow designers Ralph Eckerstrom, Bob Noorda, James Fogelman, Wally Gutches and Larry Klein, Vignelli set up the design consultancy Unimark International. Unimark was a truly global operation, with 11 offices in five different countries. Vignelli was originally based in Milan, but then moved to New York and headed up the NYC branch with Bob Noorda (p. 152).

One of its first commissions was to redesign the signage and graphics for the New York Subway system, much of which is still in place today. The pair created a modular system with square panels for arrows and line numbers in coloured circles. A bold new typeface was also introduced – Standard, the American version of Akzidenz-Grotesk. There followed a piece that many graphic designers hold up as the Holy Grail of information design – a stylized (and very stylish) redesign of the New York Subway map, similar to Harry Beck's London Underground map, featuring only 45- and 90-degree angles.

Unimark created corporate identities for an impressive list of international clients, including American Airlines, Ford, Pirelli, Jaguar, Knoll International and Unilever, but went bust in 1972. Vignelli had left in 1971 to set up Vignelli Associates with Lella, and the pair continued to run a very successful practice. Rarely straying far from his Modernist roots, Vignelli insisted, 'I like design to be semantically correct, syntactically consistent, and pragmatically understandable. I like it to be visually powerful, intellectually elegant, and above all timeless.'

Above Portrait of Vignelli by Doug Manchee, 2011.

American Airlines Annual Report **1969**

Denver

United States
Candidate
for the XII Winter
Olympic Games
1976

Massimo Vignelli

1920

1931 — Born in Milan, Italy.

1940

1950

1958 — Moves to Chicago to teach at the Institute of
Design, and work as a designer at the Container
Corporation of America.

1960 — Sets up the Vignelli Office of Design and
Architecture in Milan.

1965 — Establishes the NYC branch of Unimark
International.

1971 — Establishes Vignelli Associates with his
wife, Lella.

1980 — A retrospective exhibition of Massimo and
Lella's work is held at Parsons.

1990

2000

2007 — Publishes Vignelli: From A to Z.

2010

2014 — Dies in New York, US.

Florence Knoll, Saarinen, Mies van der Rohe,
oguchi have designed for Knoll.
Aulenti, Albinson, Caffero, Christen, Colombo,
Mangiarotti, Pearson, Pettit, Plather, Pollock,
Schultz, and Stephens still do.

Knoll International, in 28 countries, has all these furniture
and textile designs.

320 Park Avenue, New York

Knoll International

'I believe that in design
30 per cent dignity,
20 per cent beauty and
50 per cent absurdity
are necessary.'

Shigeo Fukuda

1932–2009

JAPAN

The American designer Paul Rand (p. 104) famously said of Shigeo Fukuda, 'A playful heart requires no translation', and it was Rand who was responsible for bringing Fukuda's work to the attention of a US audience when he organized an exhibition of the Japanese designer's work at New York's IBM Gallery in 1967. Rand was heavily influenced by traditional Japanese design, and Fukuda recognized these themes running through Rand's work. This led to Rand interviewing Fukuda for PBS, and in Fukuda eventually becoming the first Japanese designer to be inducted into the Art Directors Club of New York Hall of Fame.

Despite being heavily influenced by the Swiss school of graphic design, Fukuda was renowned for his playful approach to both his life and his work – perhaps something inherited from his parents, who were both toy makers. His 1999 exhibition at the Asian Art Museum in San Francisco bore the title of 'Visual Prankster: Shigeo Fukuda'.

However, his obvious sense of fun did not prevent him from tackling serious subjects through the many posters that he designed. His most famous, *Victory 1945*, shows a bullet being fired back towards the barrel of a canon. Its simplicity of line summed up the senselessness of war in a way that anyone could understand, and it won Fukuda the Grand Prize at the 1975 Warsaw Poster Contest. His 1980 poster for Amnesty International, with its clenched fist, barbed wire and letter S replaced by a shackle, also typifies his masterful way of getting a message across with minimum fuss and maximum impact, as do his 1982 *Happy Earth Day* environmental posters.

Much of Fukuda's work displays his love of creating 'illusions', clever visual twists for the viewer to unlock: 'Rather than catering to the design sensitivity of the general public, there is advancement in design if people are left to feel satisfied with their own superiority, by entrapping them with visual illusion.'

Fukuda's love of illusion did not just manifest itself in his work either. In an obituary for the *New York Times*, Steven Heller wrote of Seymour Chwast's visit to his Tokyo home: 'Mr. Fukuda was indeed a prankster throughout his life. To reach the front door of his house, on the outskirts of Tokyo, a visitor had to walk down a path to a door that appeared to be far away. In fact, appearances were deceiving because the front door was only four feet high. Inside, Mr. Fukuda would emerge from a concealed white door exactly the same colour as the wall to offer the visitor a pair of red house slippers.'

Opposite *No More*, silkscreen print, 1968.

Above Portrait of Fukuda.

VICTORY 1945

SHIGEO FUKUDA - Japan

Opposite *Victory 1945*, poster, 1975.

Below Shigeo Fukuda Exhibition poster, 1975.

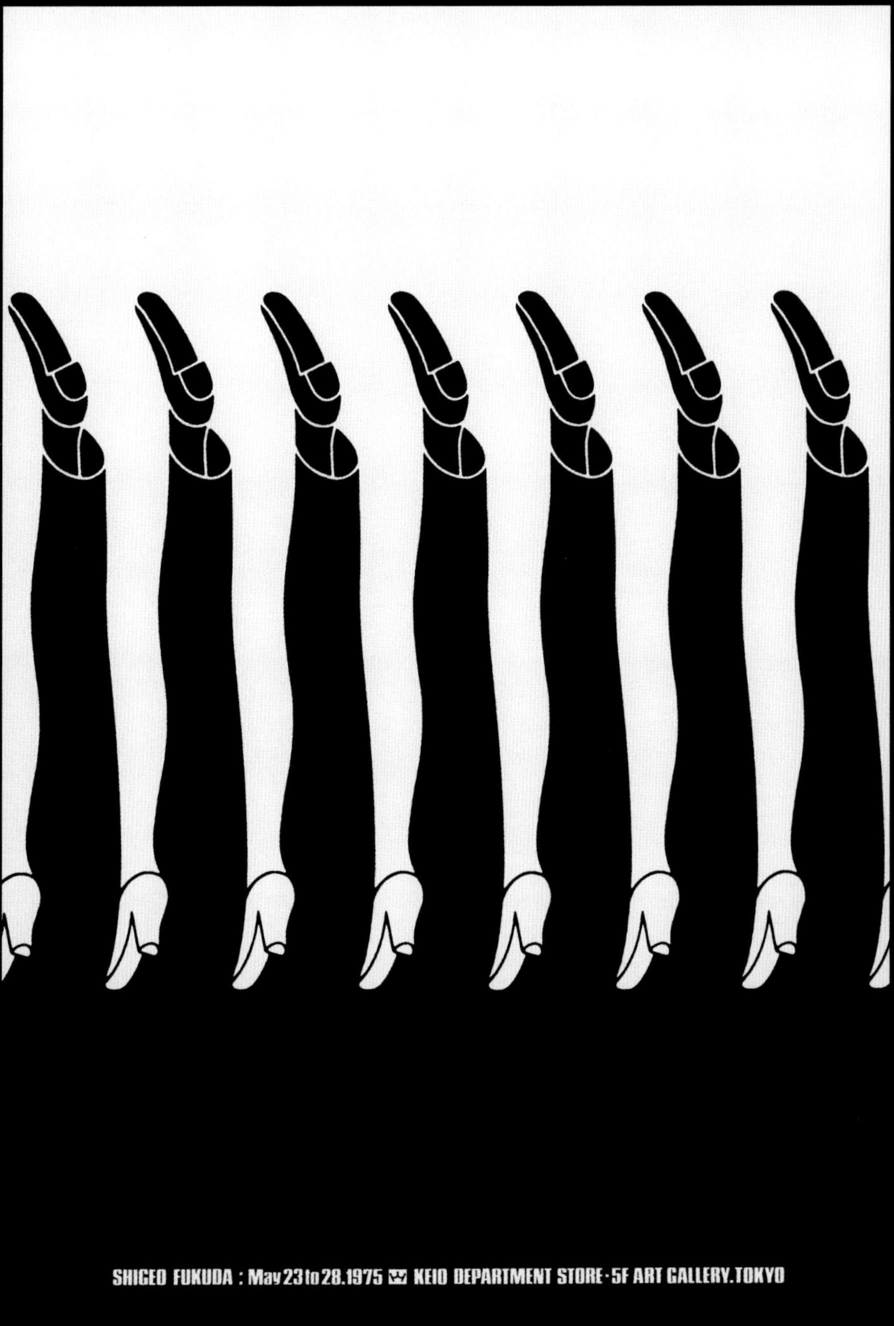

SHIGEO FUKUDA : May 23 to 28.1975 ☒ KEIO DEPARTMENT STORE·5F ART GALLERY.TOKYO

1920

1930
1932 Born in Tokyo, Japan.

1940

1950

1956 Graduates from Tokyo National University of Fine Arts and Music.

1960

1967 Exhibition at IBM Gallery in New York. Designs Montreal Expo 67 poster.

1970 Designs poster for 1970 World's Fair in Osaka.

1975 *Victory 1945* poster wins first prize at the Warsaw Poster Contest.

1980 Designs Amnesty International poster.

1987 Inducted into the Art Directors Club of New York Hall of Fame.

1990

2000

2009 Dies in Tokyo.

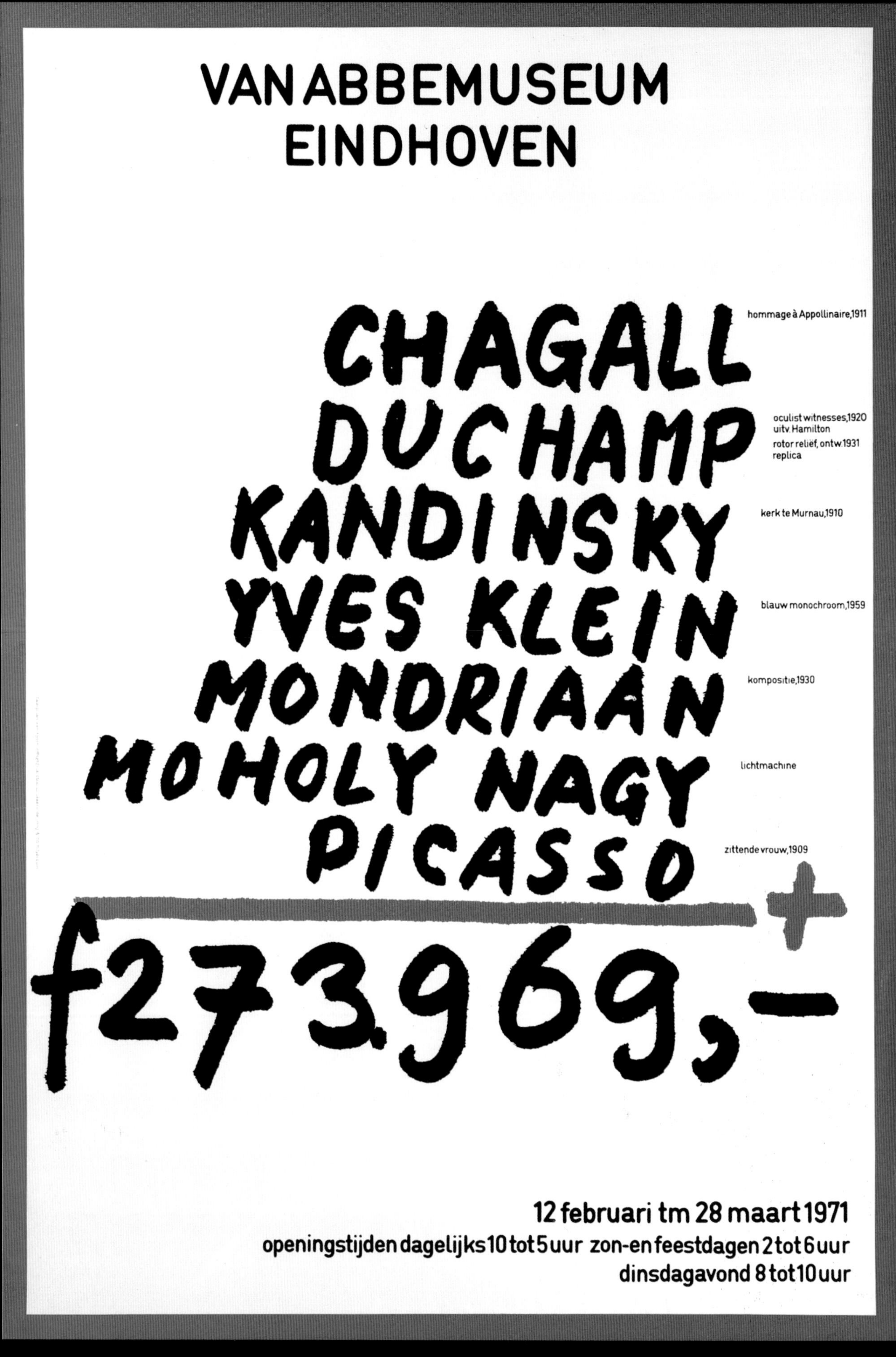

VAN ABBEMUSEUM EINDHOVEN

CHAGALL — hommage à Appollinaire,1911

DUCHAMP — oculist witnesses,1920 uitv. Hamilton / rotor relief, ontw.1931 replica

KANDINSKY — kerk te Murnau,1910

YVES KLEIN — blauw monochroom,1959

MONDRIAAN — kompositie,1930

MOHOLY NAGY — lichtmachine

PICASSO — zittende vrouw,1909

f273.969,-+

12 februari tm 28 maart 1971
openingstijden dagelijks 10 tot 5 uur zon- en feestdagen 2 tot 6 uur
dinsdagavond 8 tot 10 uur

A Selection from the Collection, poster for Van Abbemuseum Eindhoven, 1971.

'Everything is possible, you can quote everything, you can use every style, but where are the arguments that are really contributing to a fundamental change in our social conditions?'

Jan van Toorn

b. 1932

THE NETHERLANDS

Jan van Toorn is hard to classify. A successful designer, educator and museum director, who is often described as radical, he argues that communication design should challenge, rather than just accept, the fixed, ahistorical meanings of the culture industry and its powerful protagonists. Van Toorn's critical approach is rare among his contemporaries (who include Wim Crouwel and Ben Bos), and while he may enjoy a lower profile, his work is considered to be equally as important.

Early on in his career, Van Toorn was employed as an in-house designer for the Van Abbemuseum in Eindhoven. Under director Jean Leering, he produced a series of catalogues and posters, each of which was a reaction to the (often controversial) subject matter, and explored a variety of informal visual strategies and styles. This was in direct contrast to Wim Crouwel's more regimented design approach, as implemented in his work for the Stedelijk Museum, Amsterdam and the Van Abbemuseum. In 1972 the pair were involved in a well-documented public debate at the Museum Fodor in Amsterdam, with Crouwel insisting that it was not the job of the designer to interfere with the content, and Van Toorn maintaining that it was the designer's responsibility to be aware of the values produced and stressing the need for strategies and a use of language that liberate the audience – scientific objectivity that refrains from interpretation versus political subjectivity that opts for active interpretation by the spectator.

As well as interrogating content and form, Van Toorn also used his various commissions to explore editorial methods and media in what he called visual journalism.

In 1970, he became the art editor of *Dutch Art + Architecture Today* (published from 1997 to 1988 by the Netherlands Ministry for Cultural Affairs, Recreation and Social Welfare), which was notable (by clever use of perforation) for combining the magazine's cover with its outside packaging. His visual experiments for the calendars for printer Mart Spruijt (produced from 1966 to 1977) gained him widespread attention within the design community. Van Toorn also had a long-standing relationship with the Dutch Post Office (PTT), for whom he designed a number of stamps and annual reports.

A keen educator, in 1991 Van Toorn was appointed director of the Jan van Eyck Academy, Maastrict, where, as well as overseeing the academic programme combining fine art, design and theory within a common area of public activities, he initiated a provocative series of lectures, events and publications, including *And Justice for All* (1994), *Towards a Theory of the Image* (1996) and *Design beyond Design* (1998).

Van Toorn stepped down as director in 1998, but continued his own practice in Holland. According to writer Gerard Forde: 'Van Toorn remains the Brecht of graphic design, working on the line between seduction and alienation, constantly finding ways to expose rather than disguise his own role as a manipulator, continually challenging the existing networks of interpretation.'

Above Portrait of Van Toorn.

KOMPAS
3

Above *Kompas 3*, New York Fine Art
since 1945, catalogue, 1967.

Opposite top *Man and Environment*,
poster for Beyerd Cultural Centre,
Breda, from a series of eight, 1980.

Opposite bottom *February Strike of 1941
against the Deportation of the Jews*,

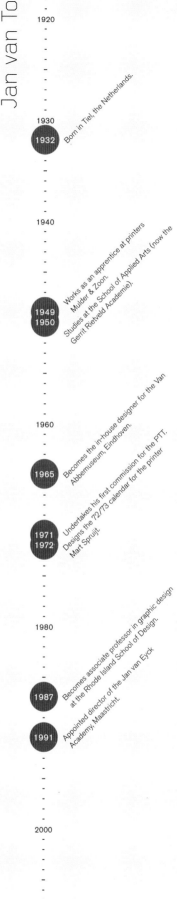

Jan van Toorn

1920

1930
1932 — Born in Tiel, the Netherlands.

1940

1949 — Works as an apprentice at printers
        Mulder & Zoon.
1950 — Studies at the School of Applied Arts (now the
        Gerrit Rietveld Academie).

1960

1965 — Becomes the in-house designer for the Van
        Abbemuseum, Eindhoven.

1971 — Undertakes his first commission for the PTT.
1972 — Designs the 72/73 calendar for the printer
        Mart Spruijt.

1980

1987 — Becomes associate professor in graphic design
        at the Rhode Island School of Design.

1991 — Appointed director of the Jan van Eyck
        Academy, Maastricht.

2000

2010

Pirelli calendar, 1968.

'I can't help thinking that books, and now perhaps websites – information – are really the proper stuff of design. All the rest is Blue Peter, playtime. It is about real text that real people have spent half their life trying to get right.'

Derek Birdsall

b. 1934

UK

Derek Birdsall is the consummate book designer, describing his craft as 'the decent setting of type and the intelligent layout of text and pictures based on a rigorous study of content'. Whether designing a modest paperback or a weighty art tome, his commitment to making reading as easy and enjoyable as possible always shines through.

Birdsall attended Wakefield College of Art and studied lettering, before winning a scholarship to study book production at the Central School of Arts and Crafts. The enterprising Birdsall had purchased his own printing press (for printing business cards and letterheads), but the composing room was out of bounds for students, which meant he would often sneak in at night to set type. He was given a thorough grounding in type and typography by luminaries such as Anthony Froshaug, Herbert Spencer and Edward Wright, only to fail his final diploma show for producing only six letterheads and three business cards ('Not enough work and the type's too small' declared Edward Bawden, the external assessor).

This proved no setback. Along with George Daulby, George Mayhew and Peter Wildbur, Birdsall set up the agency BDMW in 1959, around the same time as his contemporaries set up Fletcher/Forbes/Gill. It was an exciting time for British design, and Birdsall was an active player, helping to found the Association of Graphic Designers, which would eventually become D&AD.

Birdsall worked on a wide range of projects, including the first Pirelli calendar in 1964, promotional material for Lotus, and from 1960 book covers for Penguin, with whom he enjoyed a lasting and productive relationship. He formed Omnific in 1967, and continued working on books and art catalogues, as well as magazines such as *Nova*, *Town*, *Twen,* and *The Independent Magazine*. In 1971, Birdsall became consultant art director for Penguin Education, commissioning more than 200 entirely typographic covers from 30 different designers. In lieu of payment for a book he designed for Monty Python, he famously accepted royalties and temporary Python membership.

In 2000 Birdsall completed one of his most important commissions, a new edition of the *Book of Common Worship* (the liturgical forms and services of the Church of England). The book was a masterstroke – painstakingly set in Gill Sans, and printed in red and black, it was both beautiful to look at and, because of the thoughtful design, extremely easy to use.

Birdsall's long-awaited book *Notes on Book Design* was published in 2004 to universal acclaim. It describes the process of designing a book in an accessible and attractive way, using examples of his favourite works. He was finally recognized by the establishment in 2005, when he was awarded the Prince Philip Designers Prize.

Above Portrait of Birdsall, 1990.

Above Covers for Penguin Education
series, 1971.

Below *Book of Common Worship*, 2000.

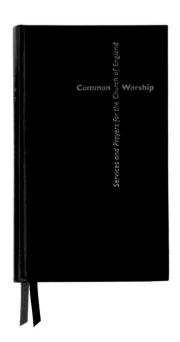

PENGUIN MODERN SOCIOLOGY READINGS

P●VERTY

EDITORS: JACK L.ROACH AND JANET K.ROACH

Derek Birdsall

1920

1930

1934 Born in West Yorkshire, UK.

1940

1950

1952 Wins a scholarship to the Central School of Arts and Crafts.

1959 Forms BDMW with George Daulby, George Mayhew and Peter Wildbur.

1960 Designs first Penguin cover.

1967 Founds Omnific studio.

1970

1980

1990

2000 New edition of Book of Common Worship is published.

2005 Awarded the Prince Phillip Designers Prize.

Awarded D&AD President's Award for Outstanding Contribution to Creativity.

2010

2012

Tokyo Map design, 1995.

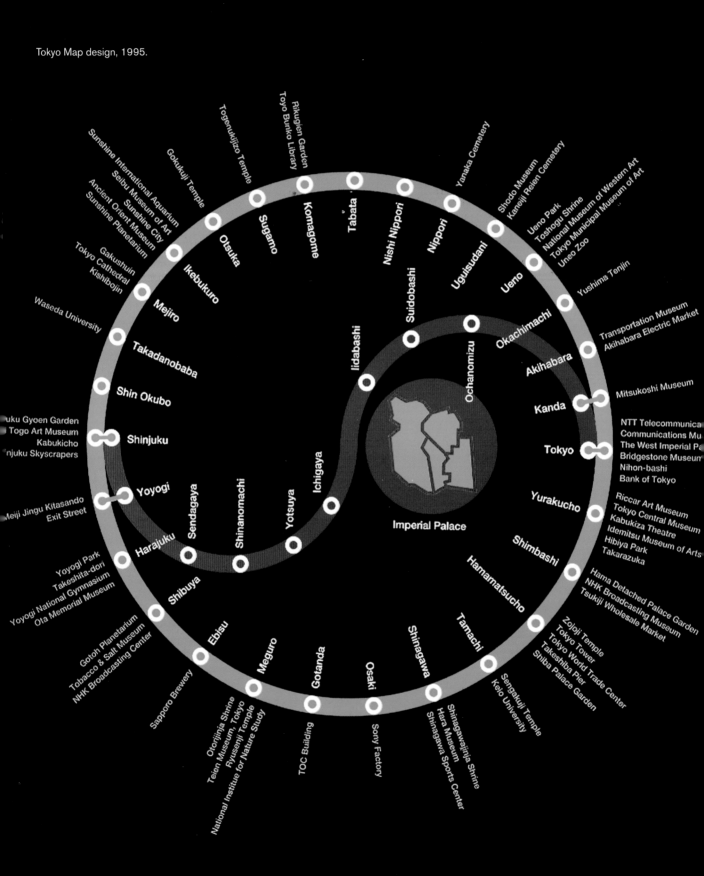

'Information design was epitomized by which map looked the best – not which took care of a lot of parallel systemic parts. That is what I thought "architecture" did and was a clearer word that had to do with systems that worked and performed.'

Richard Saul Wurman

b. 1935

USA

Now best known as the founder of TED, Richard Saul Wurman's mission to increase the public's understanding of complex data has led to him being considered one of the pioneers of modern information design, and he is credited with coining the term 'information architect'. A true polymath, he is architect, cartographer, graphic designer and educator, although it is for his books and conferences that he is most recognized.

Since his first, *Cities: A Comparison of Form and Scale*, in 1962, Wurman has written 83 books. In his highly prescient *Information Anxiety* of 1984, he anticipated the phenomenon of what we now call 'big data' and its transformation into 'big understanding'.

His self-published Access guides began with a series of travel guides, covering major cities and regions, then went on to cover other topics that sparked Wurman's interest. Full of accessible graphics, these sold in the millions (his guide to the 1984 Olympics sold 3.2 million copies alone).

His *Medical Access* (1985) and later *Understanding Healthcare* (2003) are two of the most notable, visualizing and explaining surgical procedures and diagnostic tests, and answering common medical questions. With internet access this information is available in a couple of clicks, but when *Medical Access* was published it was invaluable, taking complex information previously only available in medical textbooks and making it understandable to the man in the street.

Wurman's enquiring outlook led him to set up the first TED conference in 1984; he continued to chair the event through 2002. Each conference initially attracted exciting speakers from the fields of technology, entertainment and design, but became broader in scope over the years. TED has been described by Stefan Sagmeister (p. 268) as 'the single most important communication platform for our own field and many others, and thereby connecting design effectively to science, technology, education, politics and entertainment.' Wurman sold TED to the gaming magazine company Imagine Media in 2002, and with its mantra of 'Ideas Worth Spreading' it has since become a global phenomenon, with thousands of talks available to view for free online, and billions of viewers.

It is Wurman's unceasing curiosity and need for clarity that constantly drive him forward. 'Many of the people I speak with are really serving other gods: the God of Beauty, the God of Style, the God of Swiss Graphics, the Poster God, the God of Money, Success, Fame, Fortune, and yet there is only one god that I serve and that is the God of Understanding. If you serve that god, all the others will be taken care of.'

Above Portrait of Wurman by Melissa Mahoney.

NYC
ACCESS®

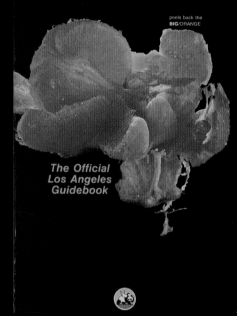

LA/ACCESS™
Richard Saul Wurman

peels back the
BIG/ORANGE

*The Official
Los Angeles
Guidebook*

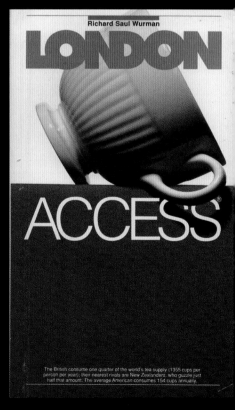

Richard Saul Wurman

LONDON

ACCESS®

The British consume one quarter of the world's tea supply (1355 cups per
person per year); their nearest rivals are New Zealanders, who guzzle just
half that amount. The average American consumes 154 cups annually.

Access Guides, book covers, London and
LA guides: photography Reven Wurman,
art direction and illustration Richard

Wurman; NYC guide: cover painting
Robert M. Kulicke, art direction and
illustration Richard Saul Wurman; 1980s

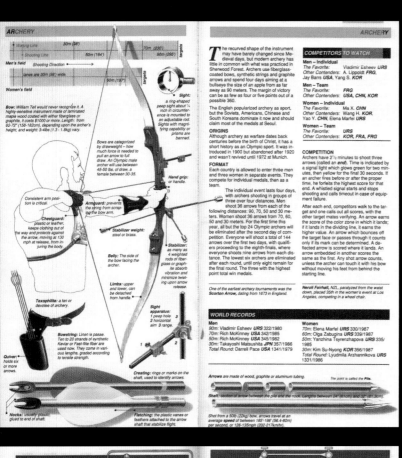

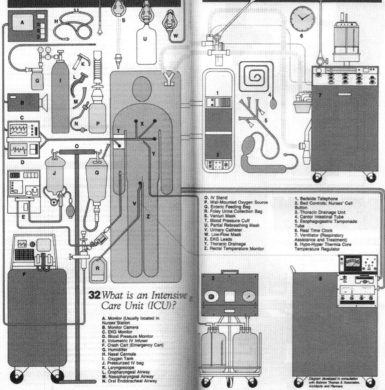

Top Archery spread from *Summer Games Access Guide*, art direction by Wurman, illustration by Michael Everitt, 1988.

Above Spread from *Medical Access*, art direction by Wurman, illustration by Nigel Holmes, 1973.

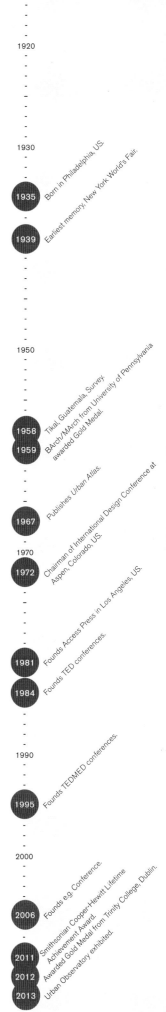

Richard Saul Wurman

- 1920
- 1930
- **1935** Born in Philadelphia, US.
- **1939** Earliest memory: New York World's Fair.
- 1950
- **1958** Tikal, Guatemala, Survey. BArch/MArch from University of Pennsylvania, awarded Gold Medal.
- **1959** Publishes *Urban Atlas*.
- **1967** Chairman of International Design Conference at Aspen, Colorado, US.
- 1970
- **1972** Founds Access Press in Los Angeles, US.
- **1981** Founds TED conferences.
- **1984**
- 1990
- **1995** Founds TEDMED conferences.
- 2000
- **2006** Founds e.g. Conference.
- **2011** Smithsonian Cooper-Hewitt Lifetime Achievement Award. Awarded Gold Medal from Trinity College, Dublin.
- **2012** Urban Observatory exhibited.
- **2013**

Japanese Culture of the Postwar Years,
1945–1995, poster, 1996.

'What I was doing constituted quite a critique of design as it existed at the time. I was going back and picking up all these things that Modernist design had discarded. People in the design community tended to see my work as "anti-design".'

Tadanori Yokoo

b. 1936

JAPAN

Sometimes referred to as 'the Japanese Andy Warhol' due to the Pop Art sensibilities of his work, Tadanori Yokoo pushed the boundaries of Japanese graphic design. In complete contrast to his contemporaries' take on Modernism, Yokoo's striking work is a riot of colour and form, bursting with iconography lifted from everything from kimono labels to children's playing cards. In addition to developing a cult following, he was honoured with a solo show at New York's Museum of Modern Art in 1972.

Adopted by a couple who owned a kimono factory, Yokoo had no formal training in art or design. Nevertheless, he went on to work for a printer, on a newspaper and then at an advertising agency. He moved to Tokyo in 1960, and soon became part of the newly formed Nippon Design Centre (p. 113). His work made an immediate impact, attracting attention from Japan's avant-garde community, including film-maker Nagisa Oshima, dancer Tatsumi Hijikata and playwright Shuji Terayama, for whom he went on to make a series of theatre production posters.

In 1967 Yokoo travelled to New York, where his entire collection of posters was purchased by the curators at MoMA (for $100 each, the same amount as a Warhol *Marilyn* poster at the time). He was then invited to take part in the 1968 'Word & Image' exhibition, and four years later was awarded a solo show there.

Growing interested in mysticism and attracted by the growing psychedelic scene, in the early 1970s Yokoo travelled extensively in India. He became a favourite with musicians such as the Beatles (in particular, John Lennon), ELP, Cat Stevens and Santana, and designed many of their LP covers.

In 1981, Yokoo had a revelation while at a Picasso retrospective in New York, deciding to leave the world of graphic design behind forever to concentrate on his art: 'It was instantaneous. It was extraordinary. When I entered that exhibition I was a graphic designer and when I left I was a painter. It was that quick. I was struck by how his whole life seemed to be led for creative ends – for self-expression.'

New York illustrator Paul Davis recognizes Yokoo's considerable contribution: 'He is unique. There isn't any other artist like him. Instead of taking a subject and just presenting it, he opens it up; and in finding so many ways to express himself and his passions, he has changed graphic design in the process.'

Above Portrait of Yokoo by Andrey Bold, 2012.

Above *Having Reached a Climax at the Age of 29 I Was Dead*, silkscreen, 1965.

Below left *Yakuza Films: One Movement of Postwar Japanese Cinema*, poster, 1968.

Below right *A la Maison de M. Civeçawa*, poster, 1965.

Tadanori Yokoo

1920

1930

1936 Born in Hyogo Prefecture, Japan.

1940

1950

1960 Becomes a member of the Nippon Design Centre.

1968 Participates in the 'Word & Image' exhibition at MoMA.

1970

1972 A solo show is held at MoMA.

1981 Retires from commercial work to become a painter.

1990

2000

2010

2012 The Tadanori Yokoo Museum of Contemporary Art opens.

O Desafio, poster, 1965.

imago apresenta
isabella
oduvaldo v. filho
sérgio brito
luiz linhares
joel barcelos
maria bethania   zé keti

o desafio

um filme de
paulo cezar saraceni

'The genius behind the geniuses.'
– Narlan Mattos

Rogério Duarte

b. 1939

BRAZIL

A true renaissance figure, Rogério Duarte is a musician, songwriter, poet, philosopher and professor, in addition to being Brazil's most revered graphic designer. Duarte was a key figure in Rio de Janeiro's counter-culture during the 1960s and was one of the founders of the avant-garde Tropicália cultural movement. As well as being an accomplished musician himself, he has designed album covers for fellow Brazilian artists such as Gilberto Gil, Gal Costa, Jorge Ben Jor, Caetano Veloso and João Gilberto.

Duarte moved from his native Bahia to Rio de Janeiro in 1960, where he took an experimental design course at the Museum of Modern Art. He worked in the studio of graphic designer Aloísio Magalhães for two years, and then with the National Union of Students as coordinator of its visual arts department. It was here that he designed the organization's *Movimento* magazine, a radical collaboration between students, intellectuals and artists, which was a precursor to the Tropicália movement that followed.

In the early part of his career, Duarte was also very much involved with Brazilian cinema, designing numerous landmark posters (including one for the 1964 film, *Black God, White Devil*), as well as directing and appearing in several films himself.

By the late 1960s Duarte was at the very heart of the Tropicália movement, a reaction against the oppressive military dictatorship that had come to power in Brazil in 1964. Through the fusion of traditional Brazilian culture and outside influences, the movement paved the way for the establishment of a new national identity via art, popular culture and, most importantly, music. Duarte designed the sleeves for the movement's record label. Its first release was a compilation by artists including Gilberto Gil and Caetano Veloso, and was considered to be the movement's musical manifesto.

Duarte also organized several high-profile art events, and in 1968 participated in the 'March of the Hundred Thousand', which took place after days of civil unrest in the capital city. He was arrested along with his brother and subsequently tortured by the military, later writing a harrowing account of his incarceration.

On his release Duarte carried on working, creating an impressive body of work, including book and newspaper designs, logos, posters and album covers. While the musical side of the Tropicália movement has been well documented, Rogério Duarte's part in it has not been. Thanks to a new generation of designers (from Brazil and beyond), however, he is now beginning to receive the recognition he deserves.

Above Portrait of Duarte.

copacabana filmes apresenta

deus e o diabo
na terra do sol

yoná magalhães
geraldo d'el rey
othon bastos **um filme de glauber rocha**
mauricio do valle **produção:luiz augusto mendes**

Deus e o Diabo na Terra do Sol,
poster, 1964.

Top *Jorge Mautner* by Jorge Mautner, album cover, 1974.

Above *Gilberto Gil* by Gilberto Gil, album cover, 1968.

1920

1930

1939   Born in Ubaíra, Brazil.

1950

1960   Moves to Rio de Janeiro.

Designs the poster for *Black God, White Devil*.

1964   Works as art director for the Vozes
        publishing house.

1966

1968   Starts designing for the Tropicália record label.

1970

1980

1990

2000

2010

Teatro San Materno, Ascona, poster for
the Spring/Summer season 2013.

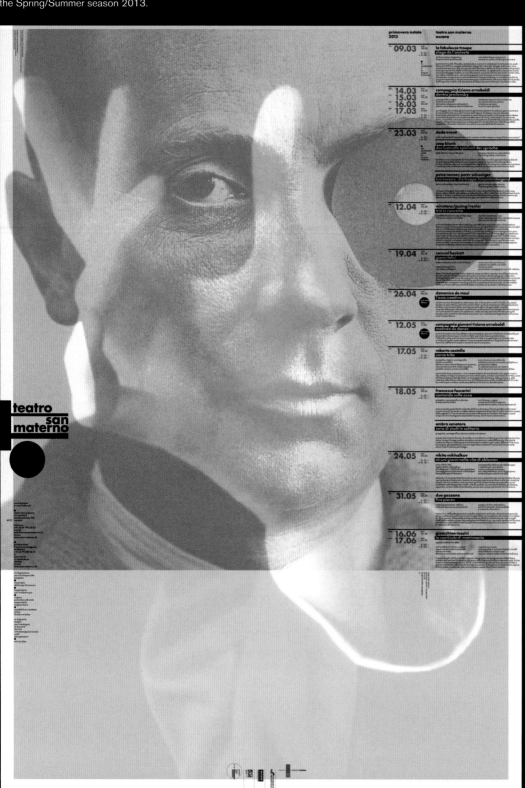

'If you keep shouting, you are not making communication any better. You are only removing talking and whispering from the system.'

Bruno Monguzzi

b. 1941

SWITZERLAND

Often described as a 'second generation Modernist', and influenced by time spent in the UK, Italy, Montreal and France, as well as his native Switzerland, Bruno Monguzzi's elegant designs have a timeless quality that sets them apart. His striking, pared-down identity (no long in use) for the Musée d'Orsay in Paris is particularly notable for its bold yet classic typographic approach.

Monguzzi grew up in the Italian-speaking region of Switzerland and studied at Geneva's School of Applied Arts. Well-schooled in the craft of design and typography, he soon found that 'a graphic design course, even in Switzerland, had little to do with communication.'

Seeking a more rounded education, he moved to London in 1960 to study at St Martins with Romek Marber, at the London School of Printing with Dennis Bailey and at the Central School of Art and Design. The designer Ken Briggs introduced him to Gestalt theory – its psychological interrogation into visual perception was highly influential on the young designer: 'It is at that point, in 1961, that I started to believe in graphic design as a problem-solving profession rather than a problem-making one.' Another big influence was the work of high-profile Americans such as Herb Lubalin, Lou Dorfsman and Lou Danziger.

Moving next to Milan, Monguzzi worked at Studio Boggeri from 1961 to 1963, where his work took on a new expressionistic side. He also credits its founder, Antonio Boggeri, for curbing his Modernist-inspired perfectionism. 'Swiss graphic design,' Boggeri once warned him, 'is often as perfect as any spider's web. But often of a useless perfection. The web is useful when broken by the entangled fly.' Monguzzi was then invited to Montreal to work on nine of the pavilions at Expo 67. In 1971 he returned to Switzerland, where he joined the

School of Applied Arts in Lugano to teach Typographic Design and the Psychology of Perception.

Monguzzi has also worked for several museums, including Lugano's Museo Cantonale d'Arte (1987 to 2004). One of his most significant commissions was for the Museé d'Orsay, the museum housed in a former railway station, which opened in 1986. Monguzzi worked with the Paris office of Jean Widmer to create a distinctive identity, comprised of a Didot uppercase 'M' and 'O', plus an apostrophe (the three elements were redrawn by Monguzzi to achieve the right proportions) divided by a line. This was applied to all of the stationery and signage, but it was Monguzzi's clever treatment of the 4-metre (13-ft)-wide poster created for the museum's opening that really stood out. Leaving the apostrophe to play centre stage along with the museum's opening date, it was an audacious treatment of the logo. As Monguzzi explains: 'The director did not want to see the building. The chief curator did not want to see works of art. So, from a "picture followed by words" poster, we arrived at a "words followed by no picture" concept. The logo and date were all that was needed. But nothing was happening, nothing was opening, nothing was beginning. I picked a Lartigue album: the image of his brother trying to take off with a glider was the answer. The fly was breaking the web.'

Above Portrait of Monguzzi, 2008.

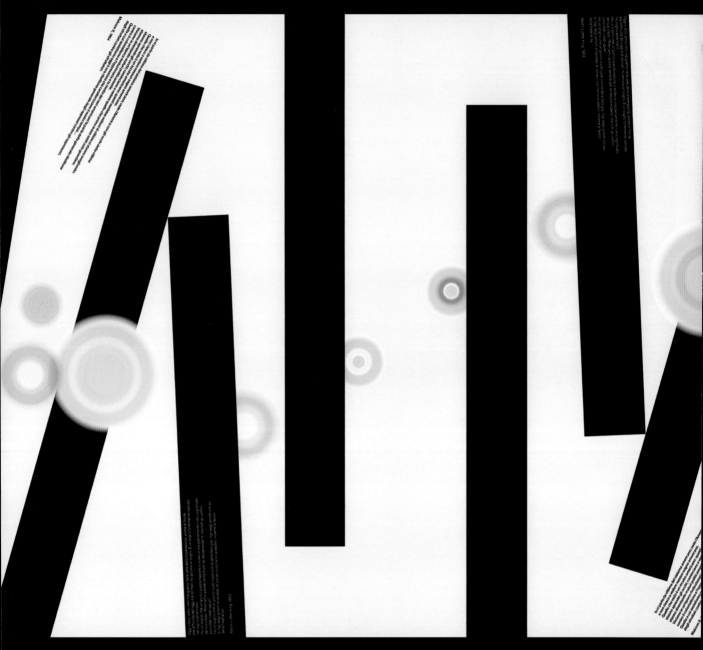

9 décembre 1986

Above *Free Freedom*, Chiasso Jazz Festival, poster, 2008.

Left Poster for the opening of the Musée d'Orsay, Paris, 1986.

Right Majakovskij, Mejerchold, Stanislavskij exhibition poster, 1975.

Bruno Monguzzi

1920

1930

1941   Born in Mendrisio, Switzerland.

1950

1956   Moves to Geneva and studies at the School of Applied Arts.

1961   Joins Studio Boggeri.

1965   Moves to Montreal to work on Expo 67.

1970

1980

1983   Wins the commission to design the identity for the Musée d'Orsay, Paris.

1987   Becomes the sole designer for Museo Cantonale d'Arte, Lugano.

1990

2000

2003   Elected Honorary Royal Designer for Industry by the Royal Society of Arts.

2011   *Bruno Monguzzi: Fifty Years of Paper*, monograph and solo travelling exhibiton (Switzerland, US, China).

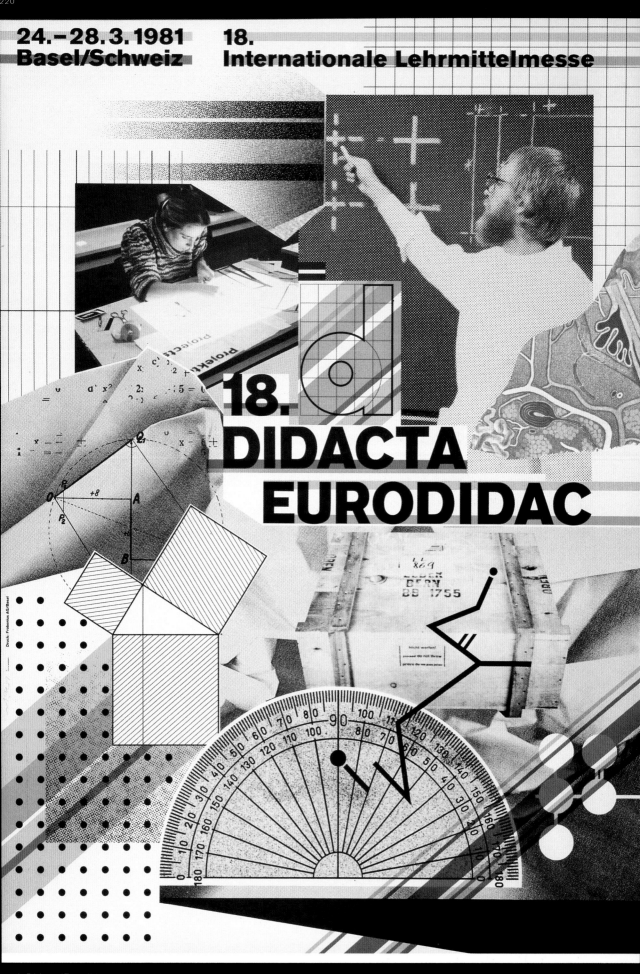

18.
DIDACTA
EURODIDAC

18th Didacta/Eurodidac, poster, 1981.

'What's the use of being legible, when nothing inspires you to take notice of it?'

Wolfgang Weingart

b. 1941

GERMANY

Weingart is often cited as a key protagonist of the New Wave of typography, but at the start of his career, he fully embraced the International Typographic Style. He then turned it on its head, pushing the boundaries of typographic design and, as a committed educator, inspiring future generations of designers to do the same.

Weingart studied graphic design at the Merz Academy in Stuttgart, southern Germany. The college printing press was his first real exposure to the printing process, and led him to take on a three-year typesetting apprenticeship at the Stuttgart printers, Ruwe. It was here that he learnt to set hot metal type expertly and where he met Ruwe's consulting designer, who would become something of a mentor. Karl August Hanke had studied at the Basel School of Design under Armin Hofman (p. 136), and encouraged Weingart to follow his dream and do the same. Weingart enrolled as an independent student in 1964, but found that Basel was not quite the inspiring place he believed it would be. He felt that the teaching had become dogmatic and dull, and questioned his decision to study there.

Weingart's talents did not go unrecognized, however, and in 1968 he was asked to teach on the typography course (taking over from Emil Ruder, p. 108). He subsequently encouraged his students to take a much more experimental approach to typography. 'I try to teach students to view typography from all angles: Type must not always be set flush left/ragged right, nor in only two type sizes, not in necessarily right-angle arrangements, nor printed in either black or red. Typography must not be dry, tightly ordered or rigid. Type may be set centre axis, ragged left/ragged right, perhaps sometimes in chaos.'

Weingart continued to practise while he taught, and this approach can be seen in his own work, although it could never be described as 'chaotic'. It pushes against conventions such as the grid, but never dispenses with them entirely. This new approach was not completely well received at Basel: 'In my presentations in 1972, there was always a group of the audience that hated it, one group that loved it, and the rest would all leave during the lecture', he admits. As well as experimenting with type, in the mid-1970s Weingart began layering multiple images using a combination of film and offset printing.

Thanks to several high-profile ex-students such as Dan Friedman and April Greiman (p. 232), Weingart's approach soon became much more mainstream, and he came to be in great demand, both as an educator and a lecturer. In 2000, his epic ten-part monograph *My Way To Typography* was published by Lars Müller.

Above *Kunstkredit Basel 1976/77*, poster, 1977.

Left *Kunstkredit Basel 1980/81*, poster, 1981.

Below *Schreibkunst*, poster, 1981.

Wolfgang Weingart

1920

1930

1941 Born in the Salem Valley, Germany.

1950

1958 Enrols at the Merz Academy in Stuttgart.

1960

1964 Begins studies at the Basel School of Design.

1968 Invited to teach typography at the Advanced Class for Graphic Design.

1970

1980

1990

My Way to Typography is published.

2000

2010

Druck: Wassermann AG Basel

Das Schweizer Plakat
1900–1984

24. Januar – 11. März 1984   Gewerbemuseum Basel

Museum für Gestaltung

Das Schweizer Plakat 1900–1984
[The Swiss Poster 1900–1984],
poster, 1981.

BUY **38**

HIT ME WITH YOUR RHYTHM STICK
IAN DURY AND THE BLOCKHEADS

THERE AIN'T HALF BEEN SOME CLEVER
BASTARDS
ID AND THE BLOCKS

'I feel really strongly about what I do, that it is for other people, that's why I don't like crediting myself on people's albums – like you've got a Nick Lowe album, it's NICK LOWE's album, not a Barney Bubbles album!'

Barney Bubbles

1942–1983

UK

The antithesis of the egocentric, headline-seeking superstar designer, Barney Bubbles was so modest about his work that he rarely used even his own pseudonym to credit it. This, on top of his complex personality and sometimes chaotic lifestyle, meant that despite his importance to so many designers in the post-punk era, his influence was unacknowledged for many years.

Colin Fulcher had a conventional suburban upbringing in London, attending the nearby Twickenham Art School. Showing obvious talent, in 1965 he went to work for the (then very hip) Conran Design Group. Two years later, Fulcher resigned, changed his name to Barney Bubbles and went on a six-month pilgrimage to San Francisco's hippy capital, Haight-Ashbury. He returned to the UK a fully fledged hippy, moving to a shared house in Notting Hill in 1968. It was here that he met Hawkwind's Nik Turner, which led to him designing the seminal mystical and sci-fi-inspired fold-out sleeve for the band's 1971 LP, *In Search of Space*. Over the following years he created a cohesive identity for the band, designing everything from posters to drum kits.

Bubbles' next milestone came when he met Jake Riviera of Stiff Records, who dragged him to a Damned concert. Bubbles never looked back, going on to become the label's in-house designer. With its cheeky 'If it ain't Stiff, it ain't worth a fuck' slogan, Stiff embodied the DIY punk ethos, and was home to bands such as The Damned, Elvis Costello and the Attractions, and Ian Dury and the Blockheads.

Stiff's innovative approach to both marketing and sleeve design allowed Bubbles total creative freedom. Effortlessly combining styles and genres, in-jokes and symbols, his playful, postmodern approach felt irreverent and exciting. For Ian Dury's 1979 LP, *Do It Yourself*, he created 31 sleeves made from different Crown Wallpaper designs, which became instant collector's items, and his design for Elvis Costello's 1979 *Armed Forces*, which could be folded in numerous different combinations, was a die-cut *tour de force.* Sleeve designs for Generation X, Billy Bragg, Dr Feelgood and the Psychedelic Furs were all released under a range of different pseudonyms.

In the late 1970s and early 80s Bubbles directed several music videos, including The Specials' *Ghost Town*, Squeeze's *Is That Love* and Fun Boy Three's *The Lunatics Have Taken Over the Asylum.* Bubbles was acutely aware of the power of this emerging medium, as he pointed out in a rare interview with *Smash Hits* in the year prior to his untimely death: 'A good video can sell a record which might not do so well. The record companies know that. I think Chrysalis would agree that The Specials' *Ghost Town* video helped sales a good deal. This year I intend to make videos which are really inexpensive but really inventive. It can be done, you know.'

Above Portrait of Bubbles, 1978.

Barney Face on White, self portrait,
1981.

Barney Bubbles

1920

1930

1940

1942 Born Colin Fulcher in Whitton, UK.

1950

1960

1965 Joins the Conran Design Group.

1969 Sets up a studio in Portobello Road, London.

1971 Designs cover artwork for Hawkwind's *In Search of Space*.

1979 Designs cover artwork for Elvis Costello's *Armed Forces*.

1983 Dies in London, UK.

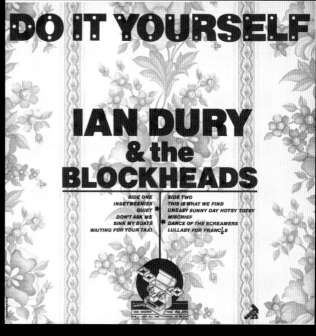

Top left *In Search of Space*
by Hawkwind, album cover,
die-cut card, 1971.

Above left *Armed Forces* by Elvis
Costello and the Attractions,
fold-out sleeve, 1979.

Top right *Do It Yourself* by Ian Dury
and the Blockheads, album sleeve,
card wallpaper sample stock, one
of 17 variants, 1979.

Above right *Armed Forces* by Elvis
Costello and the Attractions, album
cover, 1979.

Street scene showing Westminster
street signage and British Rail identity,
c. 1967.

'Simplicity is not a goal, but one arrives at simplicity in spite of oneself, as one approaches the real meaning of things.'
– Herbert Read

Design Research Unit

est. 1943

UK

Founded in 1943, the Design Research Unit (DRU) was a true pioneer – it was the first multidisciplinary consultancy in Britain, combining graphics, industrial design and architecture within the same practice. It was one of the forerunners in the field of what we now call corporate identity. Projects for clients such as British Rail, the Watney Mann brewery and the City of London left a lasting impression on the country's post-war landscape.

Founded by the critic Herbert Read and the advertising executive Marcus Brumwell, the Design Research Unit grew from the desire of a group of designers who had worked together at the Ministry of Information to shape the design landscape in the immediate post-war period. Three areas of design were established: design and fabrication, technics and research, and finance and administration.

The DRU's first corporate identity was for the film manufacturer Ilford, in 1946, an identity which was then redesigned in 1966 (incorporating the new 'sunburst' logo). In 1951, DRU was commissioned to work on the Festival of Britain, across a range of disciplines – designing signage, creating the exhibition design for the Dome of Discovery, the interior and exterior of the Regatta Restaurant and the Bailey Bridge.

In 1956, DRU started working on two major corporate identity projects. The first was for the brewery Watney Mann. Over the course of 15 years, DRU created a radical new identity, featuring the distinctive red barrel, which encompassed all of the graphics, interiors and exteriors of the brewery's pubs. This changed the face of the British public house forever.

In the same year, Misha Black embarked on a six-year consultancy project with British Railways. The corporate identity that was to follow was immense and involved 2,000 stations, 4,000 locomotives, 23,000 carriages and 45 Sealink ships. A new name – British Rail – and a new logo (designed by Gerald Barney) was implemented, along with a bespoke typeface, New Rail Alphabet, designed by former DRU member Jock Kinneir, and Margaret Calvert (p. 116). Aimed at unifying the railway network and inspiring confidence in the public, the project was one of the most ambitious corporate identities ever undertaken. The extensive brand guidelines publication that was produced as part of the project (comprising four volumes) has become something of an archetype for a new generation of graphic designers.

DRU went on to complete many other high-profile projects, two of which left a big impression on the capital. One was the identity and signage for the London Underground's Victoria Line, which opened in 1968 and included platform murals by Edward Bawden, Tom Eckersley (p. 88) and Abram Games (p. 92). The other was for the City of Westminster, for whom Misha Black created its much-loved (and reproduced) red-and-black street signs.

Above Portrait of DRU, 1968.

Above left The New Face of British Railways, exhibition at the Design Centre, 1965.

Above right London Underground signage at Oxford Circus Station, 1968.

Below ICI logo design, part of the corporate ID programme devised by Ronald Armstrong and Milner Grey, c. 1969.

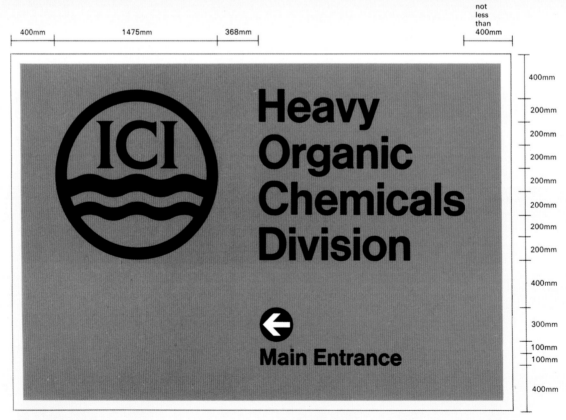

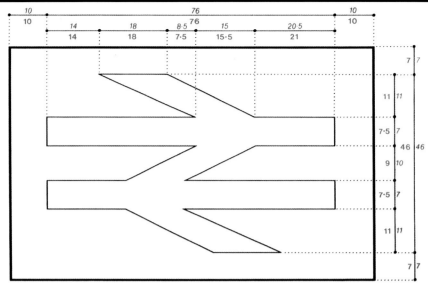

The symbol may be used with or without the rectangular box, in positive or negative form. The box bears a specific relationship to the symbol. An outline version of the symbol is also available. On no account should the proportions of symbol or box be altered to suit particular applications.

Above Recommended use of the British Rail logo (designed by Gerald Barney), *British Rail Corporate Identity Manual*, 1965.

Below Courage and Co, beer mat, corporate identity design 1949–55.

Design Research Unit

1920

1930

1940

1943 — DRU founded by Marcus Brumwell and Herbert Read, with Milner Gray and Misha Black

1951 — Designs Regatta Restaurant and displays for the Dome of Discovery for the Festival of Britain.

1956 — Starts to design corporate identity for Watney Mann brewery.

1961 — Starts to design corporate identity for British Rail.

1967 / 1968 — Richard and Su Rogers become associates. Misha Black designs the City of Westminster Street signs.

1970

1977 — Designs Silver Jubilee Walkway pavement discs.

1980

1990

2000

2004 — Merged with Scott Brownrigg.

2010

WET Magazine, April Greiman in
collaboration with Jayme Odgers, 1979.

'People say "Oh, April Greiman … she's a graphic designer", but I haven't called myself a graphic designer since 1984, when I got the Macintosh.'

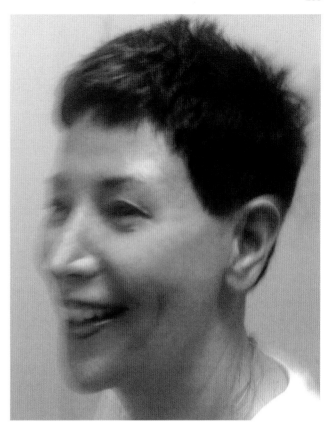

April Greiman

b. 1948

USA

Whereas some designers were wary of the Macintosh when it was first released, April Greiman was one of the first to embrace the new technology, seeing it as the future rather than a threat – a new way to explore and experiment. A hugely influential figure, Greiman saw the computer as a way of finding out what graphic design could be, as opposed to what it was already.

Greiman began her studies at the Kansas City Art Institute, then went on to attend the Basel School of Design, where she studied under Armin Hofmann and Wolfgang Weingart (pp. 136 and 220). While the teaching there was very much based on the International Style, Weingart was experimenting with a new typographic aesthetic that was much more intuitive and experimental – what was to become known as the New Wave.

After returning to the US, Greiman practised in New York for a while, but in the mid-1970s, feeling that she needed to leave her comfort zone, she moved to LA. Here she forged a partnership with the photographer Jayme Odgers, which was to lead her work in a new and exciting direction.

In 1982, the California Institute of the Arts asked Greiman to lead its graphic design programme. This gave Greiman access to the latest equipment, and she spent her spare time creating hybrid pieces, exploring emerging technologies and the interplay between analogue and digital. In 1984 she campaigned successfully for the department to change its name from Graphic Design to Visual Communication, explaining 'It's not just graphic design anymore. We just don't have a new name for it yet.'

Greiman returned to full-time practice in 1984, purchasing her first Macintosh computer the same year. In 1986 she sent shockwaves through the design community with her radical treatment of issue 133 of *Design Quarterly*, published by the Walker Arts Center. Eschewing the traditional magazine format, it was a life-sized digitized poster of a naked Greiman, overlaid with text and images that had been created using the early version of MacDraw. It was an amazing feat, given the limitations of the technology at that time, and was the subject of much debate within the industry. Suddenly designers who had done their best to ignore the new technology were made aware of its exciting possibilities.

Still practising and running her studio Made in Space, Greiman is a designer who is constantly moving forward, challenging our preconceptions about what graphic design can be, and inspiring future generations.

Above Self portrait of Greiman.

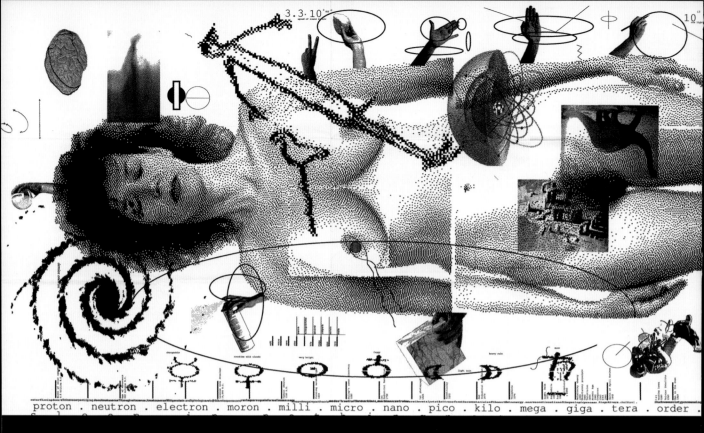

proton . neutron . electron . moron . milli . micro . nano . pico . kilo . mega . giga . tera . order

Above *Design Quarterly #133: Does It Make Sense?*, 1986.

Right 1984 Los Angeles Olympics poster, Greiman in collaboration with Jayme Odgers, 1982.

Los Angeles 1984 Olympic Games

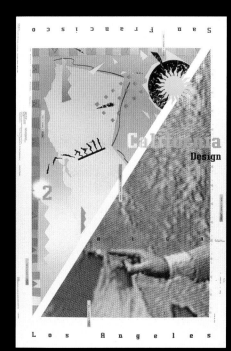

Below *AIGA, California Design 2*,
poster, 1995.

Below right *Your Turn, My Turn, 3-D,
1983*, Pacific Design Center /
Westweek, 1983.

April Greiman

1920

1930

1940

1948 Born in New York City, US.
1950

1960

1970 Enters the Basel School of Design.

1976 Moves to Los Angeles.

Becomes head of the design department at the
California Institute of the Arts.
1980
1982 Changes name of the department to
1984 Visual Communications.

1990

2000

2010

Map of Antarctica, acrylic on canvas, 2011.

'Find out what the next thing is that you can push, that you can invent, that you can be ignorant about, that you can be arrogant about, that you can fail with, and that you can be a fool with. Because in the end, that's how you grow.'

Paula Scher

b. 1948

USA

Paula Scher has a passion for typography and topology. Her forthright work is appreciated by everyone, from corporate clients such as Bloomberg, Tiffany's and Citibank, to cultural institutions such as the Public Theater and the Metropolitan Opera, while she has also exhibited her intricate typographic map paintings.

Scher cut her teeth as an in-house art director at both CBS and Atlantic Records, presiding over hundreds of LP covers every year. All the artists had artwork approval, so in effect she had two sets of people to please, which gave her invaluable experience in dealing with clients. She then set up Koppel & Scher with Terry Koppel (whom she had met at the Tyler School of Art in Philadelphia), designing everything from advertising to packaging for a wide range of clients. These included Swatch, for whom she designed a series of posters that mimicked Herbert Matter's classic Modernist posters for the Swiss National Tourist Office (p.52 and 55). Scher's mischievous sense of humour is present in much of her work, but the designer in-joke was not appreciated by everyone.

In 1991 Scher became the first woman to be made a partner at Pentagram (p. 284). She remained the only woman partner at the agency until Lisa Strausfeld was made a partner in 2002 – a development that Scher fully endorsed in 2012 when further women were made partners: 'I think more women should work on more visible projects and be recognized for it and more men should partner with and promote terrific women designers. Finally, this year, Pentagram will have four women partners. Hooray!'

While Scher's work for corporate clients such as Microsoft and Tiffany is undeniably accomplished, her work for cultural clients has also attracted admiration. One of her most enduring clients is New York's Public Theater, for whom she has designed a stunning series of posters since her first commission to design its identity in 1994. Scher's love of type – and especially big type – is reflected in her work, and nowhere more so than in her exuberant typographic interior for the New Jersey Performing Arts Center, and an equally striking exterior for its Lucent Technologies Center for Arts Education.

Scher's expansive typographic maps have gained attention. First exhibited in New York, the idiosyncratic representations of cities and countries later appeared in the 2011 book *Paula Scher: Maps*, published by Princeton Architectural Press.

While widely acknowledged by her peers, Scher's work still possesses an unashamedly populist appeal, which she is happy to embrace: 'I think I once said I'd rather be the Beatles than Philip Glass – they're both qualitative, it's just that one has a broader appreciation from audiences than the other does.'

Above *The Truth Behind the Overused Publicity Photo (circa 1985)*, self portrait of Scher, *circa* 1992.

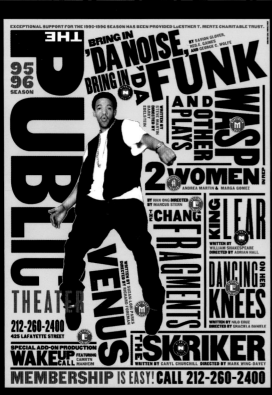

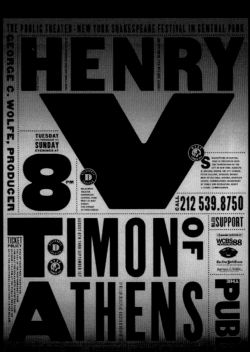

Above left New Jersey Performing Arts Center, exterior graphics, 2001.

Far left *Bring in 'Da Noise, Bring in Da' Funk*, New York Public Theater poster, 1995.

Left *Shakespeare Festival, Henry V, Timon of Athens*, New York Public Theater poster, 1996.

Above right Comedy of Errors. Love's Labour's Lost, New York Public Theater poster, 2013.

Paula Scher

1920

1930

1940

1948 Born in Virginia, US.

1950

1960

1970

1972 Becomes art director at CBS Records.

1980

1982 Forms the studio Koppel & Scher with Terry Koppel.

1991 Becomes a partner at Pentagram.
1992 Becomes an educator at the School of Visual Arts, New York.

2000

2002 Publishes her career monograph, *Make It Bigger*.

2010

a magazine about the rest of the world   una rivista che parla del resto del mondo

COL⊙RS

tribù a new york
cowboy in polonia
il re di tonga e la regina dell'aglio
(E UN principe O DUE)
colazione in tibet
(E IN EGITTO E IN RUSSIA E IN COSTA D'AVORIO)
eroi in guatemala
(E IN SUD AFRICA E IN TAILANDIA)
baci dappertutto

tribes in new york
cowboys in poland
breakfast in tibet
(AND EGYPT AND RUSSIA AND CÔTE D'IVOIRE)
king of tonga & queen of garlic
(AND A prince OR TWO)
heroes in guatemala
(AND SOUTH AFRICA AND THAILAND)
kisses everywhere

Above *It's a Baby!*, *Colors Magazine 1*,
1991.

Opposite *AIDS*, *Colors Magazine 7*,
1994.

'We live in a society and a culture and an economic model that tries to make everything look right.... But by definition, when you make something no one hates, no one loves it. So I am interested in imperfections, quirkiness, insanity, unpredictability.'

Tibor Kalman

1949–1999

HUNGARY

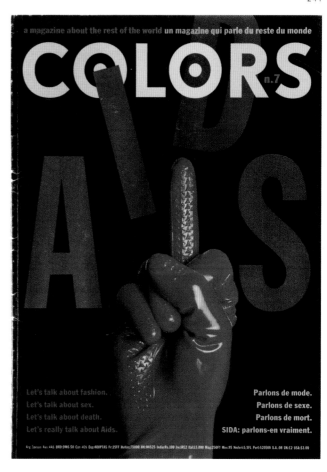

Tibor Kalman was something of a rare thing – a designer who worked for commercial clients but retained a keen sense of social responsibility; someone who was at the heart of the New York design scene, but not afraid to criticize it. Through his work for *Colors* magazine, he harnessed the power of the image, using it to both shock and encourage viewers to question their views.

Kalman moved to New York from his native Hungary as a child. He studied journalism at New York University, then worked for the bookstore Barnes & Noble, overseeing the publicity and window displays before eventually running the in-house design department. In 1979 he set up M&Co (with Carol Bokuniewicz and Liz Trovato), which soon became a successful agency, working with clients such as Talking Heads, *Artforum* and the fashionable NYC restaurant, Florent.

Kalman believed design had two functions – to make life better, and to raise awareness of social issues. In the mid-1980s he used M&Co as a platform to campaign on causes such as homelessness, and was accused by less charitable members of the design community of creating PR stunts for self-promotion.

Despite his belief that design should be used to change the world, Kalman rallied against what he saw as complacent, mediocre design, and was openly critical of those he felt were guilty of this. He also liked to take his clients out of their comfort zone – 'We're here to make

them think about design that's dangerous and unpredictable. We're here to inject art into commerce.'

In 1991, Kalman found a new outlet for his views. After helping Oliviero Toscani with a series of hard-hitting ads (dealing with subjects such as AIDS, war and racism) for the fashion retailer Benetton, he became editor-in-chief of the company's new magazine, *Colors*. Two years later, Kalman closed M&Co and moved to Rome to work full-time on *Colors*, which he described as 'the first magazine for the global village'. The magazine continued in the same controversial vein, and gave Kalman a global platform. In an issue on racism, the article 'What If' featured a series of startling transformations (courtesy of Photoshop), including a black Queen Elizabeth II, a white Spike Lee and an Asian Pope John Paul II. *Colors* was the antithesis to most fashion publications, dealing with serious issues in a refreshingly frank way, and addressing a young, international audience.

Illness forced Kalman back to New York in 1997. He set up a more modest M&Co, working only on projects that he really cared about, writing for the *New York Times* and teaching a weekly class at the School of Visual Arts right up until his death from cancer in 1999.

Arnold Schwarzenegger

Spike Lee

what if..?
e se..?

COLORS

Queen Elizabeth
Regina Elisabetta

Michael Jackson

Opposite Spreads from *Colors Magazine,*
Issue 4, 1993.

Below Advertisement for the Florent
restaurant, poster, 1987.

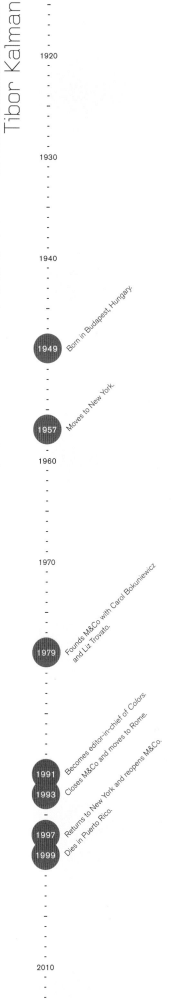

NOVEMBER

SOUP   BOUDIN & WARM TARTS

GUSTY WINDS

HIGH S UPPER 40S TO MID 50S

LOWS UPPER 30S TO MID 40S

FLORENT

OPEN 24 HOURS 989 5779

WATCH FOR HEAVY RAINS

WEAR YOUR GALOSHES

MNCO

Tibor Kalman

1920

1930

1940

1949 — Born in Budapest, Hungary.

1957 — Moves to New York.

1960

1970

1979 — Founds M&Co with Carol Bokuniewicz and Liz Trovato.

1991 — Becomes editor-in-chief of Colors. Closes M&Co and moves to Rome.

1993 — Returns to New York and reopens M&Co.

1997 —

1999 — Dies in Puerto Rico.

2010

'I think drawing is a kind of writing, where you explain many things with a very simple line, like a letter.'

Javier Mariscal

b. 1950

SPAIN

Javier Mariscal's joyful, expressive work embodies the spirit of post-Franco Spain. One of few graphic designers to cross over into designing in three dimensions, his output can truly be described as multidisciplinary. In addition to vibrant graphics (identities, books, comics and idents) he has designed furniture, wallpaper, interiors, ceramics, glass, toys, sculpture, and even an animated feature film (*Chico & Rita*, 2010).

After a short stint at the Elisava School Of Design and Engineering in Barcelona, and time spent designing comics, it was Mariscal's hand-drawn identity for the city of Barcelona that first brought him to the public's attention. With its quirky lines and bright colours, *Bar Cel Ona* (*Bar Sky Wave*), perfectly encapsulated the newfound optimism of Mariscal's adoptive home city. After 40 years of dictatorship under Franco, Spain had finally become a democracy, and joined the EU. Then, in 1986, Barcelona won the bid to host the 1992 Olympics; Mariscal's mascot – Cobi, a cheeky Catalan sheepdog – went on to become the Games' most commercially successful mascot ever, with his own TV series.

In 1980 Mariscal designed his first bar – the Duplex in Valencia – which gave rise to the colourful, wobbly-legged Duplex stool, his first piece of furniture to be put into production. With a growing reputation as a furniture designer, he was then invited to exhibit with the Memphis group in Milan. Since then, Mariscal has designed for major furniture and lighting manufacturers, including Magis, Alessi, Artemide, Cassina and Moroso.

Despite his varied output, Mariscal's graphic work has always been in great demand. He has created identities for clients as diverse as the Swedish political party Socialdemokraterna, Glasgow's Lighthouse art centre, Barcelona Zoo and London-based post-production house Framestore. His vibrant aesthetic is completely at odds with the sans serif, grid-loving, Swiss Modernist-influenced school of graphic designers, but its playful approach masks a hidden sophistication.

Mariscal seems to be able to turn his hand to anything – he has designed 12 covers for *The New Yorker*, a theme park in Japan, bags for Camper Kids and the interior of the H&M store in Barcelona. Eschewing the computer in favour of working by hand, using markers or pencils to sketch out ideas, Mariscal's work has a unique quality and an irresistible energy. While many of the restaurants and bars that he has designed may be long gone, Mariscal has left his mark on Barcelona. His sculpture, *La Gamba*, was originally created for Gambrinus, a trendy 'scene' restaurant designed by the architect Alfredo Arribas in 1988, but when the restaurant eventually closed, *La Gamba* was acquired and restored by the city council. Now, courtesy of Mariscal, visitors to Barcelona's elegant seafront are greeted by an enormous cartoon-like sculpture of a prawn with huge claws smiling down on them.

Opposite *Bar Cel Ona*, illustration, 1979.

Above Portrait of Mariscal.

Left *Chico & Rita*, film poster, 2010.

Below Scene from *Chico & Rita* film, 2010.

Opposite Poster for Vespa, 1996.

Opposite below *Cobi*, official poster for the Olympic Games, Barcelona, 1992.

Javier Mariscal

- **1920**
- **1930**
- **1940**
- **1950** — Born in Valencia, Spain.
- **1960**
- **1970**
- **1979** — Designs the Bar Cel Ona logo.
- **1980** — Designs the Duplex stool.
- **1981** — Participates in 'Memphis, an International Style' in Milan.
- **1989** — Designs Cobi, the 1992 Barcelona Olympics mascot.
  — Opens Estudio Mariscal.
- **1995** — Designs the Alexandra armchair for Moroso.
- **2000**
- **2010** — Animated feature film *Chico & Rita* is released.

Power, Corruption and Lies by
New Order, Factory album. *A Basket
of Roses* by Henri Fantin-Latour,
1890. Design: Peter Saville
Associates, 1983.

'Working with Factory there was no business model, no advertising, no marketing director, nobody committed to the notion of profitability.'

Peter Saville

b. 1955

UK

It is unlikely that Peter Saville would even consider himself to be a graphic designer, but despite his recent transition into the art world, his influence on the world of visual communication, and on the way the designed world looks today, has been immense.

Saville's first piece of work for Tony Wilson's nightclub event, 'The Factory', created while Saville was still at Manchester Polytechnic, is an early example of the 'appropriation' of images that would become an intrinsic part of his work. *FAC1*, as the poster has come to be called, combined an industrial warning sign taken from a door at art school, a carpark-yellow background and bold, sans serif type. It was both found object and a reference to early Tschichold. Together with Alan Erasmus, Saville and Wilson went on to set up Factory Records, releasing music by bands such as Joy Division (later New Order), A Certain Ratio, OMD and the Happy Mondays. While the business side of things was disorderly, Saville had total creative freedom in terms of design and budget: 'We lived out an ideal, without business calling the shots. It was a phenomenon.'

Lack of commercial constraint has proved to be a recurring theme in Saville's career, and his inability to work the traditional 9 to 5 is the stuff of legend. A brief spell at Pentagram in 1992 was the only real concession he made to working within a professional framework. Yet the focus on his refusal to conform only serves to detract from his vision, and his ability to operate beyond the traditional confines of graphic design.

Pentagram was followed by a short stint in Hollywood, after which Saville returned to the UK. In 1995 he was set up by Meiré and Meiré in a 1970s-style

Mayfair bachelor pad, the perfect backdrop for him – intellectual, world weary and resplendent in a silk dressing gown, he was a complete antidote to the 1990s buttoned-up, strategy-obsessed breed of graphic designer. As well as fashion and identity work, Saville continued producing work for New Order, and members of the new generation of Britpop, Suede and Pulp.

Recognition from the establishment finally came in 2003 with 'The Peter Saville Show', a retrospective held at London's Design Museum, and an accompanying book, *Designed by Peter Saville*. Further evidence of his acceptance came the following year when the City of Manchester appointed him its first official creative director. At the same time, a new generation of art directors, many of whom had discovered his work as students, began to reference – and sometimes commission – him.

In recent years, Saville has distanced himself somewhat from the world of graphic design, creating conceptual pieces and being represented by a gallery. The book *Peter Saville: Estate* (based on his solo exhibition at Zurich's Migros Museum for Contemporary Art) presents items from his extensive archive as a personal biography.

Above Portrait of Saville by Wolfgang Stahr, 2011.

Technique by New Order, Factory album.
Dichromat: Trevor Key and Peter Saville.
Design: Peter Saville Associates, 1989.

Below *Unknown Pleasures* by Joy
Division, Factory album. Design:
Joy Division and Peter Saville, 1979.

Bottom 'Blue Monday' by New Order
Factory single. Design: Peter Saville
and Brett Wickens, 1983.

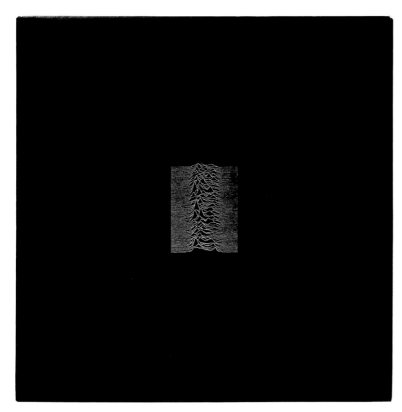

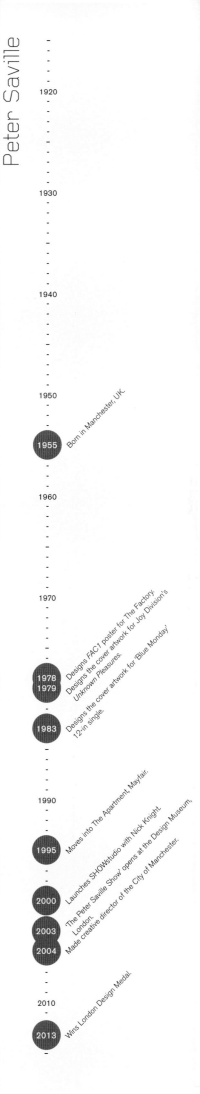

Peter Saville

1920

1930

1940

1950

1955 Born in Manchester, UK.

1960

1970

1978 Designs *FAC1* poster for The Factory.
1979 Designs the cover artwork for Joy Division's *Unknown Pleasures*.

1983 Designs the cover artwork for 'Blue Monday' 12-in single.

1990

1995 Moves into The Apartment, Mayfair.

2000 Launches SHOWstudio with Nick Knight.

2003 'The Peter Saville Show' opens at the Design Museum, London.
2004 Made creative director of the City of Manchester.

2010

2013 Wins London Design Medal.

'Design is directed toward human beings. To design is to solve human problems by identifying them and executing the best solution.'

Chermayeff & Geismar & Haviv

est. 1957

USA

Often described as one of America's most influential graphic design partnerships, Ivan Chermayeff and Tom Geismar are widely credited with revolutionizing the world of corporate identity. Their 300-plus identities for clients such as Chase Manhattan, Xerox and Pan Am form an unmistakeable part of the post-war American graphic design landscape.

Chermayeff and Geismar met when they were postgraduate students at the Yale School of Art and Architecture. After graduating, Chermayeff (who was born in London and is the son of architect Serge Chermayeff) went on to work for Alvin Lustig and at CBS, while Geismar (who originated from New Jersey) worked with the US Army's Exhibition Unit, on graphics and installations.

The pair joined with Robert Brownjohn (a former student of Serge Chermayeff, see p. 144) in 1957 to form Brownjohn, Chermayeff & Geismar. Commissions included corporate identities, book jackets and album covers, as well as the US Pavilion for the 1958 World's Fair in Brussels. Brownjohn left for London in 1960, and the studio became Chermayeff & Geismar. In 1961, its new identity for the US bank Chase Manhattan (which is still in use today) gained much attention and is credited as starting a trend for abstract logotypes.

Chermayeff & Geismar's client list reads like a *Who's Who* of corporate America – its simple but masterful identities include Pan Am (1957), Xerox (1963), Mobil (1964), the American Bicentennial (1976), PBS (1984) and Univision (1988), some of which were utilized for many years. As well as creating an incredibly diverse range of corporate identities, the studio also specialized in exhibition design, creating the US pavilions for World's Fairs of 1958 (Brussels) and 1970 (Osaka).

The studio continued to practise until 2005, when Chermayeff & Geismar set up a scaled-down studio after separating from their partners at the time, who included long-term associate Steff Geissbuhler. In 2006 there were three partners once again, when the founding pair were joined by designer Sagi Haviv. In 2013 the firm became Chermayeff & Geismar & Haviv.

Opposite Pan Am corporate branding.

Above Portrait of Geismar, Chermayeff & Haviv by Mark Craemer, 2009.

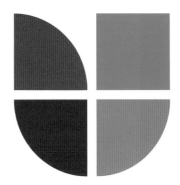

Top NBC logo, 1980.

Middle PBS logo, 1984.

Bottom Univision logo, 1989.

Opposite top Pan Am logo, 1969.

Opposite middle Mobil logo, 1964.

Opposite bottom American Revolution
Bicentennial logo, 1976.

Mobil

1920

1930

1940

1950

1957 Brownjohn, Chermayeff & Geismar established.
Designs the Pan Am corporate identity.

1960 Robert Brownjohn leaves the studio.
1961 Designs the identity for Chase Manhattan Bank.

1963 Designs the Xerox corporate identity.
1964 Designs the corporate identity for Mobil oil.

1970

1980

1990

2005 Steff Geissbuhler leaves to form C&G Partners.

2000

2010

2013 The firm becomes Chermayeff &
Geismar & Haviv.

Treasure, Cocteau Twins album cover,
back and front, 1984.

'I always start with the music, read the lyrics. Because I think it's such an otherwise simple or superficial exercise – take a fabulous image, and a bit of wonderful cutting-edge type and, oh, wonderful sleeve. But if it doesn't connect with the music, it's worthless. I think the strongest sleeves are the sum of the parts.'

Vaughan Oliver

b. 1957

UK

Oliver's name will forever be associated with the music of the indie label 4AD, and with cult bands such as the Pixies and the Cocteau Twins in particular. As with many fruitful creative partnerships, the record company's head, Ivo Watts-Russell, gave Oliver complete control over the label's artistic output, and acutely understood the value of specifying quality paper and special print processes. Oliver's treatments reflected each band's individual ethos, and while seen as extensions of the music, they stood up as unique pieces in their own right.

Oliver arrived in post-punk London after graduating in graphic design from Newcastle Polytechnic in 1979, initially working as a packaging designer. He was commissioned to design his first cover for 4AD in 1981, and the following year he set up the studio 23 Envelope with the photographer Nigel Grierson. The pair would work together for the next six years.

Oliver was essentially the in-house designer for 4AD, and worked on sleeves for its much lauded roster of indie artists, which included Lush, Ultra Vivid Scene, This Mortal Coil, the Pixies and the Cocteau Twins. While each band required a different approach, a 4AD band's artwork was instantly recognizable: 'I suppose back in the beginning the intention was to have a label identity, but there was never a house style... What we wanted was a consistency in approach. This is going back before the days when the word "branding" was used.'

When Grierson left the company in 1988, Oliver and fellow designer Chris Bigg set up v23, expanding their remit to include clients from the worlds of industrial design, fashion and publishing, including Ron Arad, John Galliano and Picador books. Their work rejected the early 1990s fascination with Modernism and neoclassicism in favour of a more expressive, layered and experimental approach, employing particular print processes, collage and calligraphy to produce a look that was often described as 'poetic' and 'esoteric'. Although it looks Photoshopped, most of Oliver's earlier work predates the computer and was created by hand.

Opposed to the elitist view of design, Oliver believed that music fans deserved beautiful and intelligently designed packaging, created with as much care as the music: '4AD was about giving the man on the street more credit than a mainstream company would... The general public is a lot brighter, more visually literate than the corporates give them credit for. I firmly believe that.'

Above Portrait of Oliver.

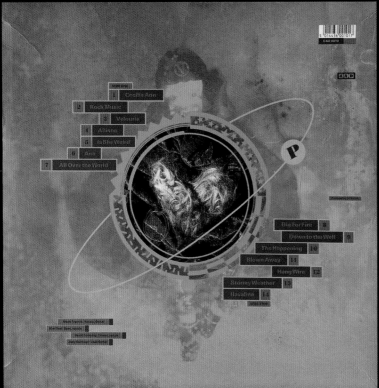

Bossanova, Pixies album cover, 1990.

Top *Ultra Vivid Scene*, Ultra Vivid Scene album cover, 1988.

Above *Doolittle*, Pixies album cover, 1989.

Vaughan Oliver

1920

1930

1940

1950

1957 Born in County Durham, UK.

1960

1970

1979 Graduates from Newcastle Polytechnic.
1981 Designs his first cover for the 4AD label.
1982 Establishes 23 Envelope.

1988 Establishes v23.

1990

2000 The monograph *Vaughan Oliver: Visceral Pleasures* is published.

2010

"James, Jennifer, Georgina" – A Story in
Postcards, 2011.

'You can find a lot on the Internet, but it is all about editing. The book as a solid container of content becomes more and more valuable.'

Irma Boom

b. 1960

THE NETHERLANDS

Irma Boom's books are quite simply objects in themselves. Everything is up for grabs – she plays with size and format, and nothing is straightforward; there are myriad spot colours, paper stocks, processes and techniques on show, yet everything is there for a reason. Well known for her no-compromise approach, she has designed over 250 books, 50 of which are in the permanent collection of MoMA.

After graduating from the AKI Art Academy in Enschede in the Netherlands, Boom worked in the Dutch Government Publishing and Printing Office in The Hague for five years. She set up her eponymous studio in 1991, working for a mixture of commercial and cultural clients.

The commission to design a commemorative book for the Dutch conglomerate SHV Holdings led to *The Think Book* – a highly acclaimed piece of work that took five years to complete, with the first three and a half of those spent searching through the company's extensive archives in Utrecht, Amsterdam, Paris, London and Vienna, and attending shareholders' meetings. There was no budget, and the brief was simply to make something unusual and to complete it by May 1996. The finished 2,136-page book was designed to be a non-linear reading experience, with no page numbers or indexing, encouraging the reader to discover the rich content for themselves. Just 4,500 copies of the book were printed, which are gradually being distributed around the world.

Not everyone was as pleased with Boom's approach. Artist Otto Treumann felt that the monograph that Boom designed in 1999 was too much about her, to which she responded: 'That makes design so interesting; you ask a designer you want to work with, because you like the design. It was my own interpretation of work, I wanted to show the best of him. I wasn't trying to be Otto Treumann; I stayed myself.'

Among the many prize-winning books that Boom has designed, *Weaving as a Metaphor*, the 2006 book about the work of textile designer Sheila Hicks (created to accompany an exhibition at the Bard Graduate Center in New York) is one of the most exquisite. Using a simple device of unfinished edges, Boom's sympathetic approach to the subject matter resulted in numerous design prizes, including the Gold Medal at the Leipzig Book Fair for 'The Most Beautiful Book in the World'.

More recent projects have included an ethereal unbound book for Chanel No. 5, which is completely embossed, and a new identity for Amsterdam's Rijksmuseum, which replaced the 32-year-old logo designed by Studio Dumbar (see p. 288). In contrast to the SHV book, at 50 × 38 mm (2 x 1½ in) *Boom* – a collection of her own works, which accompanied the 2010 retrospective 'Irma Boom: Biography in Books' at the University of Amsterdam Library – is verging on the miniscule.

Above *1001 Women from Dutch History*, 2013.

*The Architecture of the Book
(Revised & Augmented Biography
Books In Reverse Chronological
Order 2013–1986), 2013.*

18

116

138

The Road Not Taken /
Bouillon, 1999

Mantra
A 718-page book with only one
poem by Robert Frost repeated
on every right page (pages are
numbered). It smells like soup,
a reference to the work of the
artist Jop Koelewijn with whom
I made the book. If you read
the poem again and again by
turning the pages, it becomes
a mantra. The poem will take
possession of you. 'I took the
one less traveled by, And that
has made all the difference'
became a lesson for life.

454

151

Irma Boom

1920

1930

1940

1950

1960 — Born in Lochem, the Netherlands.

1970

1980

1986 — Works at the Dutch Government Publishing and Printing Office.
— Founds her studio, Irma Boom Office.

1991 — Teaches at the Jan van Eyck Akademie in Maastric
1992 — Becomes a critic at Yale University.
— Solo exhibition 'Boom Beyond Books' at the
— Solo exhibition 'Irma Boom on her Books', The

1998 — Leipziger Stadtbibliothek.
— Youngest winner of the Gutenberg Prize.

2001 — Member of the supervisory Board Gerrit
Rietveld Academy, Amsterdam.

2004 — 'Irma Boom: Book Design' exhibition at the
Museum für Gestaltung, Zurich.

2009 — 'Irma Boom: Biography in Books' exhibition at
University of Amsterdam.

2010 — 'Irma Boom: The Architecture of the Book'
exhibition at the Institut Neerlandais, Paris.

2013

SHV Think Book 1996–1896, 1996.

The Poster: Celebrating the Poster, Eastern Kentucky University, Richmond, screenprint by Arts Graphiques de France, 2000.

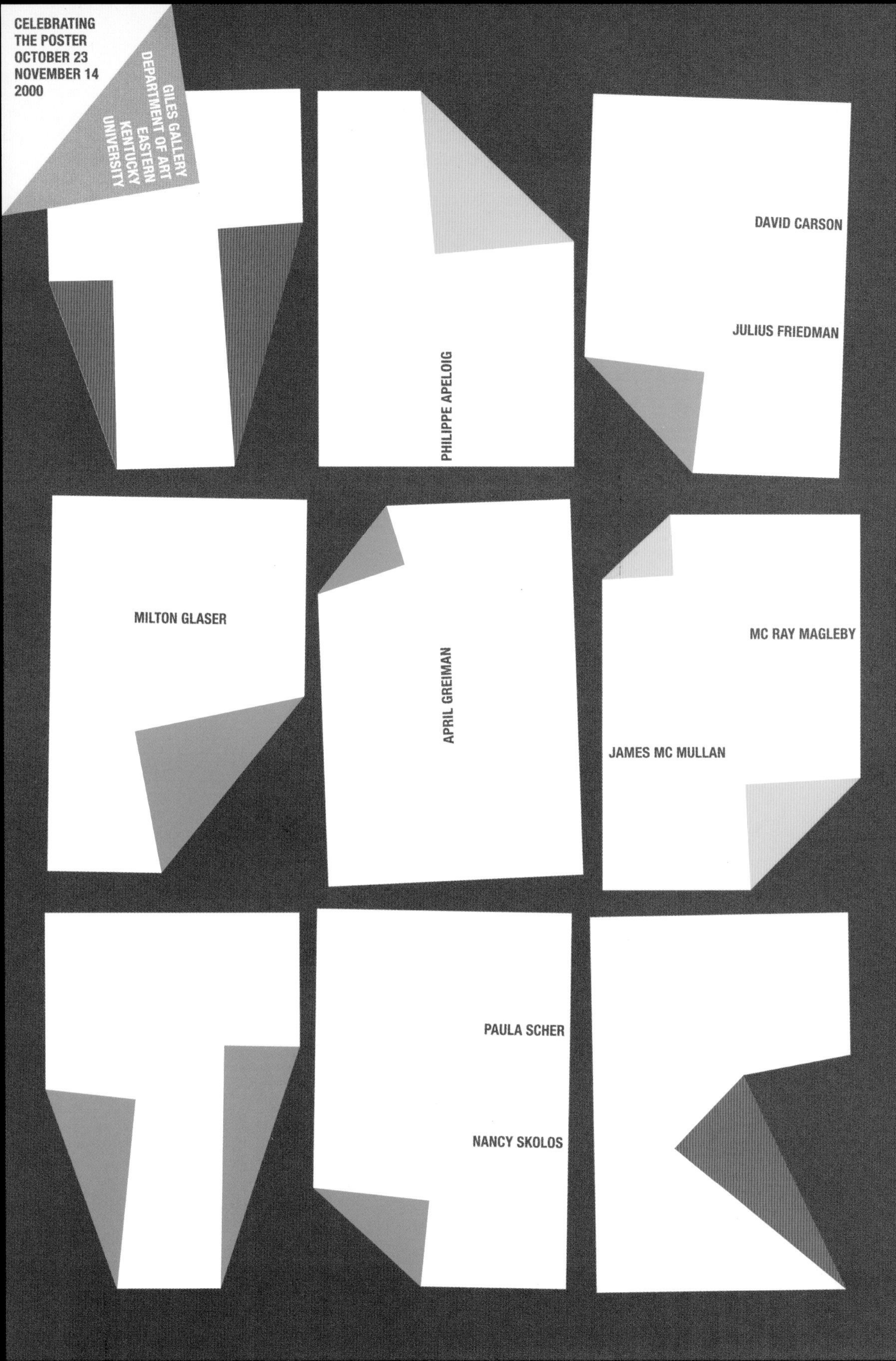

CELEBRATING
THE POSTER
OCTOBER 23
NOVEMBER 14
2000

GILES GALLERY
DEPARTMENT OF ART
EASTERN
KENTUCKY
UNIVERSITY

DAVID CARSON

JULIUS FRIEDMAN

PHILIPPE APELOIG

MILTON GLASER

APRIL GREIMAN

MC RAY MAGLEBY

JAMES MC MULLAN

PAULA SCHER

NANCY SKOLOS

'I like simple, basic use of perfect type. Letters should introduce a subtle, expressive element. They must also project analogies, or serve as metaphors, for technique, functionality, and art.'

Philippe Apeloig

b. 1962

FRANCE

There are few designers who can handle type with the assurance and flair of Philippe Apeloig. While it is true that his pieces often employ 'type as image', the type is never merely for decoration – it is always central to communicating the intended message in a meaningful and often witty way. While Apeloig's posters are clearly meticulously planned and precisely executed, they somehow still manage to exude a feeling of freshness, excitement and spontaneity.

After graduating from the École Nationale Supérieure des Arts Appliqués Duperré and the École Nationale Supérieure des Arts Décoratifs (ENSAD) in Paris, Apeloig interned twice at Total Design in Amsterdam. As his choice of internship suggests, he has always looked further than his native France for inspiration. In 1988 (courtesy of a grant from the French government) he went to work with April Greiman in Los Angeles, and after being awarded a grant by the French Academy of Art in 1993, he began two years at the Villa Medici in Rome. In 1999 he travelled to New York to set up a studio and become a professor of design at the Cooper Union School of Art. He was also made curator at the school's Herb Lubalin Center of Design and Typography, organizing a programme of exhibitions and lectures.

Cultural clients, and museums in particular, have also featured consistently in Apeloig's practice. He worked as a designer at the newly opened Musée d'Orsay in Paris between 1985 and 1987, after which he went to work at the Louvre; he was the art director there when he left in 2008. Apeloig has designed numerous posters and books, including a poster for the 2013 Saut Hermès international showjumping competition. In the same year he was given a rare honour – an extensive solo show entitled 'Typorama' at Les Arts Décoratifs, exploring the first 30 years of his work.

Although he has worked in many different formats, Apeloig seems to have an enduring affinity for the poster. An early example created for the Musée d'Orsay's inaugural exhibition 'Chicago, Birth of a Metropolis', with its 45-degree angles and wrap-around type, was the first piece that Apeloig had designed using a computer, and it hinted at the inventive approach that was to come.

His 2000 poster for 'Celebrating the Poster' at the Eastern Kentucky University (which uses folded corners to transform blank pages into different letters) is deceptively simple. An all-too-rare example of graphic design that can be appreciated by non-graphic designers, it is reminiscent of Alan Fletcher's playful approach (see p. 184). As Apeloig explains, 'To make an idea communicative, precise and concise, it is necessary to reduce, to leave behind what appears at first to be indispensable. I find a fine balance between sobriety, simplicity and complexity.'

Above Portrait of Apeloig by Mischa Halle, 2012.

bateaux

Exposition   28 juin – 5 juillet 2003

sur l' eau

rivières es   et

canaux

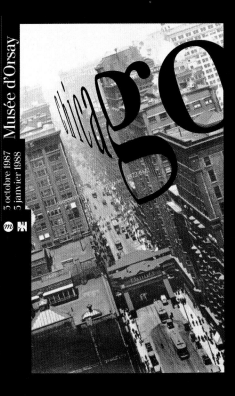

Musée d'Orsay
5 octobre 1987
5 janvier 1988

Opposite *Bateaux sur l'Eau, Rivières et Canaux*, Armada de Rouen, Voies Navigable de France, screenprint by Dubois Imagerie, 2003.

Above *Chicago. Naissance d'une Métropole 1872–1922*,

Musée D'Orsay, Paris. Printed by Jacques London/Bedos, 1987.

Below *The Roth Explosion*, Aix-en-Provence, festival of foreign literature, screenprint by Art Graphiques de France, 1999.

267

Philippe Apeloig

1920

1930

1940

1950

1960
1962 — Born in Paris, France.

1970

1980

1988 — Works with April Greiman in Los Angeles.

1990 — Takes up residency at the French Academy of Art in the Villa Medici, Rome.

1993 — Appointed artistic consultant for the Louvre.

1997 — *Au cœur du mot* (Inside the Word), published.

2001 — Appointed artistic director of the Louvre.

2003

2010

2013 — 'Typorama' exhibition held at Les Arts Décoratifs, Paris.

Sagmeister on a Binge, poster, 2003.

'Good design is design that either helps people or delights people.'

Stefan Sagmeister

b. 1962

AUSTRIA

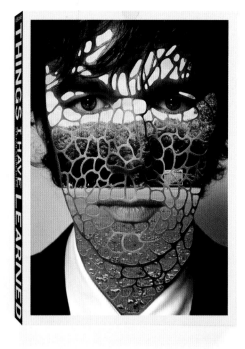

Never reticent about baring his soul or his body, Austrian-born designer Stefan Sagmeister has charmed both his clients and his many admirers throughout his career with his masterful use of materials, goofy humour and endearing honesty.

Sagmeister Inc. was set up in 1993 and, taking Tibor Kalman's advice to keep things small, consisted of Sagmeister, designer Hjalti Karlsson and an intern. Sagmeister's real passion was for music packaging; rather than viewing it as a restriction, he saw the plastic CD jewel-case format as an opportunity, gaining Grammy nominations for his work for H. P. Zinker, David Byrne, Lou Reed and the Rolling Stones, and finally winning one in 2003 for the Talking Heads' *Once in a Lifetime* box set.

As well as his own hand-drawn type, humour is rarely far from Sagmeister's work, and he has never been scared of controversy. All were present to a degree in his posters for the AIGA's talks in New York and New Orleans, but it was his 1999 poster for an AIGA event in Detroit that proved he was so much more than someone with a talent for designing cool music packaging. The much-reproduced poster, featuring lines of writing cut directly into Sagmeister's naked torso by his intern, was extremely provocative (especially as it could easily have been created using Photoshop), and continues to make waves outside the confines of the design world.

Charming and self-deprecating, Sagmeister is disarmingly honest about the challenges he faces as a graphic designer running his own studio. His book *Sagmeister: Made You Look* (2001) had the semi-ironic subtitle 'Another self-indulgent design monograph (practically everything we have ever designed including the bad stuff)'. The constant reappraisal of his work and creative processes has led to him taking a year off to work on experimental, not-for-profit projects every seven years. One of these (started during a year off in Bali) is *The Happy Film* (2010), an ambitious feature-length documentary in which Sagmeister attempts to unlock the key to his personal happiness through a series of experiments with drugs, meditation and psychotherapy.

When questioned about the use of nudity in his work, Sagmeister has admitted, 'It's just a cheap trick. It worked in the past and will probably work again in the future. Being naked is no big deal for me (studying in Vienna where many public bath places are nude or topless) but seems to get everybody's attention here in the States every time.' That was certainly true in 2012, when the announcement that Jessica Walsh had become a partner in the company took the form of a photograph of both partners standing naked, side by side in the studio, and again (alongside the rest of the staff) when their new website was relaunched in 2013.

Above *Things I Have Learned in My Life So Far*, book case, 2008.

Left *Trying to Look Good Limits My Life*, typographical installations, 2004.

Below *Set the Twilight Reeling*, Lou Reed, poster, 1996.

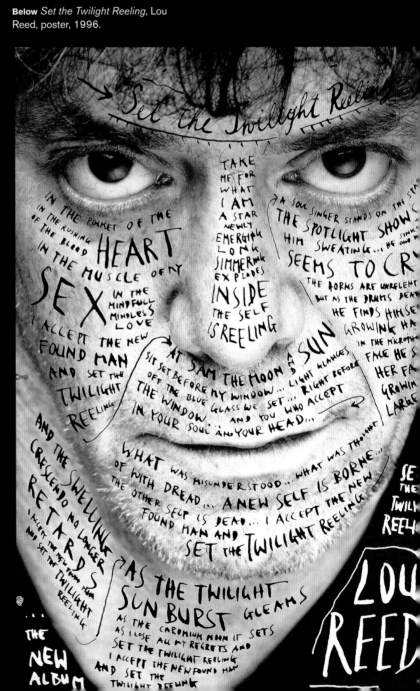

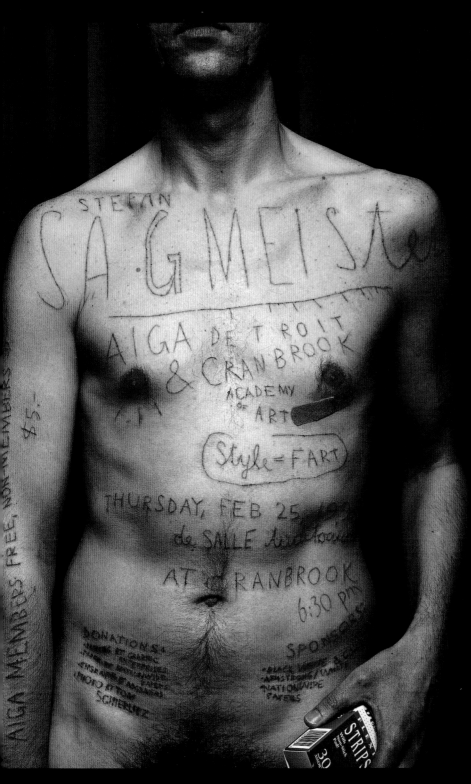

AIGA Detroit poster, 1999.

Stefan Sagmeister

1920

1930

1940

1950

1960
1962 Born in Bregenz, Austria.

1970

1980
1987 Moves to New York to study at the Pratt Institute.

1990
1993 Sets up Sagmeister Inc.

Designs poster for AIGA Detroit.

1999 *Sagmeister: Made You Look* monograph published.
2001 *Things I Have Learned in My Life So Far* published.

2008 Starts work on *The Happy Film.*
2010
2012 Sagmeister Inc. becomes Sagmeister & Walsh.

Album cover for *The Next Day* by David
Bowie, original photograph Masayoshi
Sukita, 2013.

'Design can change the world when it works in service of the right people and gets an issue on the mainstream political agenda.'

Jonathan Barnbrook

b. 1966

UK

Unusually for a graphic designer, Jonathan Barnbrook seamlessly combines typeface and graphic design with activism and social commentary. Throughout his career he has mixed client-led commercial projects with projects he carries out for causes he believes in, while at the same time gaining a cult following for his subversively named but expertly designed typefaces.

Typography is intrinsic to Barnbrook's work – he designed his first typeface, Bastard, while studying at the Royal College of Art, and his subsequent typefaces Exocet and Manson (later renamed Mason due to complaints) were distributed by Emigre in California. In 1997 Barnbrook set up VirusFonts to distribute his own typefaces, but claims this was more for publicity than commercial reasons. Barnbrook's seditious font names (which include Bourgeois, Infidel, Shock and Awe, Tourette and Moron) display his irreverent approach to what is traditionally a very stuffy area of design.

That year also saw Barnbrook collaborate with the artist Damien Hirst on his first book, *I Want To Spend The Rest Of My Life Everywhere, With Everyone, One To One, Always, Forever, Now*. A *tour de force* featuring pop-ups and special inks, and which took two years to complete, the book won a raft of awards and redefined the art monograph for a new generation. Barnbrook also worked with Hirst to create graphics for his controversial Pharmacy restaurant, which opened in 1998.

Despite maintaining a deliberately small set-up, Barnbrook is no stranger to large-scale projects. These have included the identity for Tokyo's largest post-war development, Roppongi Hills, the Los Angeles Museum of Contemporary Art and the 17th Biennale of Sydney, held in 2010. The studio's output is nothing if not varied

– other projects have included a Tokyo undertakers, advertisements for the British Heart Foundation, and an identity for make-up brand Shiseido.

Barnbrook has never shied away from involvement in politics. As well as working with *Adbusters*, he participated in the First Things First 2000 manifesto redrafted in 1999 (see p. 165) – both as a signatory and also by creating a promotional billboard that used a Tibor Kalman quote, urging 'Designers, stay away from corporations that want you to lie for them'. More recently, Barnbrook created the 2012 identity for the Occupy London movement, which was chosen by a public vote.

One of Barnbrook's most high-profile clients is David Bowie, with whom he has worked since his 2002 album, *Heathen*. Bowie was the subject of a sell-out exhibition at the V&A in 2013, and Barnbrook designed both the catalogue and the graphics for the exhibition. The same year he also designed the much-debated cover for Bowie's album *The Next Day*, which (rather aptly given that his client is the master of reinvention) reworked the cover image of Bowie's earlier *"Heroes"* album.

Above Portrait of Barnbrook by Teri Varhol.

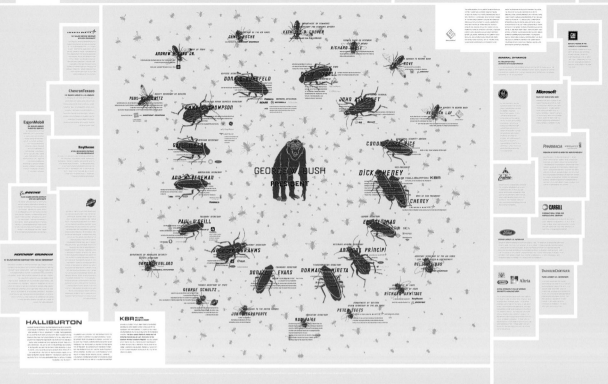

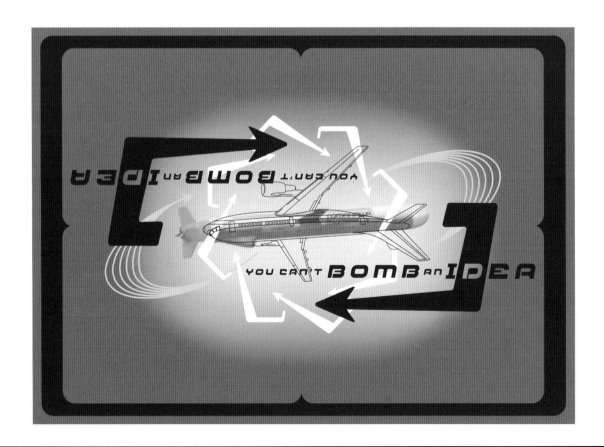

Top *The Corporate Vermin that Rules America*, poster, 2003.

Above *You Can't Bomb an Idea*, screenprint, 2004.

OCCUPY
LONDON

A A B C D E E F F G
H H I i J K K L M M M
N N O P Q Q R R S
T T U U V V W W
X X Y Y Z

1 2 3 4 5 6 7 8 9 0
1 2 3 4 5 6 7 8 9 0

Top Occupy London logo, 2012.

Above Mason typeface, licensed and released by Emigre Inc., 1992.

Jonathan Barnbrook

1920

1930

1940

1950

1960

1966 Born in Luton, UK.

1970

1980

1990 Graduates from the RCA and establishes Barnbrook Design.

1997 Establishes VirusFonts.
Becomes a primary signatory of the 'First Things First 2000' manifesto.

1999 Designs artwork for David Bowie's *Heathen*.

2002 The Design Museum holds the retrospective 'Friendly Fire'. *The Barnbrook Bible* is published.

2007 Designs logo for Occupy London.

2010

2012 Designs graphics for the V&A's 'David Bowie Is'
2013 exhibition.

Ummagumma by Pink Floyd, original
cover artwork, 1969.

'I like photography because it is a reality medium, unlike drawing which is unreal. I like to mess with reality ... to bend reality. Some of my works beg the question of is it real or not?' – Storm Thorgerson

Hipgnosis

1968–1983

UK

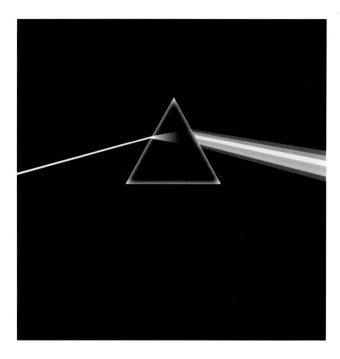

As well as nearly all of Pink Floyd's releases, Hipgnosis created equally striking LP covers for high-profile artists such as Led Zeppelin, Peter Gabriel, T-Rex, ELO, 10cc and UFO. While they will forever be associated with these high-octane pieces, though, it is the considerably lower-key, text-only, concept-driven artwork created for the English band XTC's 1978 LP *Go 2* that is revered within the design community as the consummate cover. Consisting entirely of type set in a white typewriter font on a black background, it states its purpose unequivocally: 'This is a RECORD COVER. This writing is the DESIGN upon the record cover. The DESIGN is to help SELL the RECORD.' Eventually labelling the reader 'THE VICTIM', and instructing them to 'STOP READING NOW', the artwork was witty, economical, and conceptually brilliant.

Taking their name from a piece of graffiti on their apartment door, Storm Thorgerson and Aubrey Powell saw Hipgnosis as a combination of 'hip' (representing everything young, new and cool) and 'gnostic' (relating to mystic knowledge). The pair started designing record sleeves while they were still film students at the Royal College of Art. Both had been to school with members of Pink Floyd, and their first commission was to create artwork for the group's second LP, *A Saucerful of Secrets* (1968). This was only the second LP cover that EMI had agreed could be designed out of house. Further commissions from the company followed and, after a short spell working from Powell's home, Hipgnosis opened its first studio in South Kensington.

The pair had designed many LP covers by the time *Dark Side of the Moon* was released in 1973, but it was this particular album (which went on to become one of the best-selling LPs of all time) that established them as the design group *du jour*. While perhaps the most iconic, it was fairly straightforward compared to many of their other covers – captivating (and often slightly troubling) surrealist vignettes that both shocked and amazed. Humour was never far away, and visual puns appeared regularly. The packaging itself often involved gatefolds, elaborate inner sleeves and stickers.

Predating Photoshop by several decades, the artwork featured photographic images (shot in medium format) that rarely included the artists themselves, with models and actors instead adding to the filmic quality. While these images were manipulated in the darkroom and subjected to a host of clever techniques – such as airbrushing and cut and paste – huge efforts were taken to create the original shots. For the Pink Floyd LP *Animals* (1977), a 9-m (30-ft) helium-filled balloon in the shape of a pig was floated high above Battersea Power Station, only to escape and land in a field in Kent, much to the annoyance of a local farmer who complained that it was scaring his cows.

Above *The Dark Side of the Moon* by Pink Floyd, original cover artwork, 1972.

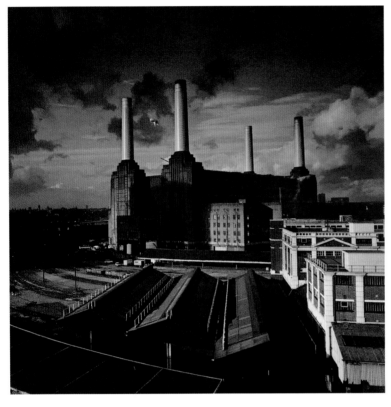

1920

1930

1940

1950

1960

1968 Designs cover artwork for Pink Floyd's *A Saucerful of Secrets.*
Opens studio space in South Kensington.

1970 Designs cover artwork for *The Dark Side of the Moon.*
Peter Christopherson joins.

1973
1974 Designs cover artwork for XTC's *Go 2.*

1978

1980

1983 Hipgnosis dissolved.

Top *Animals* by Pink Floyd, album cover, 1977.

Above *Houses of the Holy* by Led Zeppelin, album cover, 1973.

This is a RECORD COVER. This writing is the DESIGN upon the record cover. The DESIGN is to help SELL the record. We hope to draw your attention to it and encourage you to pick it up. When you have done that maybe you'll be persuaded to listen to the music - in this case XTC's Go 2 album. Then we want you to BUY it. The idea being that the more of you that buy this record the more money Virgin Records, the manager Ian Reid and XTC themselves will make. To the aforementioned this is known as PLEASURE. A good cover DESIGN is one that attracts more buyers and gives more pleasure. This writing is trying to pull you in much like an eye-catching picture. It is designed to get you to READ IT. This is called luring the VICTIM, and you are the VICTIM. But if you have a free mind you should STOP READING NOW! because all we are attempting to do is to get you to read on. Yet this is a DOUBLE BIND because if you indeed stop you'll be doing what we tell you, and if you read on you'll be doing what we've wanted all along. And the more you read on the more you're falling for this simple device of telling you exactly how a good commercial design works. They're TRICKS and this is the worst TRICK of all since it's describing the TRICK whilst trying to TRICK you, and if you've read this far then you're TRICKED but you wouldn't have known this unless you'd read this far. At least we're telling you directly instead of seducing you with a beautiful or haunting visual that may never tell you. We're letting you know that you ought to buy this record because in essence it's a PRODUCT and PRODUCTS are to be consumed and you are a consumer and this is a good PRODUCT. We could have written the band's name in special lettering so that it stood out and you'd see it before you'd read any of this writing and possibly have bought it anyway. What we are really suggesting is that you are FOOLISH to buy or not buy an album merely as a consequence of the design on its cover. This is a con because if you agree then you'll probably like this writing - which is the cover design - and hence the album inside. But we've just warned you against that. The con is a con. A good cover design could be considered as one that gets you to buy the record, but that never actually happens to YOU because YOU know it's just a design for the cover. And this is the RECORD COVER.

Go 2 by XTC, album cover, 1978.

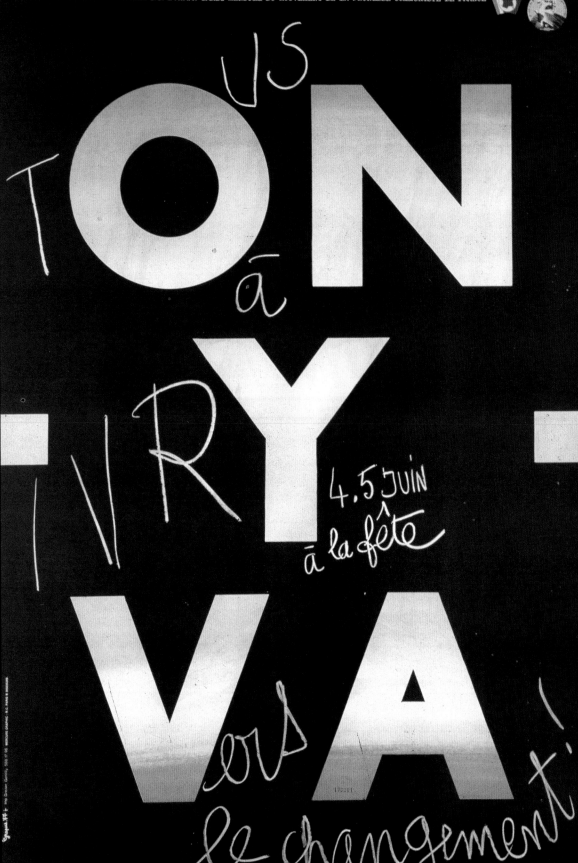

On y va, poster, 1977.

'We discovered semiology and it was very important to us. It allowed us to deconstruct images, so we could say to the political commissioning bodies: "We are going to make images for you which will have real meaning. We are going to make true political images."'

Grapus

1970–1991

FRANCE

The late 1960s saw huge political and social change in France, with 11 million students and workers protesting against Charles de Gaulle's government and its policies by holding a national strike, leading to months of demonstrations and civil unrest. It was against the backdrop of this turbulent time that the collective Grapus was formed in Paris by Pierre Bernard, François Miehe and Gérard Paris-Clavel; fiercely political, they vowed only to work for political and cultural clients who shared their left-wing ideology.

Bernard had studied in Paris under Jean Widmer. Fascinated by 20th-century Polish posters, both he and Paris-Clavel went to Warsaw to study under the great poster designer Henryk Tomaszewski. In 1968 the pair met Miehe (then still a student) at the Atelier Populaire. One of a number of studios that had been occupied during the Paris uprising, the Atelier Populaire (within the École des Beaux-Arts) was a hotbed of activity, with new protest posters silkscreened every day and flyposted across the city as 'weapons in the service of the struggle'.

Grapus was formed in 1970, in the aftermath of the uprising. Set up as a collective, with the express aim of only working for clients who shared its political views, none of its works were ever attributed to individual members. One of their first clients was the Communist Party (Grapus were all active members). Other commissions for trade unions, theatre groups,

educational institutions and good causes followed, all expressed in Grapus's energetic style, which combined arresting imagery, collage and hand-drawn type. Clients were constantly pushed to take radical directions, which although it produced exciting results, was according to Bernard not a financially astute strategy long term: 'I think it's because our attitude towards them excites them, but at the same time it makes them take risks. People don't like to take one risk after another – and if they do take a risk twice, they don't do it a third time. It's too adventurous, too difficult.'

One of the last commissions that Grapus carried out was a redesign for the Louvre, which caused much discussion within the group, as some saw the institution as being too elitist. Shortly afterwards Grapus split, with Bernard forming Atelier de Création Graphique and Paris-Clavel forming Ne Pas Piler.

Above Poster for a Grapus exhibition at the Musée de l'Affiche, Paris, 1982.

282

Left above *16 years. A Season to Celebrate*, Theatre Sartrouville poster, 1981.

Left *Liebestod an Opera,* Atelier Lyrique of the Rhine, Radio France, poster, 1981.

Right Young Communist Movement of France, 22 Spring Festivals, poster, 1976.

1920

1930

1940

1950

1960

1970 Formed by Pierre Bernard, François Miehe and Gérard Paris-Clavel.

1974 Jean-Paul Bachollet joins.
1975 Alex Jordan joins.

1980
1982 Grapus exhibition held at the Musée de l'Affiche, Paris.

1989 Creates the identity for the reopening of the Louvre.
1991 Grapus disbands.

284

A selection of logos designed by Pentagram: top row l–r: Asea Brown Boveri, 1987; Brooklyn Historical Society, 2005; Citi, 2000; Dallas Opera, 1978; Editions d'Olivier, 1991; second row l–r: Faber & Faber, 1981; The Good Diner, 1992; Heart Center, 1979; Ila, 2007; Joyco, 1999; third row l–r: Kanuhura, 2004; Landmark, 2012; Mandarin Oriental, 1985; New York Jets, 2001; Penguin Books, 2003; fourth row l–r: Qasr al Hosn, 2010; Royal Academy, London, 2012; Saks Fifth Avenue, 2007; Tactics, 1984; UCLA Architecture and Urban Design, 2007; bottom row l–r: Victoria and Albert Museum, 1989; Waller Brothers, 1979; Xinet, 2005; Yound Foundation, 2005; Zeckendorf, 2007.

'Some of us are better at bringing in business, others at keeping clients happy, and others at winning awards... While we're all paid equally, differences in profitability are often as much as three times. But we know that everyone's playing an important part.'
— Colin Forbes

Pentagram

est. 1972

UK

One of the must successful multidisciplinary design agencies ever, with clients spread across the world and 19 partners in five offices, Pentagram still adheres to the principles on which it was founded in 1972. Its unique arrangement requires all of its partners to source their own projects, manage their own teams and be financially accountable for them. The set-up allows all the benefits of a small agency (creative control and a lack of hierarchy) while taking advantage of working collectively, with resources such as administration and finance shared, and profits divided equally.

Inspired by US designers such as Robert Brownjohn and Paul Rand, Alan Fletcher, Colin Forbes and Bob Gill had been working as Fletcher | Forbes | Gill since 1962. Architect Theo Crosby joined them in 1965, and in 1972 (without Bob Gill but with Kenneth Grange and Mervyn Kurlansky), they established Pentagram, taking up residence in a disused dairy in Westbourne Grove, London. While Pentagram was run on very democratic principles, it was Colin Forbes who acted as unofficial chairman for the first 20 years, taking charge of the six-monthly partnership meetings.

Resisting the temptation to sell the company (which many similar-sized design companies did in the 1980s and '90s), Pentagram has remained independent, while growing steadily over the years. Opening offices in New York, San Francisco, Austin and Berlin and working on

a wide range of projects spanning the disciplines of architecture, interiors, product design, graphics and digital media, it has worked with an impressive range of clients from numerous different sectors.

While it is now considered very much part of the establishment, Pentagram has continued to rejuvenate itself and keep its output fresh by ensuring its new partners were mostly chosen from outside of the company (the latest exception being Natasha Jen, a former intern who was made a partner in 2012). Potential partners go through a rigorous joining procedure and are only accepted if there is a unanimous vote. They are then required to complete a two-year probationary period.

Not everyone is suited to Pentagram's idiosyncratic set-up, which requires partners to be just as focused on the financial as well as the creative aspect of their practice. John Rushworth (who joined the London office in 1989 when he was 31) is currently Pentagram's longest serving partner.

Above Portrait of the original Pentagram partners, l–r: Theo Crosby, Kenneth Grange, Colin Forbes, Mervyn Kurlansky, Alan Fletcher.

ecclesiastes
or, the preacher
with an introduction by | doris lessing

the gospel according to
john

the first book of moses, called
genesis
with an introduction by | steven rose

rossman

ruth
and esther

the gospel according to
mark
with an introduction by

proverbs
with an introduction by | charles johnson

on
with an introduction by | will self

solomon
with an introduction by | a

the book of
isaiah

the epistle of paul the apostle to the
hebrews
with an introduction by | karen armst

with an introduction by | peter

the book of
job
with an introduction by | louis de bernières

ooks of
el

the
wisd

Opposite *Pocket Canons* by Angus Hyland, book covers, 1998.

Above Redesign of *The Guardian* by David Hillman, 1988.

1920

1930

1940

1950

1960

1970

1972 Established by Alan Fletcher, Theo Crosby, Colin Forbes, Kenneth Grange and Mervyn Kurlansky.

New York office opened by Colin Forbes.

1978

1980

San Francisco office opens.

1986

1990

1992 Alan Fletcher leaves.

1993 Colin Forbes leaves.

1994 Austin office opens.

2000

2002 Berlin office opens.

2010

THE HAGUE 1995

HOLLAND DANCE FESTIVAL

muziek voor dans

4-21 oktober

AT&T DANSTHEATER

4,5 / White Oak Dance Project

Baryshnikov productions

7,8 / DonauBallett

FESTIVALKASSA (070) 346 5272

'My colleagues sometimes scold me for being an artist among designers but that is exactly what I want. I have always taken the fine arts to be a sort of breeding ground for all sorts of applied design.'

Studio Dumbar

est. 1977

THE NETHERLANDS

A key player on the Dutch design scene during the 1980s and 1990s, Gert Dumbar has always cut something of a controversial figure. Rejecting the functional, rationalist, grid-based approach that had dominated graphic design in the Netherlands for so many years, he established a new, collaborative way of working and an expressive style that had more in common with Postmodernism than the Modernist thinking which had dominated the country's graphic design for so long.

Gert Dumbar studied painting at the Royal Academy of Arts in The Hague, before going on to study graphic design at the Royal College of Art in London in the mid-1960s. After graduating, he co-founded Tel Design, and ten years later, in 1977 set up Studio Dumbar. Based in The Hague, Studio Dumbar comprised around 12 designers, plus various interns from the Cranbrook Academy and the Royal College of Art, where Dumbar returned to teach on several occasions.

Studio Dumbar was well known for its lack of bureaucracy, and its innovative multilayered designs which featured expressive typography and often encompassed illustration, photography and sculpture. Dumbar's aim was to apply a fine art approach to commercial projects, and it proved to be highly influential, gaining a huge following in the Netherlands and beyond.

As well as the more expected cultural clients (such as the Holland Dance Festival, a long-standing client for which it designed a series of striking posters), Studio Dumbar also gained commissions from many clients in the public sector, including the Dutch Police Force, Dutch Railways and the Dutch Post Office (PTT). In 1989, it created a radical identity for the PTT that coincided with its controversial privatization, and is now viewed as an exemplary example of a Postmodernist corporate identity.

While Dumbar's approach proved popular with his contemporaries, it was not something that the more established Dutch designers fully embraced, with Wim Crouwel remarking that 'Gert's views are very different to mine. I can get very wound up over his sardonic posters for Piet Zwart and Mondrian exhibitions.' However, while Dumbar might be considered by some to be anti-establishment, in 1987 he took on one of the most 'establishment' positions possible, that of the presidency of the UK's foremost membership association for graphic designers and art directors, D&AD.

Opposite Promotional poster for Holland Dance Festival, 1995.

Above Portrait of Gert Dumbar by Lex van Pieterson, 2003.

Right and below Visual identity Koninklijke
PTT Nederland, 1989.

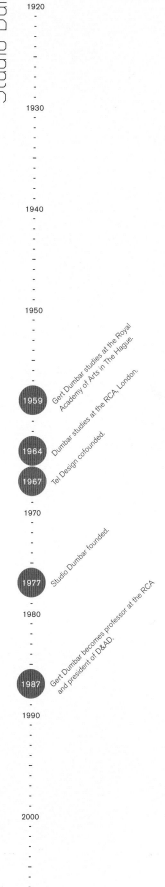

Above and left Promotional posters for International Theatre Festival, Holland Festival, 1988.

1920

1930

1940

1950

1959 Gert Dumbar studies at the Royal Academy of Arts in The Hague.

1964 Dumbar studies at the RCA, London.

1967 Tel Design cofounded.

1970

1977 Studio Dumbar founded.

1980

Gert Dumbar becomes professor at the RCA and president of D&AD.

1987

1990

2000

2010

Haçienda nightclub seventh anniversary
poster, 1989.

'Do each job better than the job before, never duplicate, not anyone else, not yourself.'

8vo

1984–2001

UK

While 8vo produced a substantial body of commercial work during its 17-year existence, it is invariably the eight issues of its complicated and hugely influential journal on typography, *Octavo,* for which it is most lauded. The trio's work was sophisticated, complex and multilayered, but despite looking digitally created (especially to designers who have never known a time pre-Photoshop), much was created by hand.

Simon Johnston and Mark Holt started working as 8vo in 1984, with Hamish Muir joining soon after. Johnston and Muir had both taken the unorthodox route of studying at the Bath Academy and then at the Basel School of Design, under Armin Hofmann and Wolfgang Weingart (p. 136 and p. 220). Mark Holt had studied in Newcastle and then spent three years in San Francisco. Michael Burke, who was made an associate in 1986, had worked extensively on the 1972 Munich Games identity with Otl Aicher (p. 140). All had a deep-rooted appreciation of Modernism and a distaste for the advertising-led, somewhat twee design prevalent in Britain in the early 1980s, believing that rigorous typography rather than the 'big idea' should form the basis of a graphic solution.

Named after an abbreviation of the book-production term 'octavo', 8vo saw themselves as outsiders; they were intense, outspoken and did not identify or engage with the design community. They were pragmatists, obsessed with detail, believing that expression should be a result of the design process, not the motivation for it.

The first issue of *Octavo* appeared in summer 1986, with serious articles on typography and pieces on Anthony Froshaug and Richard Long. Although the format remained the same (A4, 16 pages, a tracing-paper dust jacket), every issue was approached as a separate entity. Issues 1 to 3 were fairly restrained compared to much of 8vo's output; issues 4 to 6 were much more experimental, with *Octavo* 88.6 the first to be four-colour printed. Unconcerned about turning a profit, the seventh issue reportedly cost £40,000 for a run of just 5,000. Although 8vo were self-confessed 'print junkies', *Octavo* always reflected the changing print technologies of the time – the final issue took the form of a CD-rom.

Equally impressive was 8vo's commercial work for clients such as Factory Records, the Haçienda nightclub, Concord Lighting, the ICA, *NME* and the Design Museum. In 1988, Wim Crouwel (p. 156) – then director of Rotterdam's Museum Boijmans Van Beuningen – commissioned 8vo to create the visual identity for the museum (something he had done for the Stedelijk). Over the next five years they designed around 50 catalogues and 40 posters. Complex information design projects for Thames Water, Powergen, Orange and American Express followed, as well as a series of vibrant typographic campaigns for Edinburgh's Flux festival, which was to be one of 8vo's last clients.

Above *Octavo International Journal of Typography* 86.1 (first issue), front cover, 1986.

Edinburgh Fringe, Aug 98

Flux

@Queen's Hall Clerk Street
Fri 14/Sat 15 Spiritualized & Steve Martland. Sun 16 Ken Kesey & Ken Babbs. Fri 21/ Sat 22 Nick Cave. Fri 28 John Zorn. Sat 29 The Creatures.

@Jaffa Cake Grassmarket
Sun 16/Mon 17 The Jesus & Mary Chain. Tue 18 Je t'aime Gainsbourg. Thu 20 Roddy Frame. Fri 21 The Bathers, Pearl Fishers. The Swiss Family Orbison. Sat 22 Arab Strap & The Nectarine No 9. Sun 23 David Thomas & Yo La Tengo. Tue 25 P J Harvey. Thu 27 Asian Dub Foundation.

All doors 8pm
Tickets from £8
Box Office 0131 667 7776
A USP Arts Presentation

Opposite Flux New Music Festival, Edinburgh Fringe, poster, 1998.

Below Flux New Music Festival, Edinburgh Fringe, poster 1997.

Above *Hardware*, exhibition poster, 1989.

8vo

1920

1930

1940

1950

1960

1970

1980

1984   8vo established by Simon Johnston and Mark Holt.
1985   Hamish Muir joins.
1986   First issue of *Octavo* is published.

1989   1989–94 Design posters and catalogues for the Museum Boijmans Van Beuningen.

1992   Final issue of *Octavo* is published.

2001   8vo closes.

WORK
bUY
CONSUME
DIE

*Pho-Ku Corporation™ (Work Buy
Consume Die ™), poster 1995*

'It's about disinformation, because disinformation provokes more of a response than information … maybe not the one you wanted, but you'll still provoke dialogue.'

The Designers Republic (TDR)

est. 1986

UK

Based in Sheffield in the north of England, sometimes it has seemed like The Designers Republic is from another planet. Its dense, pop culture-inspired graphics (described as 'digital baroque'), Japanese texts, subverted logos and provocative slogans make it seem like they come from somewhere in the future. Simultaneously mocking and celebrating consumer culture, and presided over by outspoken leader, Ian Anderson, with its Tokyo shop (Peoples Bureau for Consumer Information) and ironic Pho-Ku alias, and mascots Sissy and Angry Man, TDR acts more like a very cool clothing or music brand than a design agency.

Despite his appearance as the consummate northerner, Anderson hails from Croydon, with no formal design training. He moved north to study philosophy at the University of Sheffield, where he started making posters and flyers for the band that he was managing. He formed TDR with Nick Phillips in 1986, early commissions included sleeves for artists such as Age of Chance and Pop Will Eat Itself, who were on the Sheffield-based Warp label, for which TDR has continued to design.

The company expanded, at its height employing 13 designers, including Michael C. Place (Build), Matt Pyke (Universal Everything) and David Bailey (Kiosk). TDR began to attract a dedicated fan base, bolstered in 1994 by a 12-page special in the magazine *Emigre*, which became its fastest-selling issue ever. In 1995 the video game Wipeout was released, featuring visuals by

TDR. Aimed squarely at the clubbing crowd, the racing game was set in 2052, and featured music from the likes of the Chemical Brothers, Leftfield and Orbital. The first non-Japanese game designed for the Sony PlayStation, Wipeout exposed TDR to an even larger, global audience.

Despite its cult status, TDR also attracted corporate clients such as Coca-Cola, MTV and Nike – all eager to buy into its unique brand of cool. Projects included designing a watch for Swatch, packaging for the original Grand Theft Auto video game, and opening a shop in Japan. Their online design forum attracted a huge amount of attention (and opinions) and its online shop sold merchandise in the form of T-shirts and posters.

In 2009, after suffering from cashflow problems, TDR went into liquidation. Anderson purchased the name, and TDR was resurrected some months later with a much reduced staff and Anderson taking a more hands-on approach. 'When I took a back seat to allow TDR to grow beyond me, it died; its creative spark was crushed,' he reflects. 'The more I took myself out of the equation to see if it could do better without me, the more obvious it became that Ian Anderson and The Designers Republic were inseparable.'

Above Portrait of Ian Anderson.

具 (27)
Ian Anderson /
The Designers Republic™
(Made——) North of Nowhere™
Jul 14 (1986——)
SoYo™ Yarkshar™

Above (Made–) North of Nowhere,
print, 2013.

The Designers Republic

- 1920
- 1930
- 1940
- 1950
- 1960
- 1970
- 1980

1986 Founded by Ian Anderson and Nick Phillips in Sheffield.

- 1990

1994 *Emigre* magazine features TDR's work.

- 2000

Opens Tokyo shop, the Peoples Bureau for Consumer Information.

2003 Co-curates Echo City, the British Pavilion at the Venice Biennale for Architecture.

2006 TDR goes into liquidation, then reopens.

2009 A 25th anniversary exhibition is held at GGG in Tokyo.

2011

'We are in constant touch with each other so the ongoing conversation shapes what we all do. When asked about how Tomato works I've always replied "it's a bit like alcoholics anonymous, it's a support system and critical forum".'
– John Warwicker

Tomato

est. 1991

UK

A collective comprising a group of friends who were graphic designers, illustrators, film-makers and techno musicians, Tomato represented a new, cross-disciplinary, collaborative way of working. Its experimental approach to type and image, fascination with new media, and seemingly effortless blend of craft and technology made a huge impact on the increasingly staid and corporate-focused graphic design landscape of the UK in the early 1990s.

Tomato was set up by John Warwicker, Steve Baker, Dirk Van Dooren, Karl Hyde, Rick Smith, Simon Taylor and Graham Wood, and, as with most collectives, it has been through several iterations since it was originally founded in 1991. This was an exciting time for graphic design, with a crossover between graphics, animation and film taking place that, before the emergence of affordable digital technology in the late 1980s, simply had not been possible.

Tomato's experimental approach ensured that it gained an immediate cult following, but, unlike some of its fellow practitioners, it also attracted high-profile corporate clients, such as Coca-Cola, Nike, Sony and Philips, as well as institutions, including the BBC and the Victoria and Albert Museum. Its dynamic, multilayered, typographic approach provided a fresh alternative to the slick, 'big idea' school of graphic design prevalent at the time.

As Warwicker explains, Tomato gained a reputation for pushing boundaries: 'The onus on everyone is to bring back something different, whether it be an improvement

in craft or something radically different, something unexpected.' Its commercial output and the individuals' personal projects fed off each other.

Tomato has always had a long-standing association with music. Warwicker was previously involved with a company producing pop promos, and two of the collective's members – Rick Smith and Karl Hyde (along with DJ Darren Emerson) – founded the techno band Underworld. After an Underworld track was featured on the *Trainspotting* soundtrack, the band became massively popular in addition to its big club following, selling millions of records and touring extensively. Underworld's distinctive visuals (which appeared in print, on screen and on stage) became synonymous with the band's unique blend of dance and techno. Equally at home on the small screen as in a club, nowhere was the seamless blend of type, image and sound more potent than in the videos made by Tomato for Underworld's epic dance tracks.

Opposite *Cowgirl/Dirty Epic* by Underworld, record sleeve, 1994.

Above Portrait of Tomato, photographer unknown, 2009.

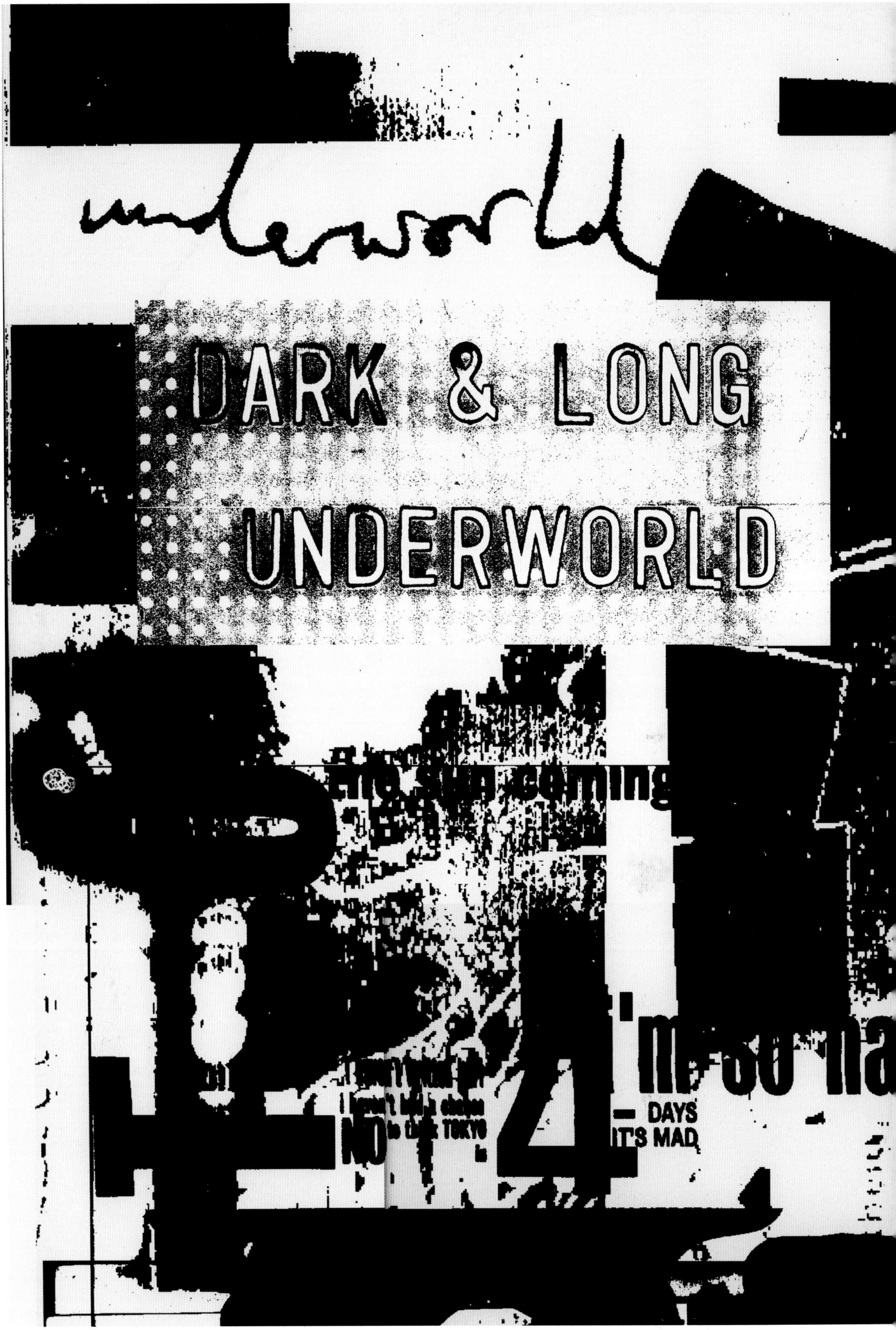

underworld

DARK & LONG

UNDERWORLD

the sun coming

I'm so ha

I won't wait
I won't think about
to think TOKYO
NO
— DAYS
IT'S MAD

Dark and Long by Underworld,
single sleeve, 1994.

Tomato

1920

1930

1940

1950

1960

1970

1980

1991 Founded in London.

Publishes five-year retrospective *Process*.

1996 Tomato Films founded.

1998 Tomato Interactive founded.
1999 *Mmm… Skyscraper I Love You* published.
2000

2010

Balenciaga Spring / Summer 2002
invitation card, after campaign
photography by Inez van Lamsweerde
and Vinoodh Matadin, 2001.

'An image never interests us as such. Its relevance lies in the fact that it contains the sum of preceding dialogues, stories, experiences with various interlocutors, and the fact that it induces a questioning of these pre-existing values. A good image should be in between two others, a previous one and another to come.'

M/M Paris

est. 1992

FRANCE

Since the partnership's inception in the early 1990s, M/M Paris has moved effortlessly between the music, fashion and art worlds, blending the commercial with the cultural to great effect. Featuring custom typefaces and hand-drawn alphabets, and using illustration and collage, their work is layered, complex and often mysterious. M/M Paris has collaborators rather than clients – 'We are designers, but as we define that role, not just as a vector for someone's ideas' – all of whom are high-profile, and many of whom have been working with the duo for years.

Mathias Augustyniak and Michael Amzalag first met while studying at the École National Supérieure des Arts Décoratifs in Paris. Somewhat dismayed by the college's ideology ('It was a utopian approach to graphic design. We knew it was a dead end.') they came to a definite conclusion: 'There is no such place called art or culture, it's all interwoven.'

Augustyniak went on to study at the Royal College of Art in London, and on his return to France in 1992 the pair established M/M Paris. Initially working for clients in the music industry, commissions for fashion clients such as Yohji Yamamoto, Jil Sander and Martine Sitbon soon followed. In 1995, the pair met photographers Inez van Lamsweerde and Vinoodh Matadin, and completed the first of many collaborations, the most high-profile of which was for Björk's 2001 LP, *Verspertine*.

Since then, M/M Paris has worked with the fashion designers Stella McCartney and Nicolas Ghesquière, as well as a host of international artists and curators, including Hans Ulrich Obrist, Philippe Parreno and Pierre Huyghe. The gallery space has been a constant for M/M Paris too, whether designing gallery identities, catalogues or exhibition graphics, curating shows, or featuring as the subject matter themselves. M/M's catholic approach has led to great demand for them as art directors for magazines such as *Paris Vogue*, *Arena Homme+*, *Purple* and *Interview*.

In 2012, to coincide with their 20th anniversary, a 528-page monograph – *M to M of M/M (Paris)* – was published by Thames & Hudson. Twelve years in the making, it is a testament to the pair's shared artistic vision. As Augustyniak remarks: 'Oliver Zahm [*Purple*] came up with the perfect metaphor for our working relationship. He said one is the bone, the other is the muscle. To me, it's the most accurate description of how we work.'

Above Portraits of Mathias Augustyniak and Michael Amzalag by Inez van Lamsweerde and Vinoodh Matadin.

Opposite top *The Alphamen*, originally photographed by Inez van Lamsweerde and Vinoodh Matadin for *V Man* premiere issue F/W 2003/04.

Below *Medúlla* by Björk, album sleeve, photography by Inez van Lamsweerde and Vinoodh Matadin, One Little Indian Records, 2004.

Opposite bottom *Icônes, Indices, Symboles*, exhibition view, Chapelle des Jésuites, Festival International de l'Affiche et des Arts Graphiques, Chaumont, France, 2003.

The Alphamen • M/M (Paris) • Inez van Lamsweerde & Vinoodh Matadin

1920

1930

1940

1950

1960

1970

1980

1988   Augustyniak and Amzalag meet at the École National Supérieure des Arts Décoratifs, Paris.

1990   M/M Paris is established.

1992   First collaboration with Inez van Lamsweerde and Vinoodh Matadin.

1995   Appointed as art directors for Paris Vogue.

2001   Appointed as art directors for Interview magazine.

2009   M to M of M/M (Paris) published.

2012

Further Reading

General

Eskilson, Stephen J. *Graphic Design: A History,* 2nd edition (Laurence King Publishing, 2012).

Heller, Steven and Véronique Vienne. *100 Ideas that Changed Graphic Design,* (Laurence King Publishing, 2012).

Hollis, Richard. *Swiss Graphic Design; The Origins and Growth of an International Style, 1920–1965,* (Laurence King Publishing, 2006).

— *Graphic Design: A Concise History (World of Art),* revised edition (Thames & Hudson, 2001).

Meggs, Philip B. and Alston W. Purvis. *Meggs' History of Graphic Design,* 5th edition (John Wiley & Sons, 2011).

Purvis, Alston W. and Cees W. de Jong. *Dutch Graphic Design: A Century of Innovation,* (Thames & Hudson, 2006).

Remington, R. Roger and Lisa Bodenstedt. *American Modernism: Graphic Design 1920 to 1960* (Laurence King Publishing, 2003).

By Designer

8vo – On the Outside, Mark Holt and Hamish Muir (Lars Müller Publishers, 2005).

Otl Aicher, Markus Rathgeb (Phaidon, 2007).

Typorama: The Graphic Work of Philippe Apeloig, Philippe Apeloig (Thames & Hudson, 2013).

Gerd Arntz. Graphic Designer, Ed Annink (010 Publishers, 2010).

Saul Bass: A Life in Film & Design, Jennifer Bass and Pat Kirkham (Laurence King Publishing, 2011).

Barnbrook Bible: The Graphic Design of Jonathan Barnbrook (Booth-Clibborn Editions, Jun 2007).

Lester Beall: Trailblazer of American Graphic Design, R. Roger Remington (W. W. Norton & Company, 1996).

Notes on Book Design, Derek Birdsall (Yale University Press, 2004).

Irma Boom: The Architecture of the Book, 2nd edition (Lecturis BV, 2013).

Josef Müller-Brockmann, Kerry William Purcell (Phaidon Press, 2006).

Alexey Brodovitch, Kerry William Purcell (Phaidon Press, 2002).

Robert Brownjohn: Sex and Typography, Emily King (Laurence King Publishing, 2005).

Reasons to be Cheerful: The Life and Work of Barney Bubbles, Paul Gorman (Adelita, 2010).

Design and Science: The Life and Work of Will Burtin, R. Roger Remington and Robert Fripp (Lund Humphries, 2007).

A. M. Cassandre: Oeuvres graphiques modernes 1923–1939, Anne-Marie Sauvage (Bibliothèque Nationale de France, 2005).

Design Research Unit: 1942–72, Michelle Cotton (Verlag der Buchhandlung Walther König, 2012).

Dorfsman & CBS, Dick Hess and Marion Muller (Rizzoli International Publications, 1990).

Marginàlia 1, Rogério Duarte (BOM DIA BOA TARDE BOA NOITE, 2013).

The Art of Looking Sideways, Alan Fletcher (Phaidon Press, 2001).

Shigeo Fukuda: Master Works (Firefly Books, 2005).

Abram Games, Graphic Designer: Maximum Meaning, Minimum Means, Catherine Moriarty, June Rose and Naomi Games (Lund Humphries, 2003).

Ken Garland, Structure and Substance, Adrian Shaughnessy (Unit Editions, 2012).

Art Work, David Gentleman (Ebury Press, 2002).

Graphic Design, Milton Glaser (Gerald Duckworth & Co Ltd, 2012).

Something from Nothing: The Design Process, April Greiman and Aris Janigian (Rotovision, 2002).

Franco Grignani, Alterazioni Ottico Mentali, 1929–1999 (Allemandi, 2014).

FHK Henrion, The Complete Designer, Adrian Shaughnessy (Unit Editions, 2013).

Graphic Design Manual, Armin Hofmann (Niggli Verlag, 2009).

Max Huber, Stanislaus von Moos (Phaidon Press, 2011).

Tibor Kalman, Perverse Optimist, Michael Beirut, Peter Hall and Tibor Kalman (Booth-Clibborn Editions, 1998).

Lora Lamm: Graphic Design in Milan 1953–1963, Lora Lamm and Nicoletta Cavadini (Silvana, 2013).

Herb Lubalin, American Graphic Designer, 1918—81, Adrian Shaughnessy (Unit Editions, 2012).

M to M of M/M (Paris), Emily King (Thames & Hudson, 2012).

Mariscal, Drawing Life (Phaidon Press, 2009).

Massin, Laetitia Wolff (Phaidon Press, 2007).

Bruno Monguzzi: Fifty Years of Paper: 1961–2011, Bruno Monguzzi (Skira Editore, 2012).

Pentagram Marks: 400 Symbols and Logotypes (Laurence King Publishing, 2010).

Vaughan Oliver: Visceral Pleasures, Rick Poynor (Booth-Clibborn Editions, 2000).

Cipe Pineles: A Life of Design, Martha Scotford (WW Norton, 1998).

Paul Rand: A Designer's Art, Paul Rand (Yale University Press, 1985).

Typographie: A Manual of Design, 7th revised edition, Emil Ruder (Verlag Niggli AG, 2001).

Things I Have Learned in My Life So Far, updated edition, Stefan Sagmeister (Abrams, 2013).

Designed by Peter Saville, Emily King (ed.) (Frieze, 2003).

Make it Bigger, Paula Scher (Princeton Architectural Press, 2005).

Zéró: Hans Schleger – a Life of Design, Pat Schleger (Lund Humphries, 2001).

Jan van Toorn: Critical Practice (Graphic Design in the Netherlands), Rick Poynor (010 Publishers, 2005).

Jan Tschichold: A Life in Typography, Ruari McLean (Lund Humphries, 1997).

Unimark International: The Design of Business and the Business of Design, Janet Conradi (Lars Müller Publishers, 2009).

Weingart: Typography – My Way to Typography, Wolfgang Weingart (Lars Müller Publishers, 1999).

Tadanori Yokoo – The Complete Posters (Kokusho Kanko Kai, 2011).

The Vignelli Canon, Massimo Vignelli (Lars Müller Publishers, 2010).

Index

Picture Credits

a = above, c = centre, b = below, l = left, r = right

8; 9 Collection Stedelijk Museum, Amsterdam. © DACS 2014; 9; 10 Digital image, The Museum of Modern Art, New York/Scala, Florence. © DACS 2014; 11a Collection Stedelijk Museum, Amsterdam. © DACS 2014; 11b Collection Stedelijk Museum, Amsterdam. © DACS 2014; 12 Museum für Gestaltung, Zurich; 13 © Topfoto; 14 Museum für Gestaltung, Zurich; 15l Digital image, The Museum of Modern Art, New York/ Scala, Florence; 15r Museum für Gestaltung, Zurich; 16; 17; 18; 19a; 19bl; 19br Collection Stedelijk Museum, Amsterdam; 20; 21 Reproduced with permission of the Ladislav Sutnar family; 22 © 2014. Digital image, The Museum of Modern Art, New York/Scala, Florence / Reproduced with permission of the Ladislav Sutnar family; 23a Reproduced with permission of the Ladislav Sutnar family; 23b Photo: Matt Flynn © Smithsonian Institution. © 2014. Cooper-Hewitt, National Design Museum, Smithsonian Institution/Art Resource, NY/Scala, Florence. Reproduced with permission of the Ladislav Sutnar family; 24 Courtesy of Hearst Communications, Inc & the Estate of Alexey Brodovitch; 25 Time & Life Pictures/Getty Images; 26a Courtesy of Hearst Communications, Inc, the estate of Alexey Brodovitch & the estate of Herbert Matter; 26b Courtesy of Hearst Communications, Inc & the estate of Alexey Brodovitch; 27 Courtesy of Hearst Communications, Inc. & the estate of Alexey Brodovitch; 28 © TfL from the London Transport Museum collection & by kind permission of Pat Schleger; 29 By kind permission of Pat Schleger; 30a © TfL from the London Transport Museum & by kind permission of Pat Schleger; 30b Courtesy the Shell Art Collection & by kind permission of Pat Schleger; 31 © Royal Mail Group Ltd 2014, courtesy of The British Postal Museum & Archive & by kind permission of Pat Schleger; 32 Photo Scala, Florence/BPK, Bildagentur für Kunst, Kultur und Geschichte, Berlin. © DACS 2014; 33; 34a; 34b; 35 The Municipal Museum of the Hague, the Netherlands. © DACS 2014; 36 Bauhaus-Archiv Berlin, Foto: Markus Hawlik. © DACS 2014; 37 Time Life Pictures/Getty Images; 38 Museum für Gestaltung, Zurich. © DACS 2014; 39a Bauhaus-Archiv Berlin. © DACS 2014; 39b © 2014. Photo Fine Art Images/Heritage Images/Scala, Florence. © DACS 2014; 40 © Mouron, Cassandre. Lic 2013-08-08-01. www.cassandre-france.com; 41 Roger Viollet/Getty Images; 42; 43a; 43b © Mouron, Cassandre. Lic 2013-08-08-01. www.cassandre-france.com; 44 Photo Scala, Florence / BPK, Agency for Art, Culture & History, Berlin; 45 The Art Archive; 46a Museum für Gestaltung, Zurich; 46b International Dada Archive, University of Iowa Libraries; 47 Photo: Dietmar Katz/Scala, Florence/BPK, Bildagentur für Kunst, Kultur und Geschichte, Berlin; 48 Courtesy of Pfizer, Inc. RIT Graphic Design Archives, Wallace Library, Rochester Institute of Technology. © Dumbarton Arts, LLC/VAGA, NY/DACS, London 2014; 49 Courtesy of the estate of Lester Beall. 50 © Dumbarton Arts, LLC/VAGA, NY/DACS, London 2014; 51 a © Swim Ink 2, LLC/CORBIS. © Dumbarton Arts, LLC/VAGA, NY/DACS, London 2014; 51b Digital image, The Museum of Modern Art, New York/Scala, Florence. © Dumbarton Arts, LLC/VAGA, NY/DACS, London 2014; 52 Courtesy of the Estate of Herbert Matter, Photo: Museum für Gestaltung, Zürich; 53 Courtesy of the estate of Herbert Matter; 54 Courtesy of the estate of Herbert Matter & Knoll International; 55a Courtesy of the estate of Herbert Matter, Photo: Museum für Gestaltung, Zürich; 55b Courtesy of the Estate of Herbert Matter, Photo: Museum für Gestaltung, Zürich; 56 © 2014. Digital image, The Museum of Modern Art, New York/Scala, Florence; 57 The Art Archive / Mondadori Portfolio / Mario De Biasi; 58-9 © Bruno Munari. Maurizio Corraini s.r.l. All rights reserved; 59a Courtesy of Penguin Books; 59 b © Bruno Munari. Maurizio Corraini s.r.l. All rights reserved; 60 Museum für Gestaltung, Zurich. © DACS 2014; 61 akg-images / Imagno / Franz Hubmann; 62l; 62r; 63 Museum für Gestaltung, Zurich. © DACS 2014; 64 Courtesy of the estate of Will Burtin & Pfizer, Inc. RIT Graphic Design Archives, Wallace Library. Rochester Institute of Technology; 65 Charles Bonnay/Getty Images; 66 Courtesy of International Business Machines Corporation, © International Business Machines Corporation & the estate of Will Burtin. Image: RIT Graphic Design Archives, Wallace Library. Rochester Institute of Technology; 67a; 67bl; 67br Courtesy the estate of Will Burtin. RIT Graphic Design Archives, Wallace Library. Rochester Institute of Technology; 67bl Courtesy of the estate of Will Burtin & Pfizer, Inc. RIT Graphic Design Archives, Wallace Library. Rochester Institute of Technology; 68; 69; 70a; 70b Courtesy of the estate of Franco Grignani. Manuela Grignani Archivio (Daniela Grignani); 71a Logo courtesy of the Woolmark Company & the estate of Franco Grignani. Manuela Grignani Archivio (Daniela Grignani); 71b Courtesy of the estate of Franco Grignani. Manuela Grignani Archivio (Daniela Grignani); 72; 73 Museum für Gestaltung, Zurich; 74; 75a; 75b Museum für Gestaltung, Zurich; 76 Courtesy of the estate of Cipe Pineles/Photographed by Anton Bruehel. A Condé Nast Publication; 77 Image courtesy of AIGA, the professional association for design. www.aiga.org/medalist-cipepineles, & the estate of Cipe Pineles; 78 Courtesy of the estate of Cipe Pineles. Photographed by Carmen Schiavone background by Bob Cato, A Condé Nast Publication; 79a Courtesy of the estate of Cipe Pineles, Hearst Inc, & the Rochester Institute of Technology. Photograph by Ben Somoroff; 79b Courtesy of the estate of Cipe Pineles & Hearst Inc; 80 Associazione Archivio Storico Olivetti, Ivrea, Italy. Permission for use by the Lionni family; 81 Permission for use by the Lionni family; 82 Digital image, The Museum of Modern Art, New York/Scala, Florence. Permission for use by the Lionni family; 83a © renewed 1987 by Leo Lionni. Permission for use by the Lionni family; 83bl Digital image, The Museum of Modern Art, New York/Scala, Florence. Permission for use by the Lionni family; 83 br Digital image, The Museum of Modern Art, New York/Scala, Florence & additional permission for use by the Lionni family; 84 Digital image, The Museum of Modern Art, New York/ Scala, Florence; 85; 86 Associazione Archivio Storico Olivetti, Ivrea, Italy; 87a Museum für Gestaltung, Zurich; 87b Digital image, The Museum of Modern Art, New York/Scala, Florence; 88 With thanks to the estate of Tom Eckersley. © TfL from the London Transport Museum collection; 89 REX/Janine Wiedel; 90a With thanks to the estate of Tom Eckersley.© TfL from the London Transport Museum collection; 90b With thanks to the estate of Tom Eckersley/ University of the Arts London/Archives & Special Collections Centre; 91 With thanks to the estate of Tom Eckersley. © Royal Mail Group Ltd 2014, courtesy of The British Postal Museum & Archive; 92; 93; 94a © Estate of Abram Games; 94b © Estate of Abram Games & TfL from the London Transport Museum collection; 95 © Estate of Abram Games; 96; 97; 98; 99; 100 Museum für Gestaltung, Zurich. © DACS 2014; 101 Josef Müller-Brockmann Archive, ch-unterengstringen; 102 Museum für Gestaltung, Zurich. © DACS 2014; 103a Museum für Gestaltung, Zurich. © DACS 2014; 103b Museum für Gestaltung, Zurich. © DACS 2014; 104 The Paul Rand Revocable Trust. Digital image, The Museum of Modern Art, New York/Scala/Courtesy of International Business Machines Corporation, © International Business Machines Corporation; 105 The Paul Rand Revocable Trust. Photo by Sally Anderson-Bruce of New Milford, CT./Paul Rand papers, 1942–1998 (inclusive), 1964–1996 (bulk). Manuscripts & Archives, Yale University; 106 The Paul Rand Revocable Trust. Photo: Matt Flynn © Smithsonian Institution. Photo Art Resource/ Scala, Florence; 107a The Paul Rand Revocable Trust; 107c The Paul Rand Revocable Trust; 107b Paul Rand Revocable Trust. © 2014 Laurence King Publishing. All rights reserved, the UPS brandmark & the color brown are trademarks of United Parcel Service of America, Inc; 108; 109; 110; 111a; 111b Museum für Gestaltung, Zurich; 112 Digital image, The Museum of Modern Art, New York/Scala, Florence; 113; 114a; 114 b; 115 Museum für Gestaltung, Zurich; 116a Courtesy of Margaret Calvert; 116 b Design by Fletcher | Forbes | Gill, courtesy of Margaret Calvert; 118 a & c Courtesy of Margaret Calvert; 118b Courtesy of A2-TYPE; 119a Courtesy of Margaret Calvert; 119 c and b Courtesy of A2-TYPE; 120; 121 Getty Images. Courtesy of CBS Broadcasting Inc; 122 Courtesy of CBS Broadcasting Inc. Photo: © Patti McConville / Alamy; 123a Courtesy of CBS Broadcasting Inc; 123b Photo courtesy the AIGA Design Archives. Courtesy of CBS Broadcasting Inc; 124; 125; 126; 127b; 127a; 127ar Courtesy of the Herb Lubalin Study Center of Design &Typography; 128; 129; 130; 131a Museum für Gestaltung, Zurich; 131b; 132; 133; 134; 135a; 135b © 2014 Estate of Saul Bass, All Rights Reserved; 136; 137; 138; 139l; 139r Museum für Gestaltung, Zurich; 140; 141; 142a; 142bl; 142br; 143 © HfG-Archiv, Ulmer Museum, Ulm & by permission of Florian Aicher; 144 © 1963 Danjaq, LLC & United Artists Corp. All Rights Reserved; 145 Getty Images; 146 Digital image, The Museum of Modern Art, New York/Scala, Florence; 147 Gift of Eliza Brownjohn; 148 Massin, 1965; 149 © Sophie Bassouls/Sygma/ Corbis; 150-1 Massin, 1954; 150 b Massin, 1950; 151b Massin, 1964; 152 Pirelli Historical Archive; 153 CDPG/Aiap; Center of Documentation on Graphic Design Aiap. Photo by Luca Pitoni (graphic designer/photographer), 2006; 154a CDPG/Aiap Center of Documentation on Graphic Design Aiap; 154b Bob Noorda (Noorda Design). CDPG/Aiap Center of Documentation on Graphic Design Aiap; 155a © Jon Hicks/Corbis; 155bl Bob Noorda (Noorda Design). Photo: Pirelli Historical Archive; 155br Bob Noorda (Noorda Design). CDPG/Aiap Center of Documentation on Graphic Design Aiap; 156 Collection Stedelijk Museum, Amsterdam; 157 © Vincent Mentzel&by permission of Wim Crouwel; 158a Collection Stedelijk Museum, Amsterdam; 158b; 159b; 159a Collection Stedelijk Museum, Amsterdam; 160 Museum für Gestaltung, Zurich; 161 Archivio Storico Pirelli, Milan; 162; 163a Museum für Gestaltung, Zurich; 163bl; 163br Archivio Storico Pirelli, Milan; 164; 165; 166; 167a; 167b Courtesy of Ken Garland; 168 © Milton Glaser; 169 © Michael Somoroff; 170 © Milton Glaser; 171a Digital image, The Museum of Modern Art, New York/Scala, Florence; 171b © Milton Glaser; 172a Courtesy of David Gentleman & Stop the War Coalition; 172b Courtesy of David Gentleman & BSC; 173 Courtesy of David Gentleman; 174 Courtesy of David Gentleman & The National Trust (commissioned by Ted Fawcett); 175a Courtesy of David Gentleman & Transport for London; 175bl Courtesy of David Gentleman & Transport for London; 175br *A Special Relationship*, by David Gentleman published by Faber, 1987; 176 Museum für Gestaltung, Zurich; 177 © 2014. Photo Scala, Florence/BPK, Bildagentur für Kunst, Kultur und Geschichte, Berlin; 178a Graphische Sammlung der Schweizerischen Nationalbibliothek, Design-Archiv Karl Gerstner; 179a; 179b Graphische Sammlung der Schweizerischen Nationalbibliothek, Design-Archiv Karl Gerstner; 180; 181; 182; 183a; 183b Museum für Gestaltung, Zurich; 184 © TfL from the London Transport Museum collection & the estate of Alan Fletcher, designed by Alan Fletcher, 1993; 185 By permission of the estate of Alan Fletcher. Photo © Jennie Mayle; 186 By permission of the estate of Alan Fletcher; 187a By permission of the estate of Alan Fletcher, designed by Alan Fletcher, 1990; 187b By permission of the Victoria and Albert Museum & the estate of Alan Fletcher; 188 Digital image, The Museum of Modern Art, New York/Scala, Florence.1: 59 x 46 ¾" (149.9 x 118.7 cm) .2: 58 7/8 x 45¾" (149.5 x 116.2 cm). Gift of the designer. Acc. n.: 371.2004.1-2; 189 The Vignelli Archive/© Doug Manchee; 190a Massimo & Lella Vignelli papers, Vignelli Center for Design Studies, Rochester, NY. Courtesy American Airlines; 190b Unimark International records, Vignelli Center for Design Studies, Rochester, NY; 191 Massimo & Lella Vignelli papers, Vignelli Center for Design Studies, Rochester, NY; 192 By kind permission of the estate of Shigeo Fukuda, Digital image, The Museum of Modern Art, New York/Scala, Florence. Silkscreen dimensions: 40½ x 28¾" (103 x 72.5 cm) Gift of the designer MoMA Number: 475.1987; 193 © Kazumi Kurigami; 194; 195 By kind permission of the estate of Shigeo Fukuda; 196 Special Collections of the University of Amsterdam, archive of Jan van Toorn. © DACS 2014; 197 Courtesy of Jan van Toorn; 198; 199a; 199b Special Collections of the University of Amsterdam, archive of Jan van Toorn. © DACS 2014; 200; 201; 202al; 202ar; 203-4b; 203a By permission of Derek Birdsall; 204 By permission of & designed by Richard Saul Wurman; 205 Photo by Melissa Mahoney; 206; 207 By permission of Richard Saul Wurman; 208 Museum für Gestaltung, Zurich; 209 © Andrey Bold; 210a; 210bl; 210br; 211; Museum für Gestaltung, Zurich; 212; 213; 214;215; 216 Courtesy Bruno Monguzzi; 217; Photo: © Matteo Monguzzi, 2008; 218; 219 Courtesy Bruno Monguzzi; 220; 221; 222; 223 By kind permission of Wolfgang Weingart, Museum für Gestaltung, Zurich; 224 © Estate Of Barney Bubbles; 225 Photo: B.Syme/ © Barney Bubbles Estate; 226; 227 © Estate Of Barney Bubbles; 228; 229; 230al; 230ar; 230b; 231a; 231b; © Scott Brownrigg; 232 © April Greiman & Jayme Odgers; 233; 234-5 © April Greiman; 234b © April Greiman & Jayme Odgers; 235 © April Greiman; 236; 237; 238 Paula Scher/ Pentagram; 239a Paula Scher/Pentagram/photo Peter Mauss; 238; 239 Paula Scher/Pentagram; 240 Photo: *COLORS Magazine* #1 /Oliviero Toscani; 241 Photo: *COLORS Magazine #7/* Pieter Hugo; 242 Racial retouching by Site One N.Y. Original photo by Ronald Woolf/Globe Photos. Excerpted from *COLORS Magazine*, issue # 4, Spring-Summer 1993; 243 The estate of Tibor Kalman; 244; 225; 226; 227 © Estudio Mariscal; 248 Design Peter Saville Associates. *A Basket of Roses* Henri Fantin-Latour 1890; 249 © Wolfgang Stahr; 250 Dichromat Trevor Key & Peter Saville Design Peter Saville Associates; 251a Design Joy Division & Peter Saville; 251b Design Peter Saville & Brett Wickens; 252; 253; 254; 255 Courtesy of Chermayeff & Geismar & Haviv; 256 Concept, art direction & design: Vaughan Oliver & 4AD. Photography Nigel Grierson; 257 Photo: Giles Revell; 258a Art Direction & design Vaughan Oliver & 4AD. Photography Simon Larbalestier. Design Assistance. Chris Bigg. Model-making Pirate; 259a Art direction & design Vaughan Oliver & 4AD; 259b Art direction & design Vaughan Oliver & 4AD. Photography Simon Larbalestier; 261; 263 Courtesy of Irma Boom; 264 © Design Philippe Apeloig. © ADAGP, Paris & DACS,

London 2014; 265 © Mischa Halle; 266; 267 © ADAGP, Paris & DACS, London 2014. Design Philippe Apeloig; 268 Sagmeister & Walsh. Art Direction & Design: Stefan Sagmeister, Additional Design: Matthias Ernstberger Client: DDD gallery, Osaka & GGG gallery, Tokyo; 269 Sagmeister & Walsh. Art Direction & Design: Stefan Sagmeister. Additional Design & Photography: Matthias Ernstberger & Henry Leutwyler. Illustration: Yuki Muramatsu, Stephan Walter Production: Anet Sirna-Bruder Client: Abrams Inc; 270l Sagmeister & Walsh. Art Direction & Design: Stefan Sagmeister, Additional Design & Photography: Matthias Ernstberger, Client: Art Grandeur Nature, Size: 5 billboards; 270r Sagmeister & Walsh.,Art Direction & Design: Stefan Sagmeister, Photography: Timothy Greenfield Sanders, Client Warner Bros. Music Inc; 271 Sagmeister & Walsh. Art Direction: Stefan Sagmeister Photography: Tom Schierlitz Client: AIGA Detroit; 272 © Barnbrook; 273 © Teri Varhol; 274; 275 © Barnbrook; 276 Courtesy of Aubrey Powell. Ummagumma – Design & Photography Storm Thorgerson & Aubrey Powell at Hipgnosis/@ Pink Floyd Music Ltd; 277 Courtesy of Aubrey Powell. Dark Side Of The Moon – Design Storm Thorgerson & Aubrey Powell at Hipgnosis / Graphics George Hardie/@ Pink Floyd Music Ltd; 278a Courtesy of Aubrey Powell. Design Roger Waters/Photography Aubrey Powell at Hipgnosis/@ Pink Floyd Music Ltd; 278b Courtesy of Aubrey Powell. Design Storm Thorgerson & Aubrey Powell at Hipgnosis/Photography Aubrey Powell/@ Mythgem Ltd; 279 Courtesy of Aubrey Powell. Design Hipgnosis @ Hipgnosis; 280; 281; 282; 283 © Grapus. Municipal archives of Aubervilliers; 284; 285; 286 © Pentagram; 287 © Guardian News & Media Ltd; 288 Studio Dumbar, Photography Deen van Meer; 289 Studio Dumbar, Photography Lex van Pieterson; 290 Studio Dumbar, Photography Lex van Pieterson (outdoor), Gerrit Schreurs (manual); 291 Studio Dumbar, Photography Lex van Pieterson; 292 © 8vo. 60 x 40 inches (4-sheet) Silk-screened, 4 special colours (including a luminescent glow-in-the-dark ink) Client: Factory Records Design: 8vo; 293 © 8vo. A4 (29.7 x 21 cm) Offset litho; trace jacket printed black + one special colour; hard cover printed black only Client: Eight Five Zero Publishing Design: 8vo; 294 © 8vo. 60 x 40 inches (four-sheet) Offset litho, four-colour process Client: USP Arts. Design: 8vo; 295a © 8vo. A1 (84.1 x 59.4 cm) Offset litho, two colours; black + special blue. Client: Museum Boymans-van Beuningen, Rotterdam. Design: 8vo; 295b © 8vo. 60 x 40 inches (four-sheet) Silk-screened, three special colours. Client: USP Arts. Design: 8vo; 296; 287; 298; 299 All images courtesy of TDR; 300; 301; 302; 303 All images Tomato (Rick. Smith, Karl Hyde & Darren Emerson trading as Smith Hyde Productions); 304 Courtesy mmparis.com; 305 Photo by Inez van Lamsweerde & Vinoodh Matadin; 306; 307 Courtesy mmparis.com.

The Author

Caroline Roberts is a journalist and author who writes mainly about the graphic arts. She is the co-author of *New Book Design, Cut & Paste: 21st-Century Collage* and most recently *50 Years of Illustration*. She has been editor of *Grafik* magazine since 2001.

Caroline would like to thank Emily Louise Higgins, who helped with the early stages of research for this book.